PIERRE-AUGUSTE RENOIR

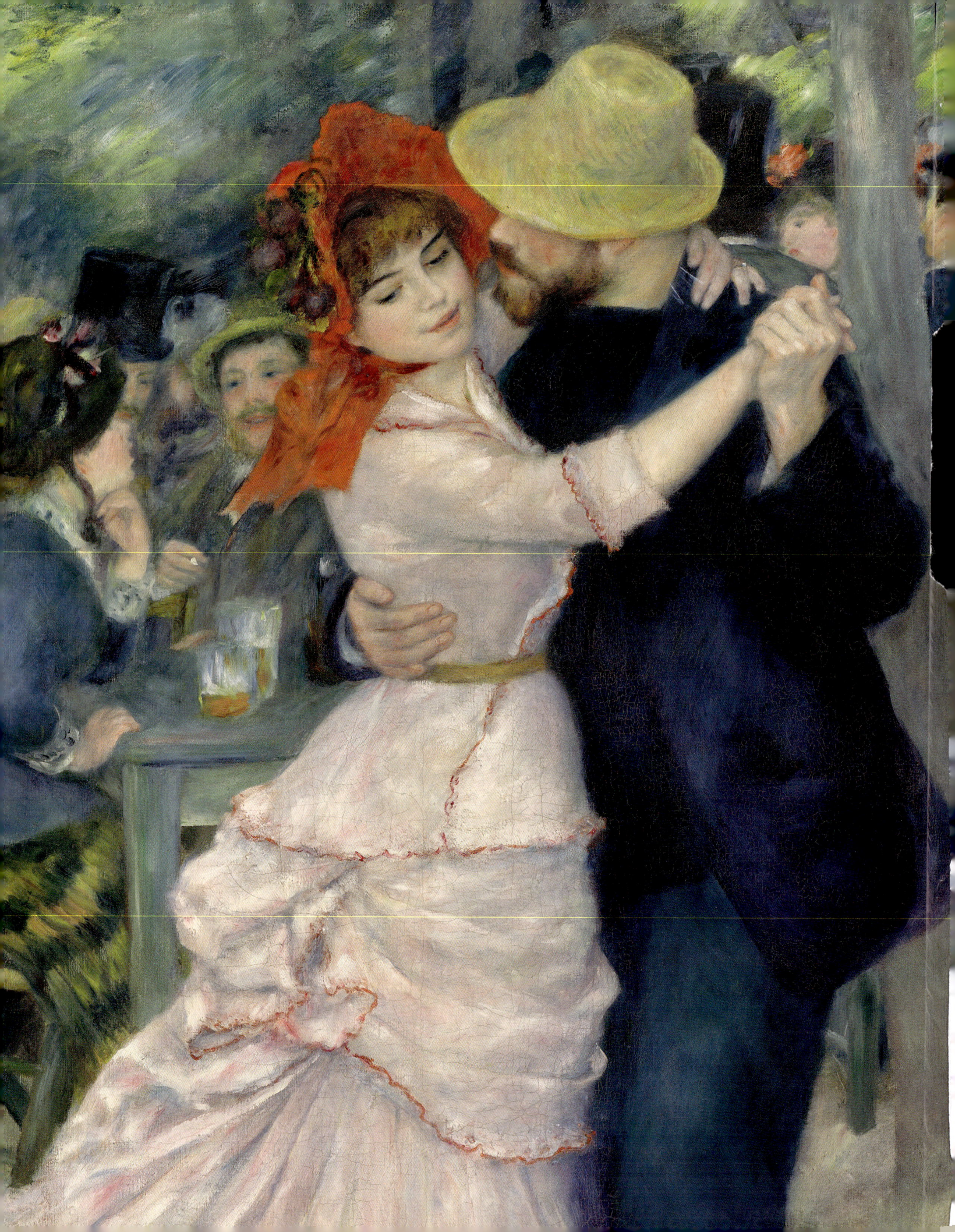

ART MASTERS

PIERRE-AUGUSTE RENOIR

THOMAS STEVENS

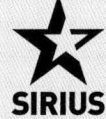

SIRIUS

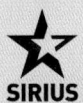

SIRIUS

This edition published in 2024 by Sirius Publishing, a division of
Arcturus Publishing Limited,
26/27 Bickels Yard, 151–153 Bermondsey Street,
London SE1 3HA

ISBN: 978-1-3988-5099-6
AD006176UK

Printed in China

In 1864, Renoir won acceptance by the Salon and exhibited his painting *La Esmeralda*, inspired by Victor Hugo's *The Hunchback of Notre Dame*. But unlike modern galleries, where paintings are given equal prominence, the Salon displayed only the best-regarded pictures at eyeline. Renoir found that his painting was tucked away, as he put it: 'My poor canvas was put under the moulding or under awning, so it would go as unnoticed as possible.'

Renoir and his contemporaries soon discovered that the juries making the awards and the critics writing the newspaper reviews were very conservative in their tastes. This resistance to art that was new or challenging would ultimately prompt the young artists to set up their own rival, more forward-thinking exhibition.

MEETING MANET

The same year, Renoir met an artist who was to have a profound influence on his work. Édouard Manet was nine years older than Renoir and had come to national attention in 1863 when, along with a number of other artists including Camille Pissarro, James McNeill Whistler and Gustave Courbet, he had his work rejected by the Salon. Every year the Salon dismissed over two-thirds of the paintings it received, and the dejected artists went away and tried again. But this year was different – the artists challenged the rejection. Their protests eventually reached the ears of Emperor Napoleon III, whose concern about the public reaction to the situation prompted him to decree that there would be a second exhibition for the rejected works – the so-called Salon des Refusés ('Exhibition of Rejects').

It was at the Salon des Refusés, amid much public ridicule, that Manet had exhibited *Le Déjeuner sur l'Herbe* in 1863. This large painting shows a picnic in a wooded glade. Two fully dressed men lounge alongside a naked woman whose gaze is turned casually yet curiously towards the viewer. In the background, another semi-naked woman bathes in a stream. The depiction of a naked female figure sitting with fully dressed men caused a scandal when the painting was first shown. But the writer Émile Zola described it as Manet's 'greatest work' and it inspired imitations by other artists, including Claude Monet and Pablo Picasso.

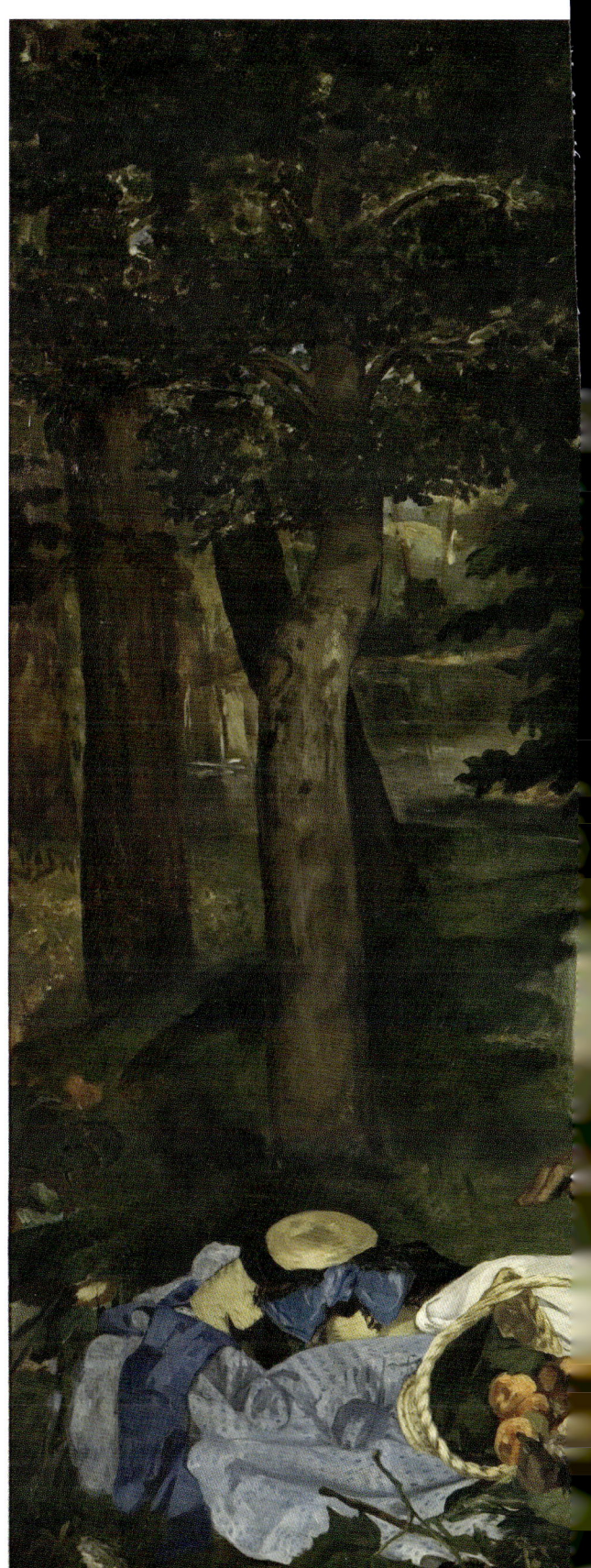

Le Déjeuner sur l'Herbe, *Édouard Manet, 1862–3. The public were unaccustomed to encountering nudes outside a classical setting, and the sight of a female figure entirely unashamed in the company of men in modern dress met with a shocked reaction. Manet's comparative lack of perspective and abrupt contrasts, rather than the more conventional subtle graduations of tone, were also unfamiliar and caused further criticism.*

ART SCHOOL
AND THE SALON

At the age of twenty-one, Renoir
entered the studio of the Swiss
artist Charles Gleyre, who had
been a student of Neoclassical
painter Jean-Auguste-Dominique
Ingres (1780–1867). Gleyre's
academic teaching style did not
suit Renoir at the time, so he
sought out kindred spirits and
found them in fellow students
Frédéric Bazille, Alfred Sisley
and Claude Monet. Through
Monet, Renoir also encountered
Paul Cézanne and Camille
Pissarro, who were studying at
the Académie Suisse, a similar
teaching atelier to Gleyre's.

In 1862, Renoir enrolled at
the École des Beaux-Arts, the
government-funded art school
of Paris, where he studied
drawing and anatomy. 'I was
a very diligent student . . .'
Renoir would later say, 'but
I never obtained the slightest
honourable mention.' According
to some sources, Renoir had no
fixed address during his early
career; he lodged with friends
and sought out commissions for
portraits, but often didn't earn
enough money to buy paint or food.

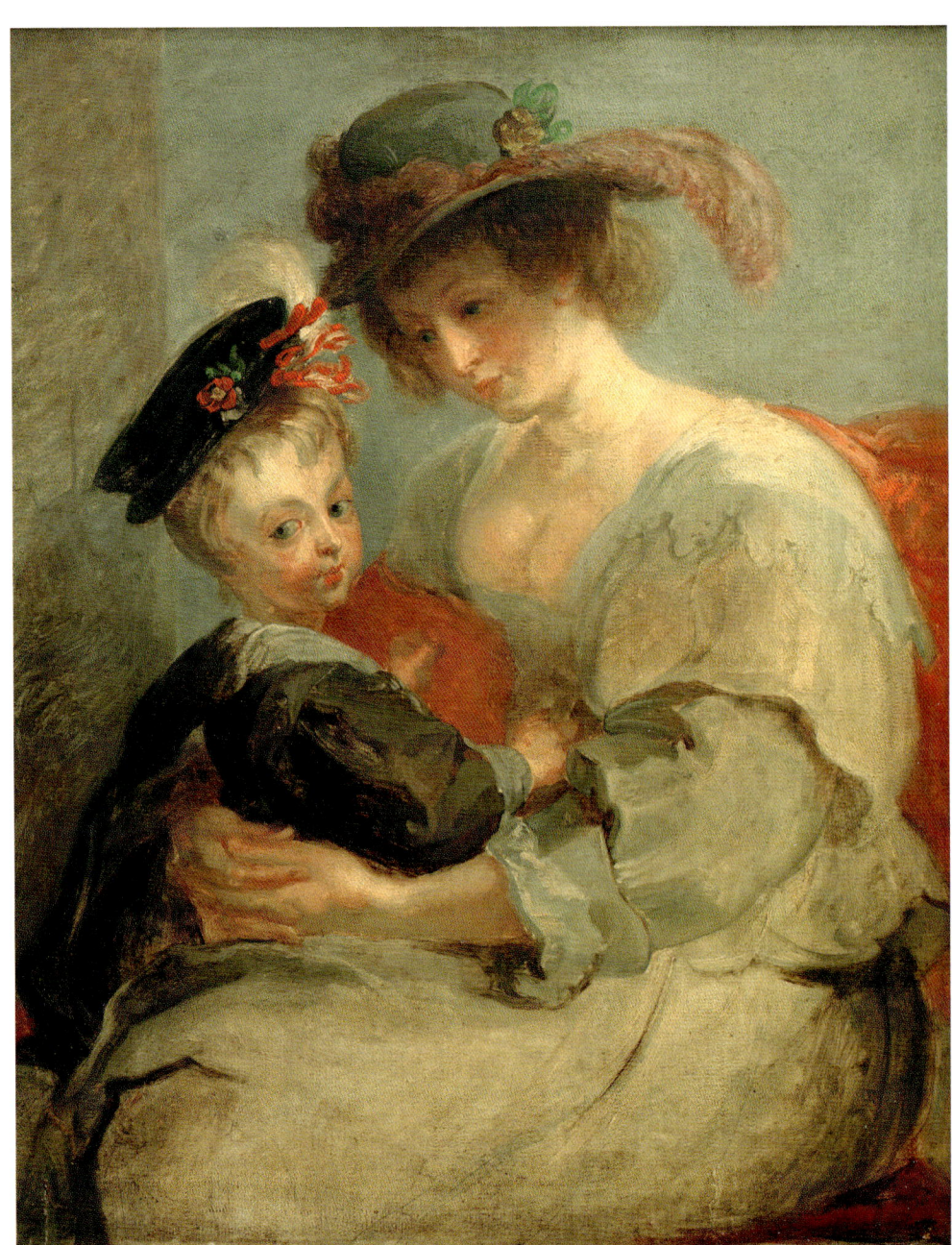

Portrait of Hélène Fourment with
Her Son, 1860–64. *Renoir's careful
reworkings of paintings in the Louvre
taught him much in the way of
technique. He later turned away
from Impressionism towards a more
classical style. Rubens remained a
lifelong influence.*

At that time, success for aspiring artists depended on being accepted by the Salon,
the official art exhibition of the Académie des Beaux Arts in Paris. First held in
1667, the Salon was the most prestigious art exhibition in France and possibly in
all of Europe. Artists who won a Salon medal were likely to forge successful careers
and win high-paying commissions from government and upper-class patrons, but
those who didn't win were left to the mercy of the critics, whose reviews could be
unsparing. As Renoir put it in 1881: 'There are hardly fifteen connoisseurs in Paris
capable of liking a painter without the Salon. There are 80,000 of them who won't
even buy a nose [of a painting] if the painter is not in the Salon.'

A DEVELOPING TALENT

Renoir attended the local Catholic school, but left in 1854 at the age of thirteen to become apprentice to a porcelain painter. He learned to copy floral designs on to plates and cups, but lost his job when the mechanization of porcelain decoration arrived. He soon found employment doing other kinds of decorative painting on fans, and on screens for shops, restaurants and private homes; he also painted religious hangings for churches.

Renoir enrolled for free drawing classes at a city-sponsored art school run by Louis-Denis Caillouette, a sculptor. Caillouette taught his students the fundamentals of art by encouraging them to make copies of works of the great masters. In 1860, Renoir began to study and reproduce some of the great works hanging in the Louvre. He spent much of his time browsing the galleries, sketchbook in hand, studying the art and honing his skills. Some of his paintings from these early years survive, most notably a copy of Peter Paul Rubens' portrait of his wife, *Hélène Fourment and Her Children*, made between 1860 and 1864 (see facing page). Renoir also produced still lifes and portraits, including one of his mother in 1860, and painted some fleeting scenes of Parisians at leisure that hint at the style and content of his later, more famous Impressionist works.

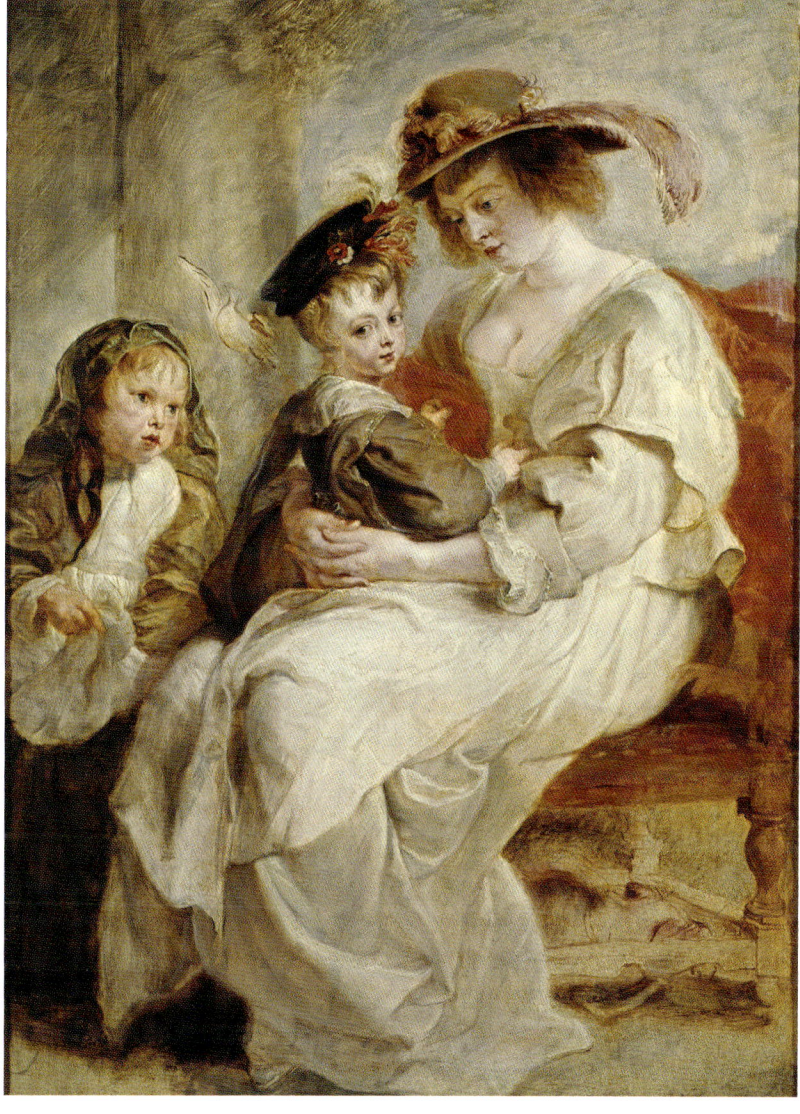

Hélène Fourment and Her Children, *Peter Paul Rubens, c.1636. Rubens (1577–1640) remained a highly influential artist long after his death. From a privileged background, he became court page to a countess at the age of thirteen, but turned instead to art and travelled to Italy and Spain to learn from the works of Renaissance and classical masters. He became a court painter in the Netherlands and later combined his work with a diplomatic career. During some months spent in England, he fulfilled a number of commissions for King Charles I. Helena Fourment was Rubens' second wife and she is portrayed here with her son Frans (b.1633) and daughter Clara Johanna (b.1632).*

CHAPTER 1
From Artisan to Artist

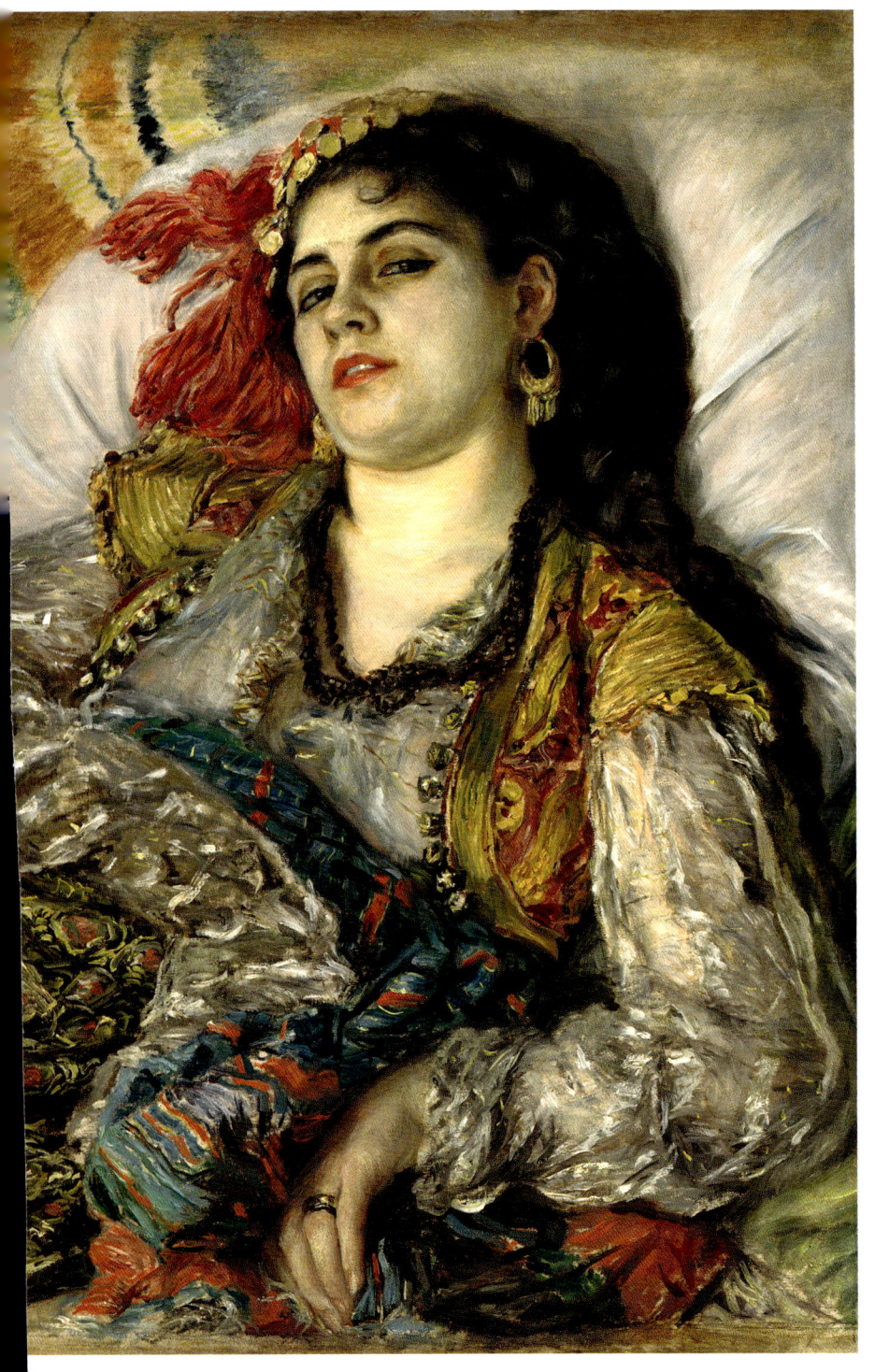

While many of the Impressionists could trace a noble lineage back through the centuries, Renoir's genealogy was shrouded in mystery. His grandfather, a foundling, had been left on the steps of the cathedral in Limoges in 1773. Adopted by the local Renouard family, who named him François, he received little education and grew up to be a craftsman – a maker of wooden shoes. When he married in 1796, at the age of twenty-three, he could neither read nor write so had to speak his name to the official scribe, who wrote it down phonetically as 'Renoir'.

In time, François Renoir had his own family. His oldest child, Leonard, was born in 1799 and became a tailor in Limoges; he eventually married a dressmaker's assistant. Leonard and his wife had seven children, five of whom survived infancy. Pierre-Auguste was the fourth of the five, born on 25 February 1841.

When Pierre-Auguste (known simply as 'Auguste') was four years old, François died and the Renoir family moved to Paris. Leonard set up a tailoring business at their home in the heart of the city. Its location, just a short walk from the Louvre where free admission was available to the general public at weekends, may have played a part in shaping Auguste Renoir's future.

Odalisque, 1870. A reclining woman in surroundings which suggest an exotic harem was a traditional subject for artists. The pose appears to have been influenced by Delacroix's Women of Algiers in Their Apartment, 1834. *When he painted this, Renoir had never been to Algiers. The model was Lise Tréhot, daughter of a French postmaster. Renoir used Islamic-inspired textiles and ceramics to create a sultry, slightly decadent atmosphere.*

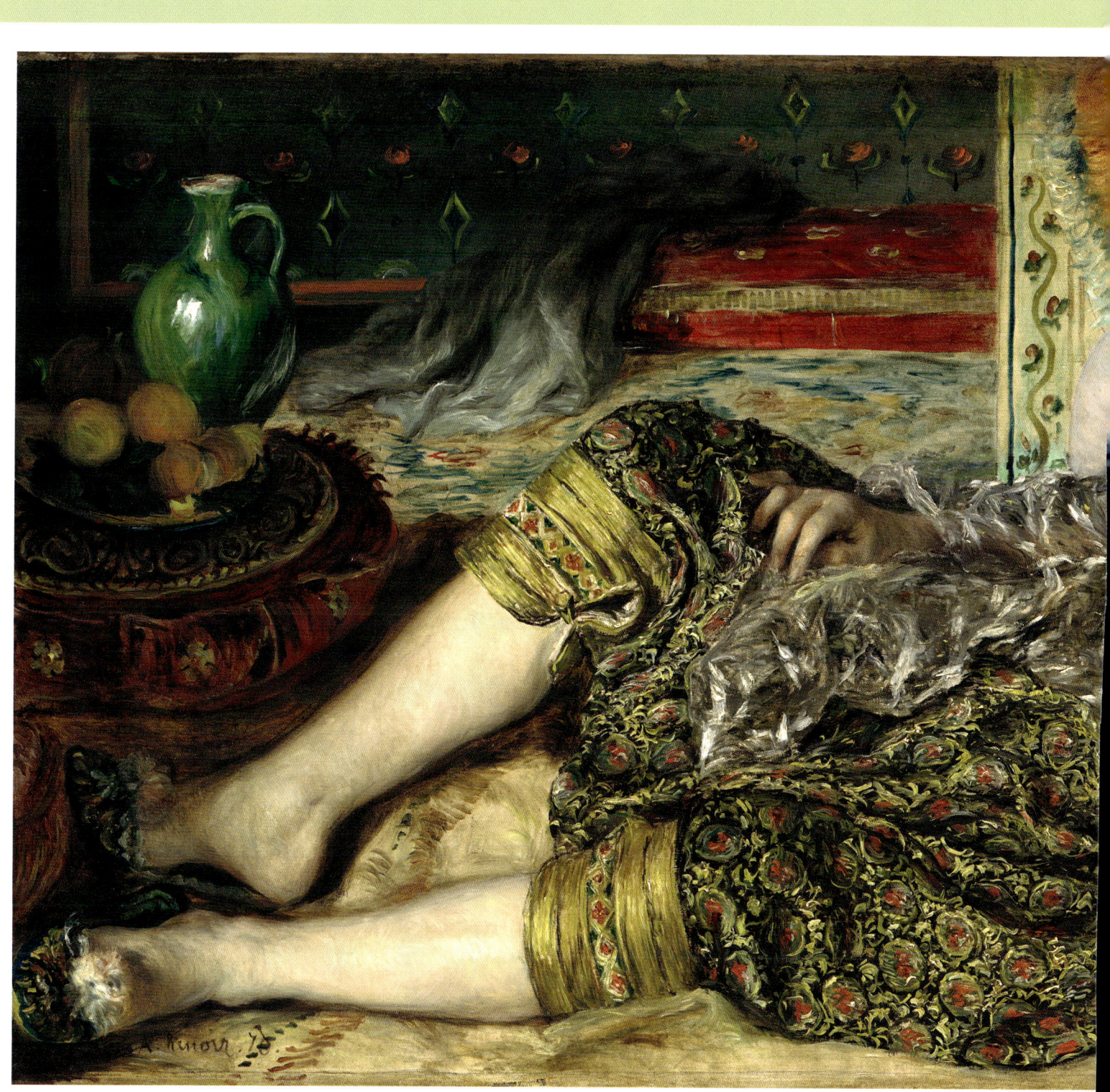

INTRODUCTION

'ONE MUST FROM TIME TO TIME ATTEMPT THINGS THAT ARE BEYOND ONE'S CAPACITY.'

Pierre-Auguste Renoir

Born in 1841 into a working-class family, Pierre-Auguste Renoir would go on to become one of the most celebrated French artists of the late nineteenth century. But although he is now lauded for his contributions to Impressionism and for the more classically styled works of his later years, success was a long time coming.

In the early years, Renoir struggled as an artist, eking out meagre finances, taking commissions where he could and living just ahead of his creditors. Poverty dogged his tracks and he frequently depended on colleagues and friends for support. But he was determined to become an artist and, with Claude Monet, was a founding member of the Impressionist movement which began in France during the 1860s. Renoir's keen eye for beauty and colour, together with his skill at depicting the play of light and shadow, is evident in some of Impressionism's most famous paintings. Like many revolutionary ideas, the new art movement was initially ridiculed and dismissed by critics and the establishment. By the time it entered the mainstream, Renoir had moved on to a more monumental style influenced by High Renaissance art. His paintings from this era would in turn influence the style of avant garde artists such as Henri Matisse and Pablo Picasso.

Throughout his life, Renoir's artistic vision remained resolutely individualistic as he combined classical influences with Impressionism to render portraits, still lifes, landscapes, cityscapes and engaging scenes of domestic life. In middle age he developed rheumatoid arthritis, which gradually paralyzed his fingers and made it difficult for him to hold a paintbrush. Despite this, he continued to paint almost every day and his art remained upbeat, glowing with tone and colour.

Renoir was astonishingly prolific, creating more than 4,500 works of art, just over 4,000 of which were in oils. His children inherited his legacy of experimentation and applied it to other disciplines: his eldest son Pierre (1885–1952) became a successful stage and screen actor, while his youngest, Jean (1901–69), became a celebrated film director.

In the early part of the twentieth century, criticism of the style of Renoir's later works featuring highly-coloured, fleshy nudes began to mount. As a result, his artistic reputation suffered in comparison with that of other Impressionists such as Monet and Cézanne (who also feature in *The Great Artists* series). Nevertheless Renoir's joyous, life-affirming paintings mean that he remains one of the world's best-loved artists.

The Grand Boulevards, 1875. *Renoir's view of Paris rejuvenated with splendid new boulevards is painted with the innovative Impressionist style of fleeting brushstrokes which suggest movement and transient light. The foliage is given light and shade without any attempt to describe the specific type of tree.*

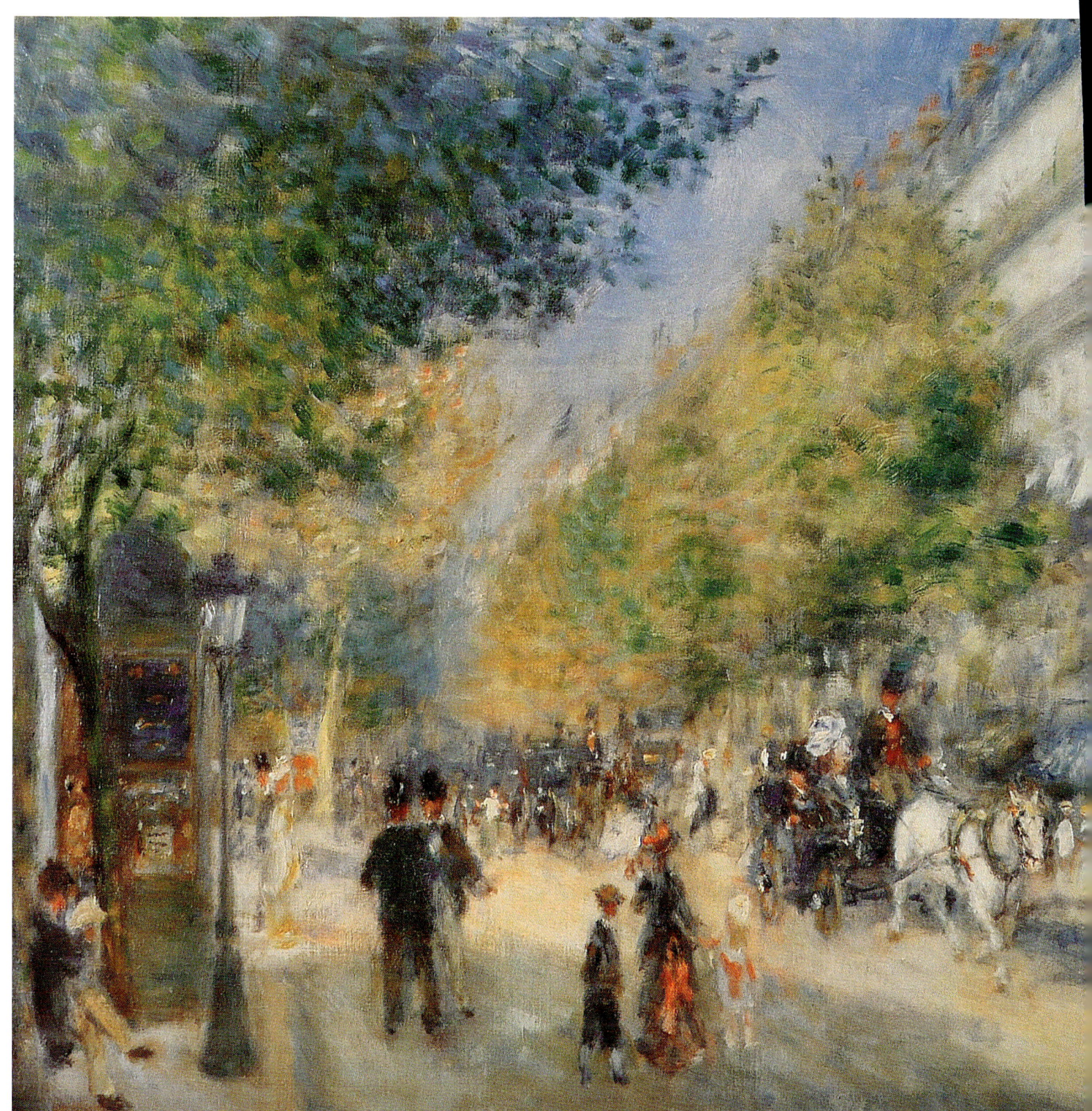

CONTENTS

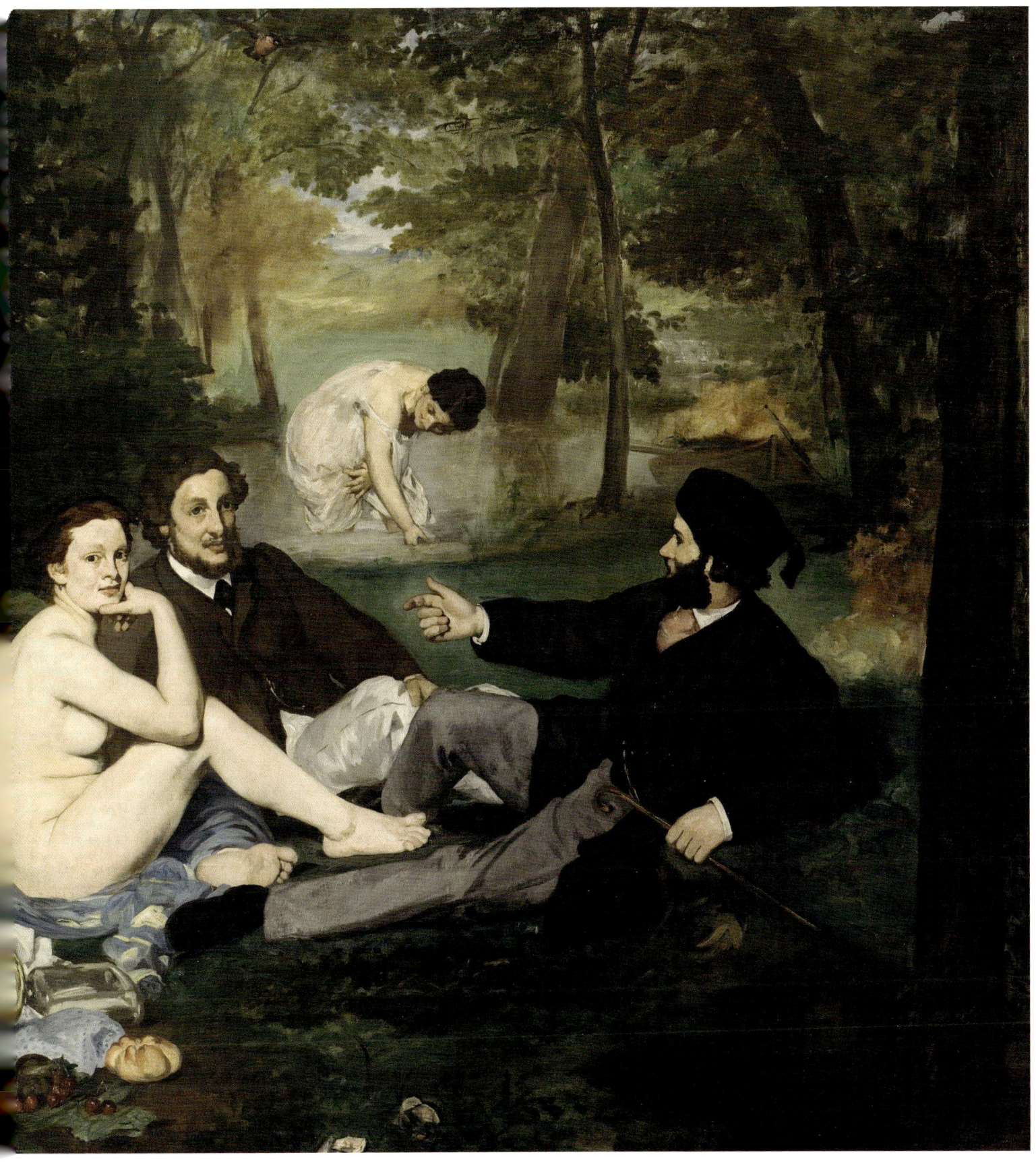

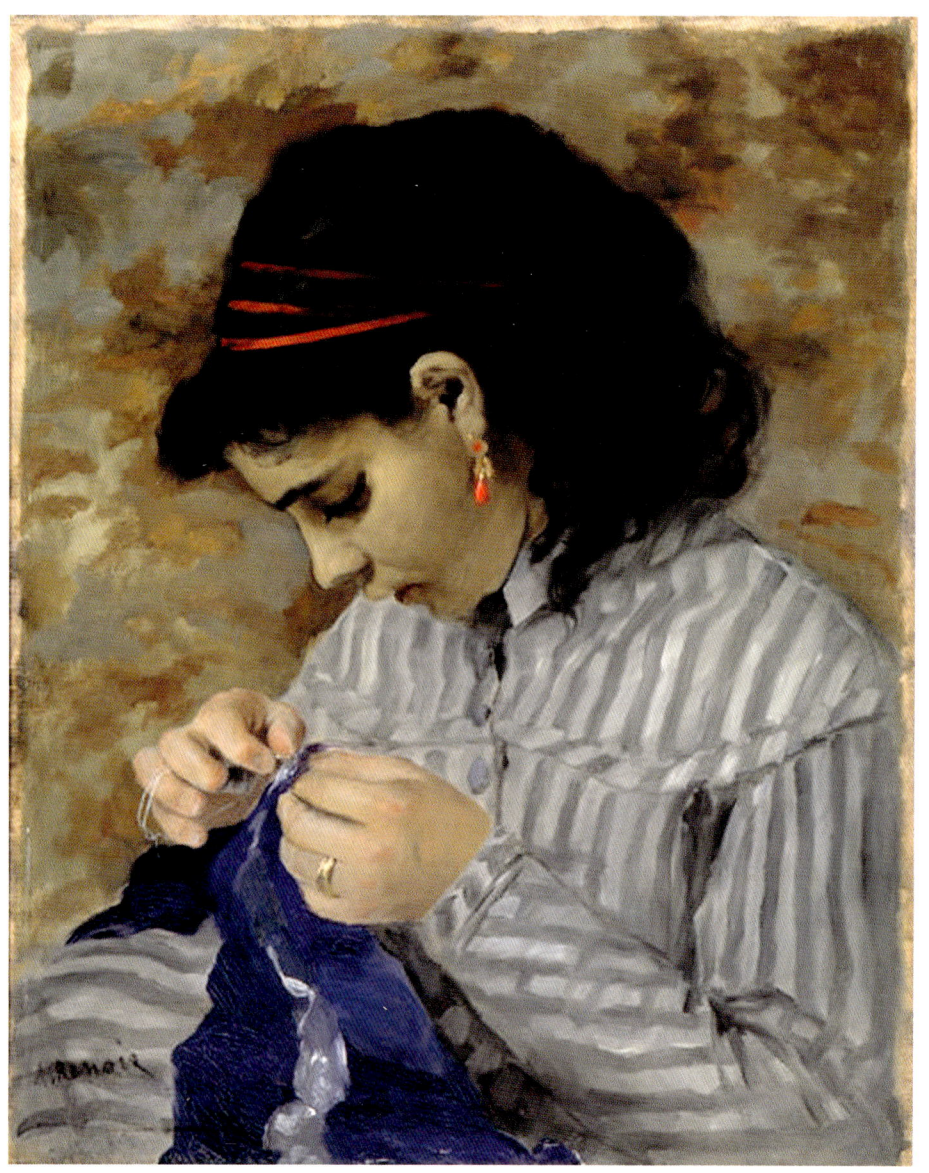

Lise Sewing, c.1866. In this apparently unposed portrait, Renoir shows his model totally absorbed in her work. The details of her clothing, red earring and red-striped ribbon in her hair are set against a background made up of loose brushstrokes in blue, brown and grey.

While the painting's insouciant tone and the clothed/unclothed nature of its subject matter sparked controversy, Renoir and his contemporaries were impressed by Manet's artistic risk-taking. Here a casual 'everyday' scene was presented at a size and scale usually reserved for religious or historical works. It was outwardly realistic yet much of it seemed artificial. The skewed perspective makes the woman in the background appear too large, there is an absence of shadow and detailing, and much of the paint has been roughly applied with obvious brushstrokes.

This was a modern painting, both in style and content, though it clearly owed a debt to the great masters, particularly to Titian's *Pastoral Concert* painted around 1509, where naked, nymph-like women are accompanied by men in courtly dress. *Le Déjeuner sur l'Herbe* exerted a huge influence on Renoir. This, he decided, was what he wanted to do – paint everyday life in a way that acknowledged great art from history but which was also entirely new.

Of course, artists had always painted everyday scenes, but they tended to be formally composed and rigidly stylized. Renoir and his contemporaries wanted to capture the moment as it really happened, naturalistically, with blurred movement and no great distinction between subject and background.

Over the next few years Manet would become the unofficial leader of the group later dubbed the Impressionists. A number of Renoir's paintings from this period are heavily influenced by Manet in terms of their casual subject matter, composition and approach.

Although he was regarded as a major talent by his contemporaries, Renoir was less successful at convincing the Salon judges and, more importantly, the buying public of his artistic worth. Even paintings that had been accepted by the Salon, such as *Lise with a Parasol* (see opposite), were generally derided by the critics and remained unsold.

Around this time, the core of the future Impressionist group, including Renoir, Manet, Bazille, Cézanne, Monet, Pissarro, Sisley and Edgar Degas, began to meet twice weekly at Café Guerbois on Avenue de Clichy in Paris. Here these non-conformist friends (or bohemians, as they came to be known) would eat, drink, argue and hammer out ideas for the new, revolutionary artistic style. They were joined by the writer Émile Zola, who would do much to champion Impressionism in the difficult years ahead. But the two most notable female Impressionist artists, Berthe Morisot and Mary Cassatt, didn't join them, because even in bohemian circles the social strictures of the day prevented 'respectable' women from socializing with men in cafés.

MOVING AROUND

Renoir's commitment to an artistic future was severely tested throughout the 1860s. Without the money to rent his own home and studio, he spent much of the decade lodging with and painting alongside some of his artist friends, including Sisley and Bazille. Born into a wealthy Protestant family in Montpellier, Bazille had given up his medical studies to concentrate on painting. He was generous with his wealth and keen to support struggling fellow artists.

In 1864, Bazille wrote in a letter to his parents: 'I am housing one of my friends . . . who does not have an art studio at the moment. Renoir, that is his name, is very hard-working. He uses my models, and even helps me to pay for them, partly.'

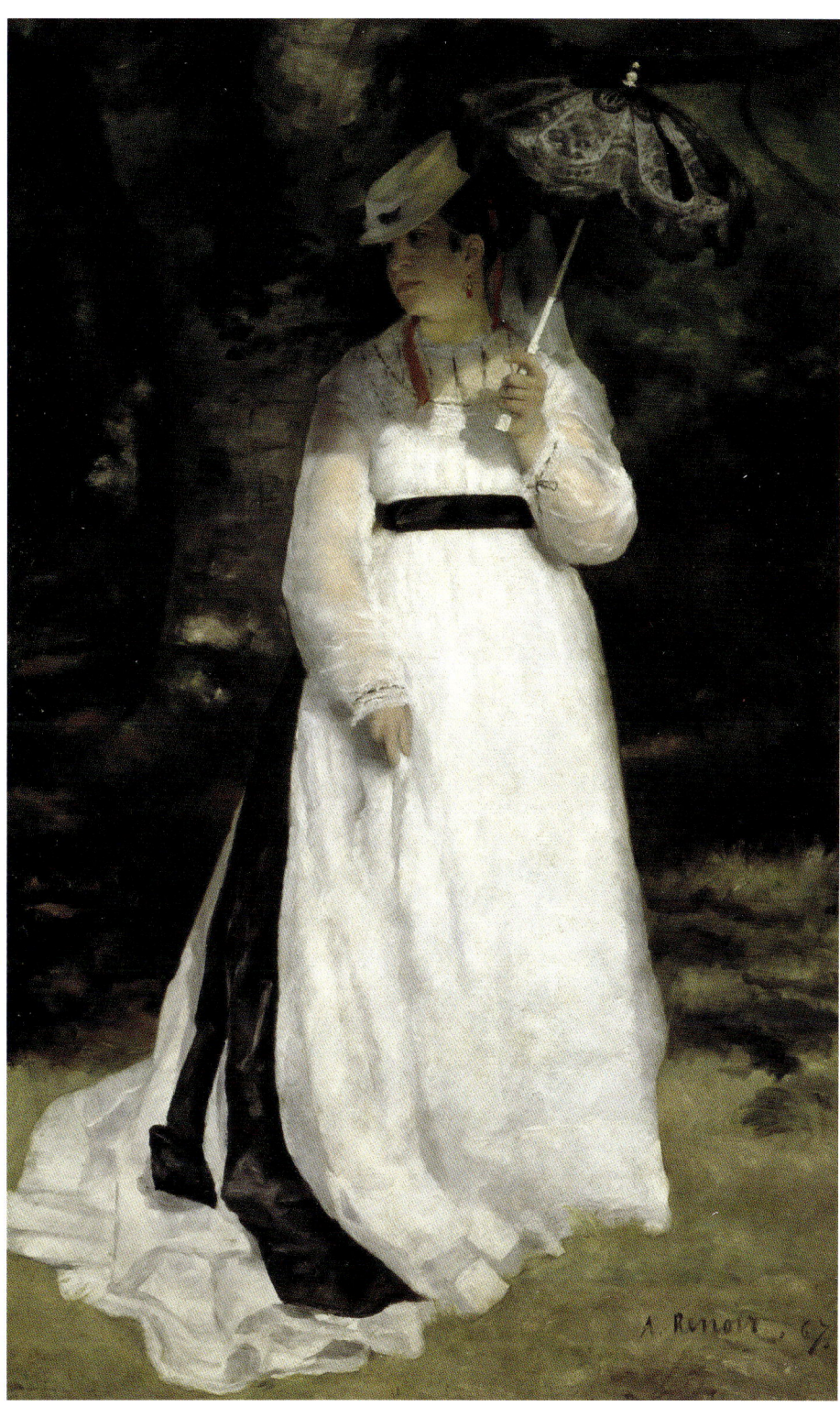

Lise with a Parasol, *1867. In Renoir's first life-sized painting executed en plein air, the subject is shown in fashionable dress in the forest of Fontainebleau, close to Paris. When the painting was exhibited at the Salon in 1868, several critics remarked upon the influence of Manet, some with approval but others more critically.*

'WITHOUT HIM, I WOULD HAVE
GIVEN UP.'

Pierre-Auguste Renoir on Claude Monet

If no models were available, Bazille and
Renoir would paint each other, as they did in
1867 (see opposite). Bazille also helped Monet,
whose financial position was perhaps even more
precarious than Renoir's, as from 1867 he had a
mistress and child to support. Renoir commented at
the time: 'We don't eat every day. But, all the same,
I am pleased because as far as painting goes, Monet
is good company. I am doing next to nothing
because I have very little paint. Things may get
better this month.'

In 1869, despite the practical hardships and
a shortage of paint, Renoir and Monet produced
two of the first true Impressionist paintings – near
identical views of La Grenouillère, 'The Frog Pond',
a popular boating and bathing resort on the Seine,
near Bougival, to the west of Paris. Both Renoir's
La Grenouillère and Monet's *Bain à la Grenouillère*
(see pages 50–51) contain all the elements of what
would soon come to be called Impressionism:
an outdoor scene; an everyday subject rendered
in short, sharp, visible brushstrokes which give
a slightly blurred 'impression' rather than precise
detail of form; an open composition with events
seemingly happening beyond the edges of the
frame; a sense of movement; a concentration on
the portrayal of light (particularly reflection); and,
above all, the notion of a fleeting moment captured.

The close friendship between the two artists was
of vital importance during these years of obscurity
and poverty. Later, Renoir would write of his
gratitude for Monet's support during these dark
days: 'I have always given in to my destiny, I never
had the temperament of a fighter and I would many
times have given up altogether, if my old friend
Monet, who did have the temperament of a fighter,
hadn't given me a hand and lifted me back up.'

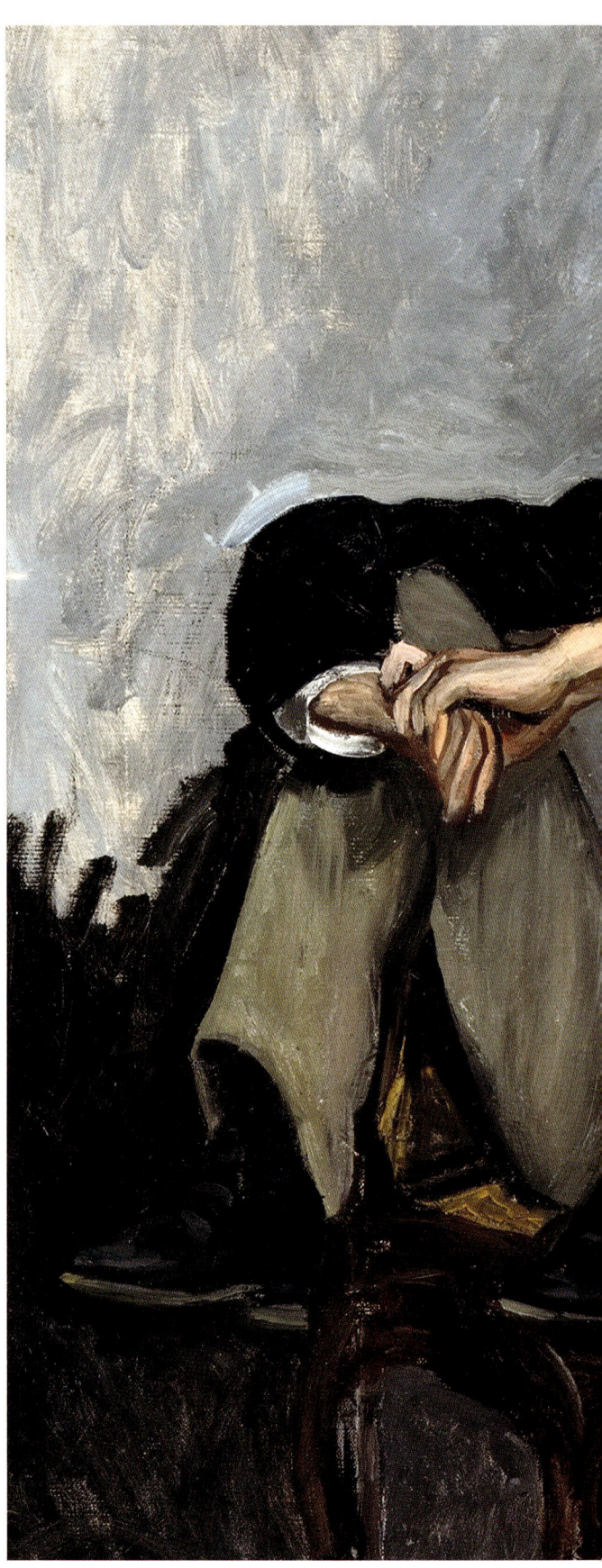

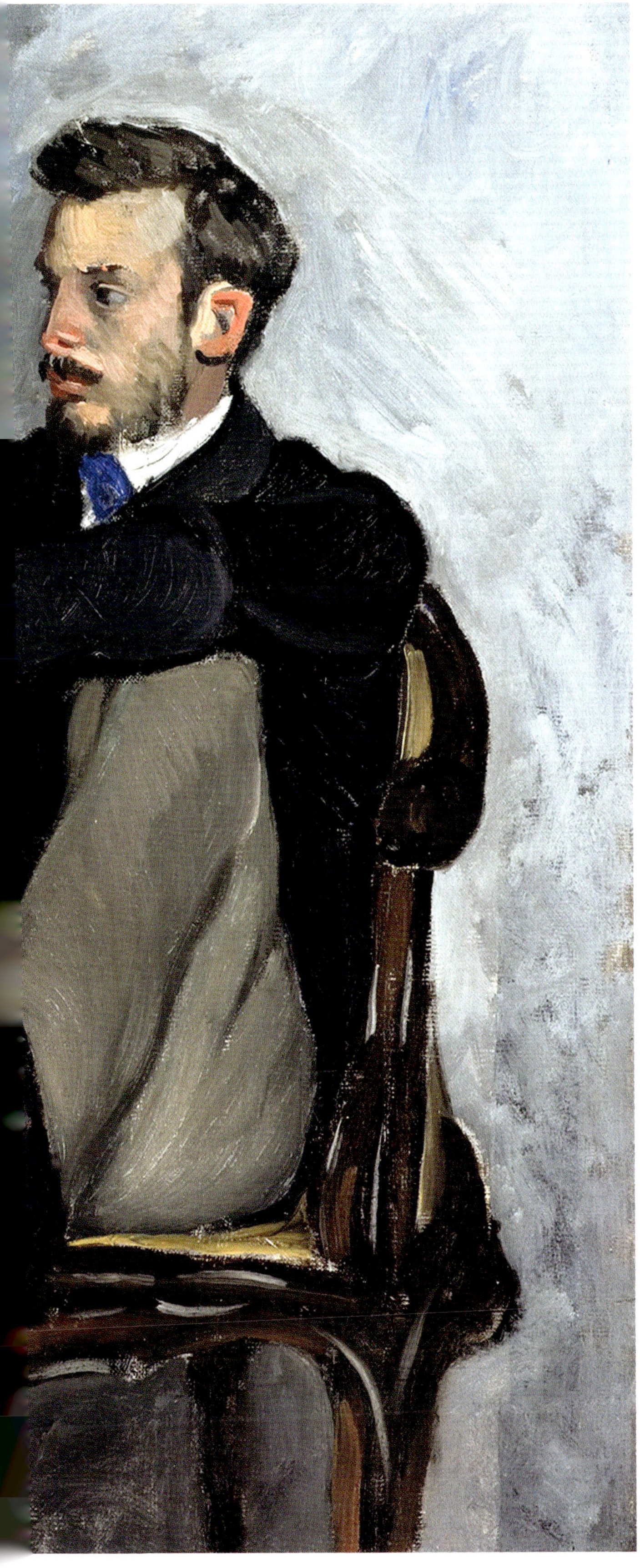

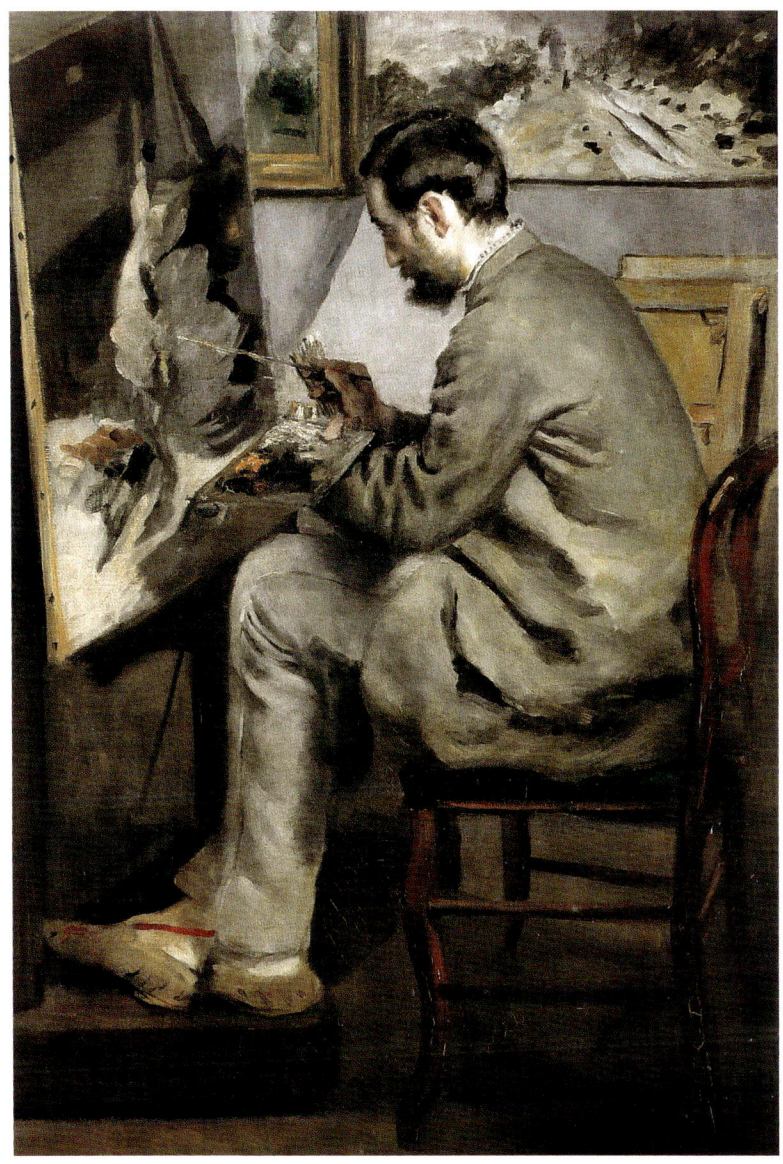

Above: Frédéric Bazille at His Easel, *1867. Renoir's painting of his friend is more fully realized than Bazille's (left). Above the artist's head can be seen the bottom portion of a Monet painting,* Honfleur in the Snow. *Monet had given this to Bazille as a present.*

Left: Portrait of Auguste Renoir, *Frédéric Bazille, 1867. While Bazille's portrait shows the young Renoir in a relaxed pose, the subject's gaze appears to be intent upon something outside the picture frame.*

THE FOREST OF FONTAINEBLEAU

At the beginning of the nineteenth century, landscape painting in France adhered to ancient classical tradition under the strict eye of the Royal Academy of Art. This powerful body gave instruction, held exhibitions and provided venues where artists could promote their work and find patrons. The academy required artists to present idealized landscapes that would serve as backdrops for historical or mythical scenes.

The Prix de Rome, inaugurated in 1663, was a scholarship that gave young artists the opportunity to win a three to five year stay at the Villa Medici in Rome, where they would study the classical method. But the award had unintended consequences. It prompted a huge new interest in landscape painting as a genre in its own right, and young artists began to look towards the naturalistic tradition of Dutch and Flemish artists instead of to the classical example.

By the 1860s, it was generally agreed by the intellectual establishment that France's landscape painting was unrivalled in the world. With an expanded rail network and the invention of the paint tube (which made it easier to carry equipment around), artists could freely explore the countryside in search of natural inspiration. Just 64 km (40 miles) from Paris, the forest of Fontainebleau provided 170 sq km (66 sq miles) of woodland, meadow, marsh and

The Gust of Wind, *Gustave Courbet, c.1865. While Courbet's painting is partially based on sketches he made in the forest of Fontainebleau, the scene is an imagined view combining different elements rather than depicting a specific location.*

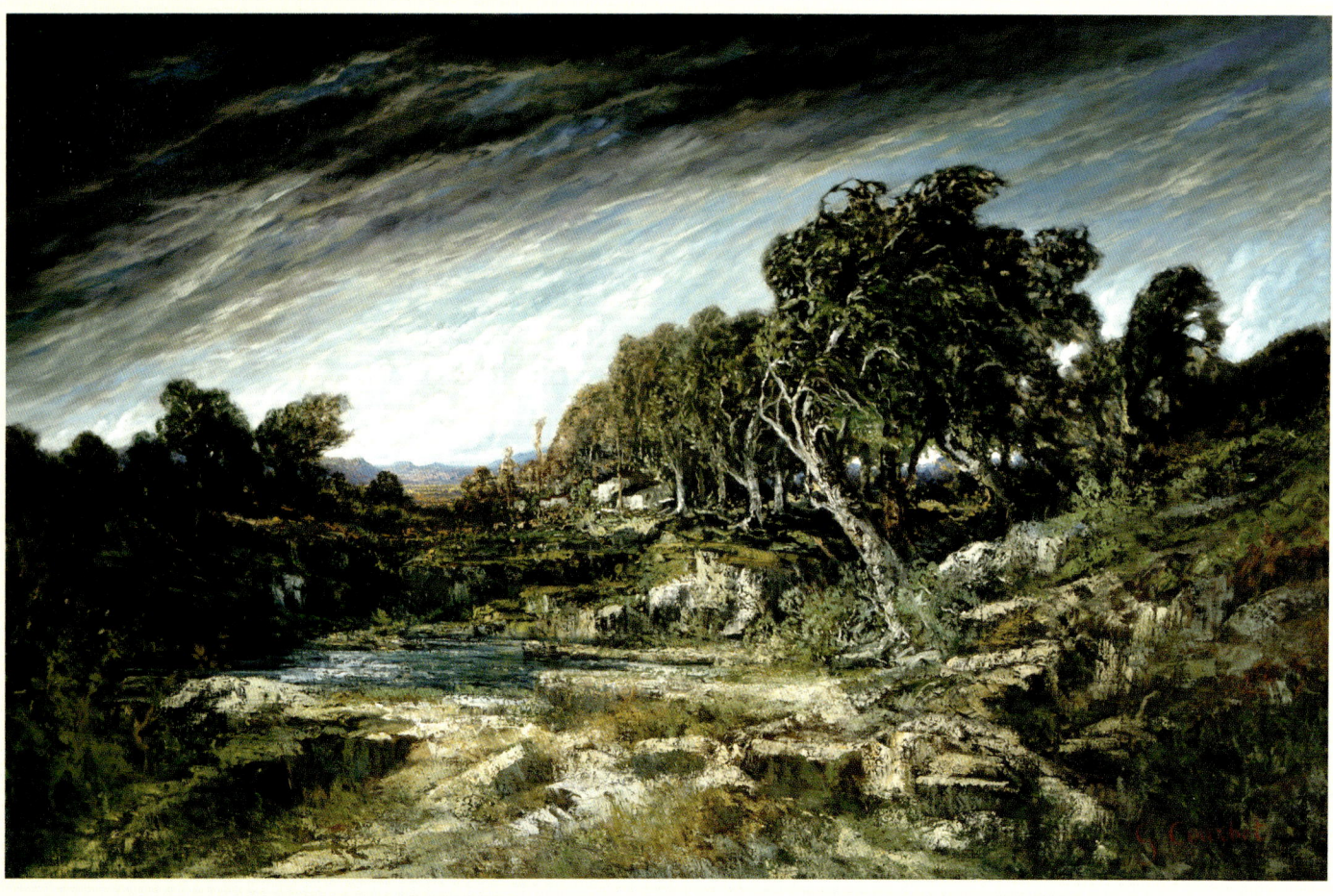

rocks – ideal subjects for rural scenes which could be exhibited and sold at the Salon and in the new galleries and auction rooms springing up in the capital.

In a village near the forest, an inexpensive hostelry called Auberge Ganne provided convivial accommodation and became very popular with artists. The name of the village, Barbizon, was given to a group who would influence the Impressionists. The Barbizon school painted directly from nature and made it their main subject instead of simply a backdrop. Artists belonging to the school included Théodore Rousseau (1812–67), Jean-Baptiste-Camille Corot (1796–1875), Charles-François Daubigny (1817–78), Jean-François Millet (1814–75) and Narcisse Virgilio Diaz de la Peña (1807–76).

Another artist who painted scenes of the forest was Gustave Courbet (1819–77). Like Millet, he portrayed peasants working on the land and, in common with most artistic innovators at the time, his art was rejected by the establishment. Courbet responded by setting up a temporary gallery of his own called the Pavilion of Realism, where he showed forty of his paintings.

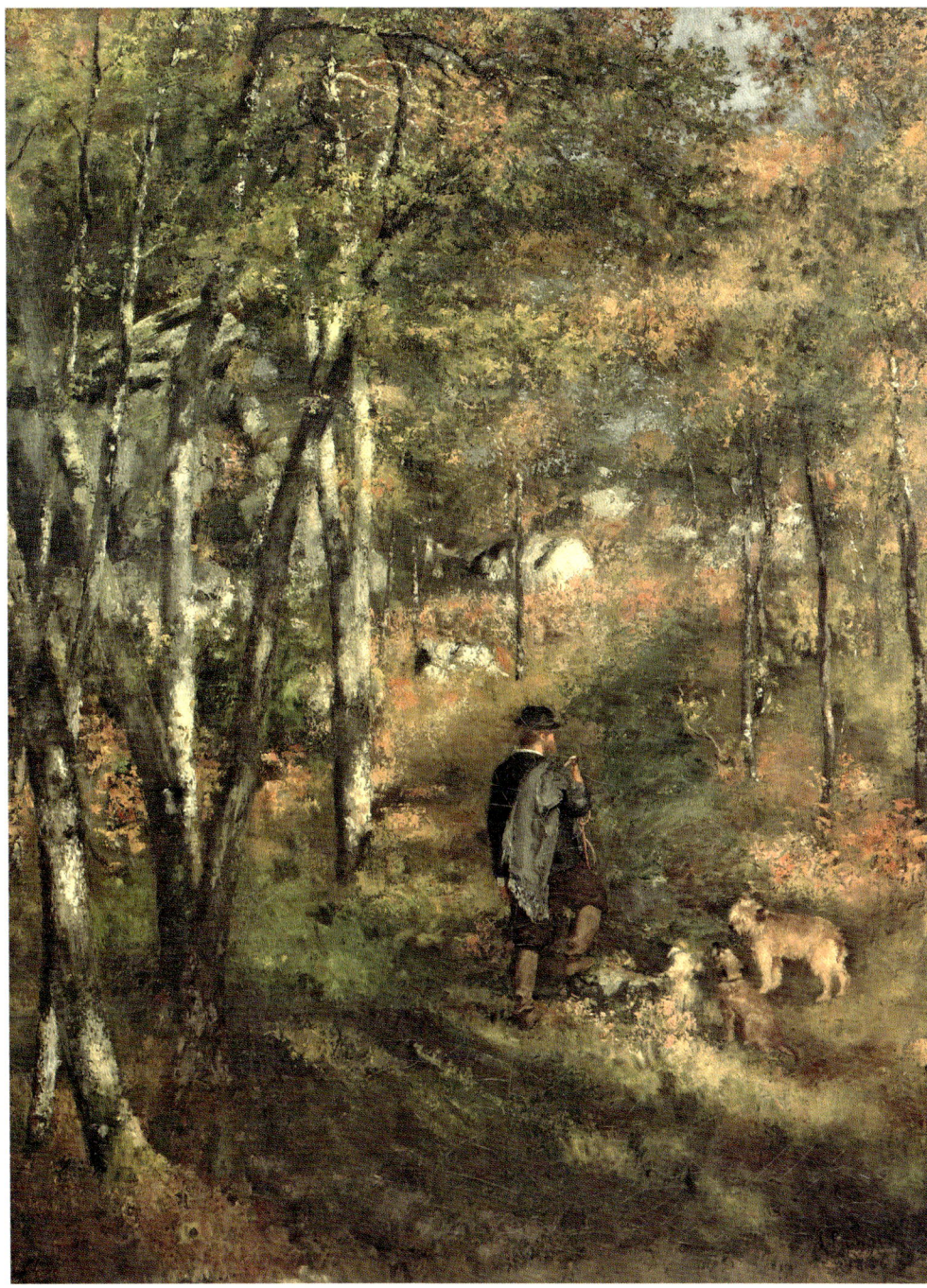

While Courbet painted landscapes, seascapes and still lifes, his interest in social issues marked him out for the most attention (generally unfavourable for much of his life). But the Impressionists were inspired by his courage and by his spontaneous application of paint. In the 1860s, when Bazille, Renoir, Sisley and Monet set out for Fontainebleau in their turn, their ideas about capturing the fleeting effects of nature were prompted by the innovations of Courbet and this earlier generation of artists.

Jules Le Coeur in the Forest of Fontainebleau, 1866. *Renoir's painting of his friend was made for the Le Coeur family, who had a house in Marlotte at the edge of the forest. Painted in the Realist style, it shows Le Coeur in rich russet and green surroundings. The path leads the viewer's eye up the gentle hill he is about to climb.*

IMPRESSIONISM: A DIFFERENT WAY OF SEEING

Impressionism, the first distinctly modern movement in art, was characterized by scenes from modern life painted in pure, bright colours. The Impressionists found that instead of painting in a studio, they could best capture the naturalistic effects they wanted by working out of doors (*en plein air*), using loose, rapid dabs of paint to render the fleeting quality of light. Almost from the start of his career, Renoir was in the midst of it all. His most famous works, including *La Loge* (1874), *Lunch at the Restaurant Fournaise* (1875), *The Swing* (1876) and *Dance at the Moulin de la Galette* (1876), are among the movement's most celebrated.

It's difficult to appreciate the extent to which Impressionism shocked the art world when it first emerged. To our eyes, many of the paintings seem tame, old-fashioned even; their popularity and accessibility have made them overly familiar compared to the more radical works that followed. But in the beginning, the movement provoked fury among metropolitan art critics. A cartoon published in the Parisian magazine *Le Charivari* in 1877 shows a policeman trying to shield a pregnant woman from the horrors of the third Impressionist show, saying: 'Lady, it would be unwise to enter!' Misunderstanding the Impressionists' deliberate avoidance of clarity of form, critics lambasted the works for their unfinished and amateurish appearance.

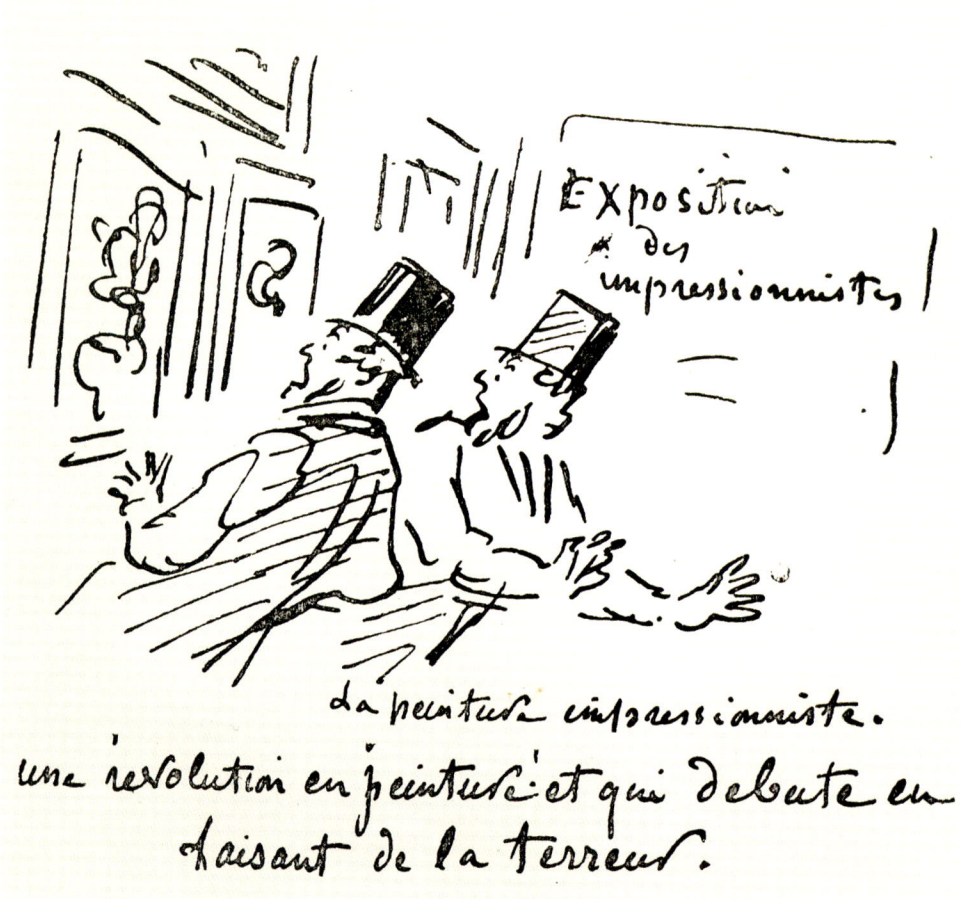

A cartoon from 1874 by Cham (Amédée Charles Henri de Noé) pokes fun at the 'terror' engendered by Impressionism – a revolution in painting.

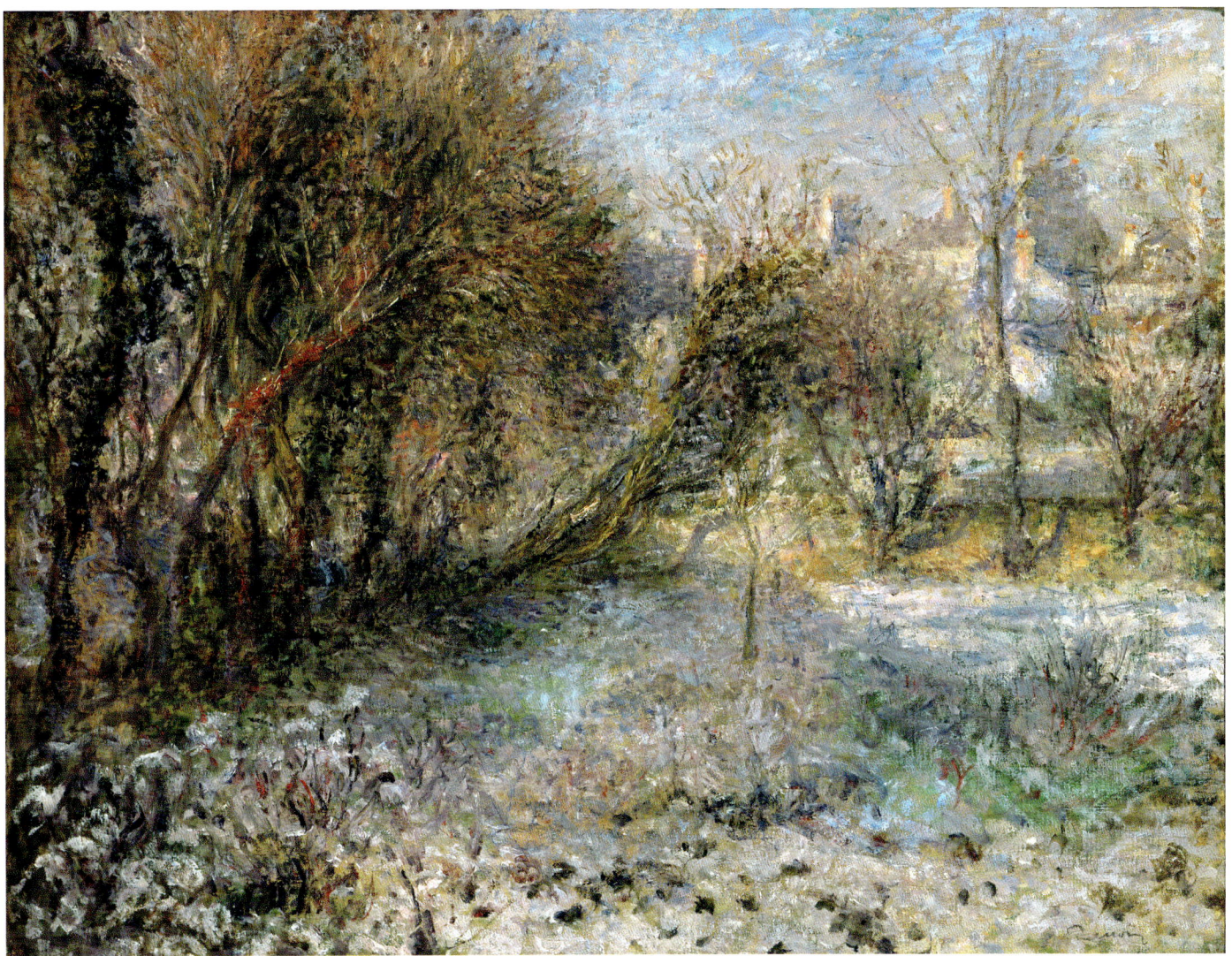

In Romanticism and Neoclassicism, two styles which had dominated the first half of the nineteenth century, paintings were carefully constructed and featured 'serious' subjects such as religious or mythological scenes, great figures from history, and so on. They were usually painted indoors, with a controlled light source, and every detail was exquisitely rendered. In contrast, the Impressionists focused on seemingly frivolous subjects such as children at play, social gatherings and nature, and often painted *en plein air* in an attempt to approximate the unpredictable effects of natural light. Scenes seemed almost haphazardly constructed, with glimpsed events taking place beyond the bounds of the picture frame. The brushwork was often visible and sparse, with figures painted using just a few strokes to give an idea, or 'impression', of the character.

In the 1860s and 1870s, Renoir's works exemplified this approach. They are shimmering scenes of everyday life, full of movement, gaiety and light as if captured in a blurred snapshot. This new style of painting would slowly gain a large and appreciative audience until, by the early years of the twentieth century, Impressionism had become the orthodoxy against which to rebel.

Snow-covered Landscape, 1875. Renoir disliked the cold and produced few snowy scenes, but he managed to complete this painting in the harsh winter of 1874–5. The sunlight is pale and the trees and bushes cast shadows on the ground. The whole is painted with a typical Impressionist approach using short, swift brushstrokes and pure, bright colours.

In Summer (The Bohemian), 1868. While this painting shows the influence of Delacroix and Courbet, the loosely painted background is in the Impressionist style. The green of the foliage and its reflected light complement the red of Lise's hairband and striped skirt.

Renoir had met the architect-turned-artist Jules Le Coeur (see page 19) at Gleyre's studio in 1864. Born into a wealthy family, Le Coeur had decided at the age of thirty to give up his well-paid job and retrain as an artist. The two men became close and Renoir often stayed at the Le Coeur family home in Paris, painting in the studio there. He also travelled with Le Coeur to a house he rented in Marlotte, on the edge of the forest of Fontainebleau, southeast of the city (see pages 18–19). This forest was an ideal subject for the *plein air* studies the Impressionists favoured – Renoir once remarked, 'I like a painting which makes me want to take a stroll in it'. He didn't restrict himself to landscapes, however, also completing portraits of Le Coeur's mother, brother and mother-in-law, as well as Jules himself. Surprisingly, for the next twenty years, Renoir would earn most of his money from portrait painting.

FIRST LOVE AND SECRET CHILD

In 1866, Le Coeur introduced Renoir to eighteen-year-old Lise Tréhot who would become the artist's principal model for the next six years. She appeared in more than twenty paintings, including *In Summer* (1868), *Bather with a Griffon Dog* (1870) and *Woman of Algiers* (or *Odalisque*) (see pages 8–9), all of which were accepted by the Salon. Lise was also Renoir's lover and in 1868 gave birth to a son, Pierre, who died in infancy; two years later she bore a daughter, Jeanne, who the couple gave up for adoption.

Although Renoir continued to support Jeanne throughout her life, he never publicly acknowledged her existence. Only a few trusted friends were told the secret so they could carry messages and money to Jeanne on Renoir's behalf. He made sure his daughter never risked discovery by writing to his home address, but arranged for her to contact him through an intermediary.

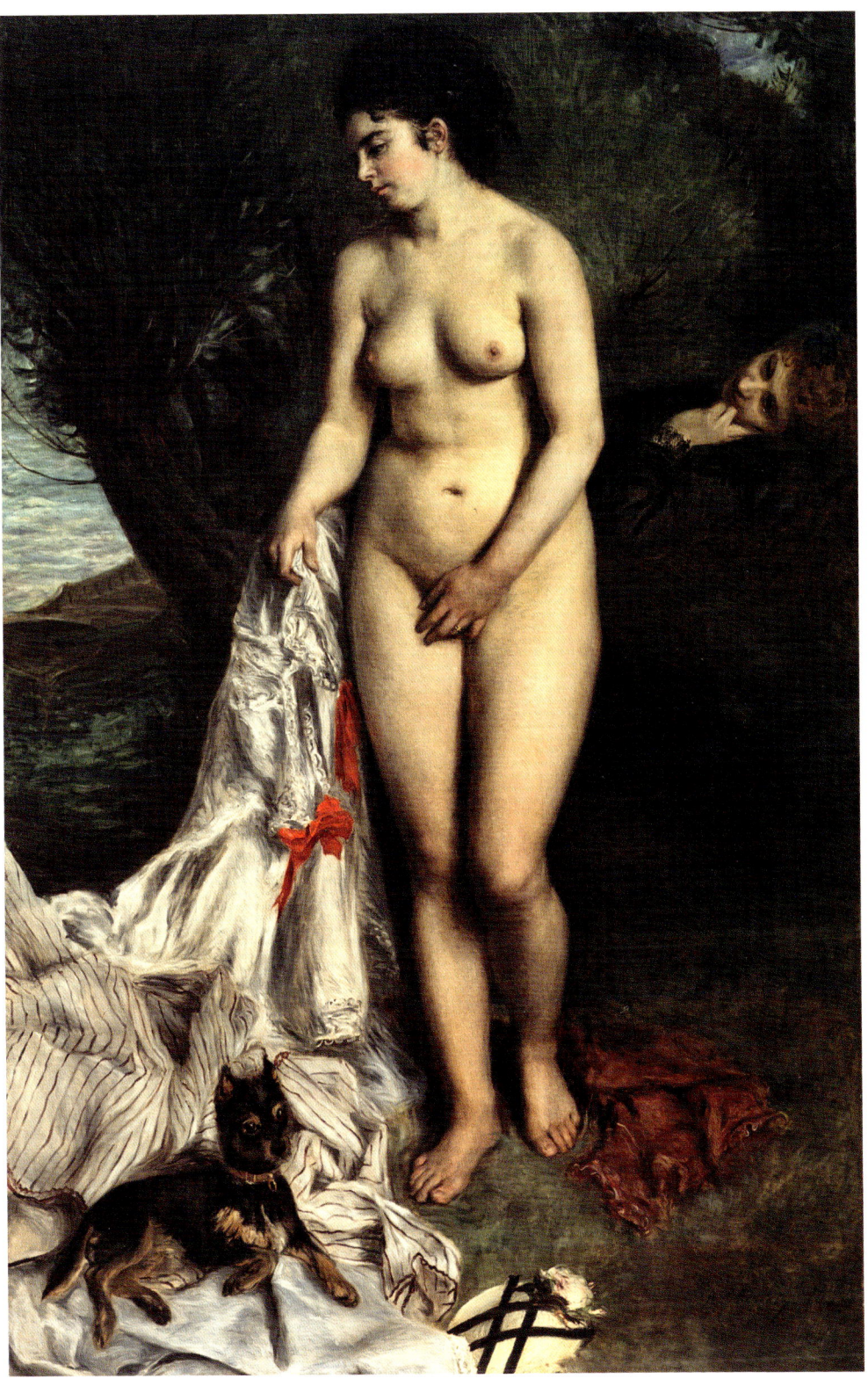

Bather with a Griffon Dog, 1870. Here Lise is portrayed more formally as a studio nude against a landscape. The influence of Courbet shows in the composition, the handling of the paint and the inclusion of a dog (one of his favourite animals). Renoir submitted the painting to the Salon of 1870, where it was accepted.

WAR

In July 1870, the Franco-Prussian War began. The group of young artists broke up as some of them enlisted to fight and others took refuge abroad. Tragically, Bazille – in Renoir's words, 'that pure-hearted gentle knight' – died in battle. The war ended in the devastating defeat of France and the overthrow of the empire of Napoleon III. France became a republic once more (the Third Republic) and its people counted the cost of a war that had resulted in a huge number of casualties – more than 138,000 killed and an even greater number wounded.

Renoir spent four months in a cavalry regiment in southwest France. He fell ill with dysentry, an infection which would kill many men during the war, but recovered and eventually returned to Paris.

In 1873 he moved to a small rented apartment in the Batignolles area of Paris, near Montmartre, with his younger brother Edmond (his relationship with Lise had ended the previous year when she left him for a wealthy architect). Renoir presented Lise with the first and last portraits he had painted of her, which she kept until her death in 1922. It appears that she and Renoir never contacted each other again.

The Swing, 1876. *Renoir made this painting in the garden of a house he was renting in Montmartre while working on* Dance at the Moulin de la Galette. *Both paintings feature a scene in dappled sunlight.* The Swing *is a disarmingly intimate piece. The woman is thought to be either the actress Jeanne Samary or the model Marguerite (Margot) Legrand; the men are believed to be Renoir's brother Edmond and the painter Norbert Goeneutte.*

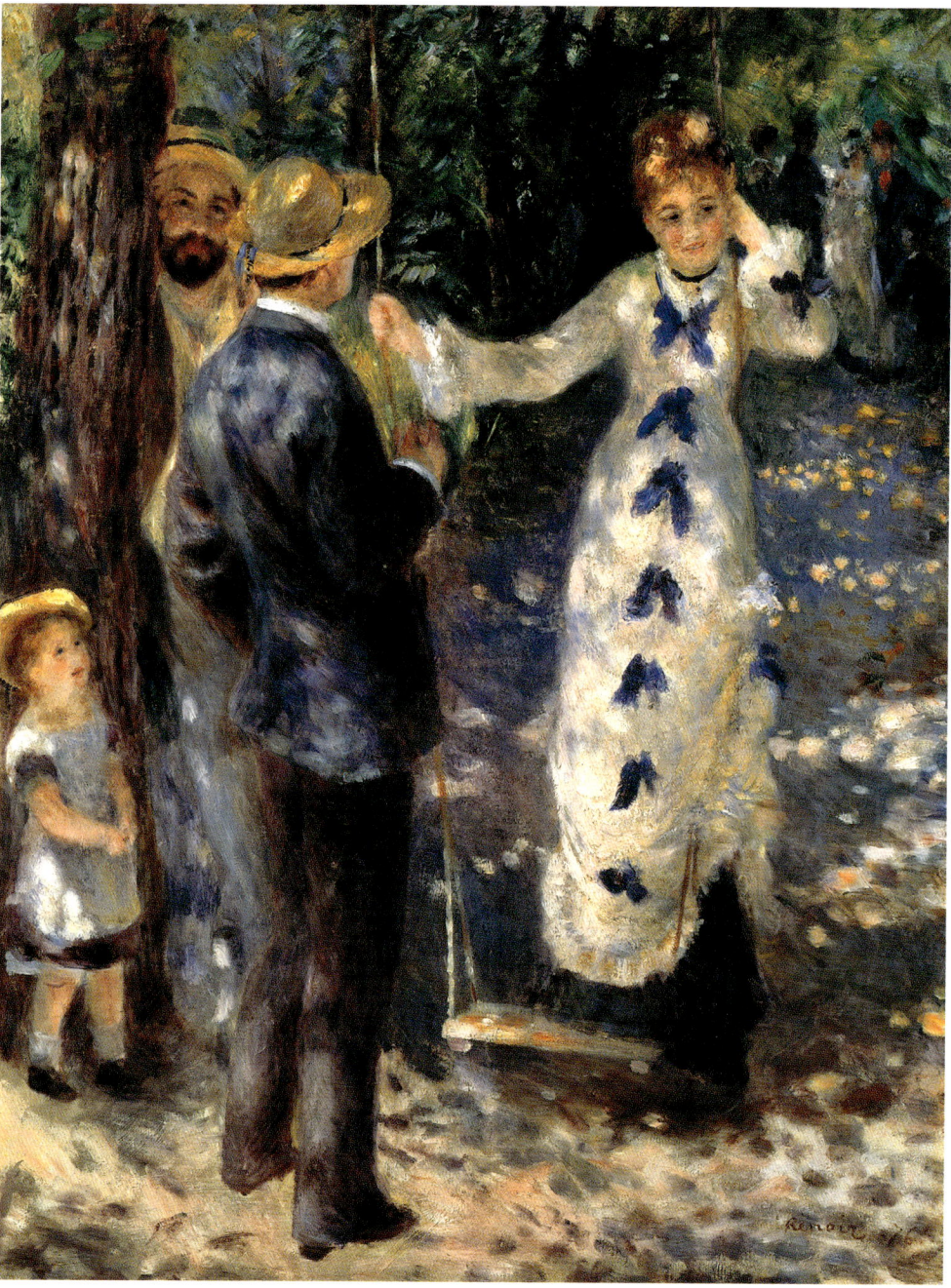

Renoir's close relationship with Jules Le Coeur and his family came to a sudden end in 1874, although the reasons why are unclear. Following the war, France was required to pay reparations to Prussia, which depressed the French economy and severely affected the art market. In such uncertain times, people were even less disposed to splash out on works of art in the new, strange Impressionistic style.

Despite his financial struggles and artistic challenges, Renoir's paintings remained joyful, many of them vibrantly recording scenes from modern daily life. Works such as *The Swing* and *Dance at the Moulin de la Galette* (see pages 32–3) are a testament to the artist's optimistic spirit.

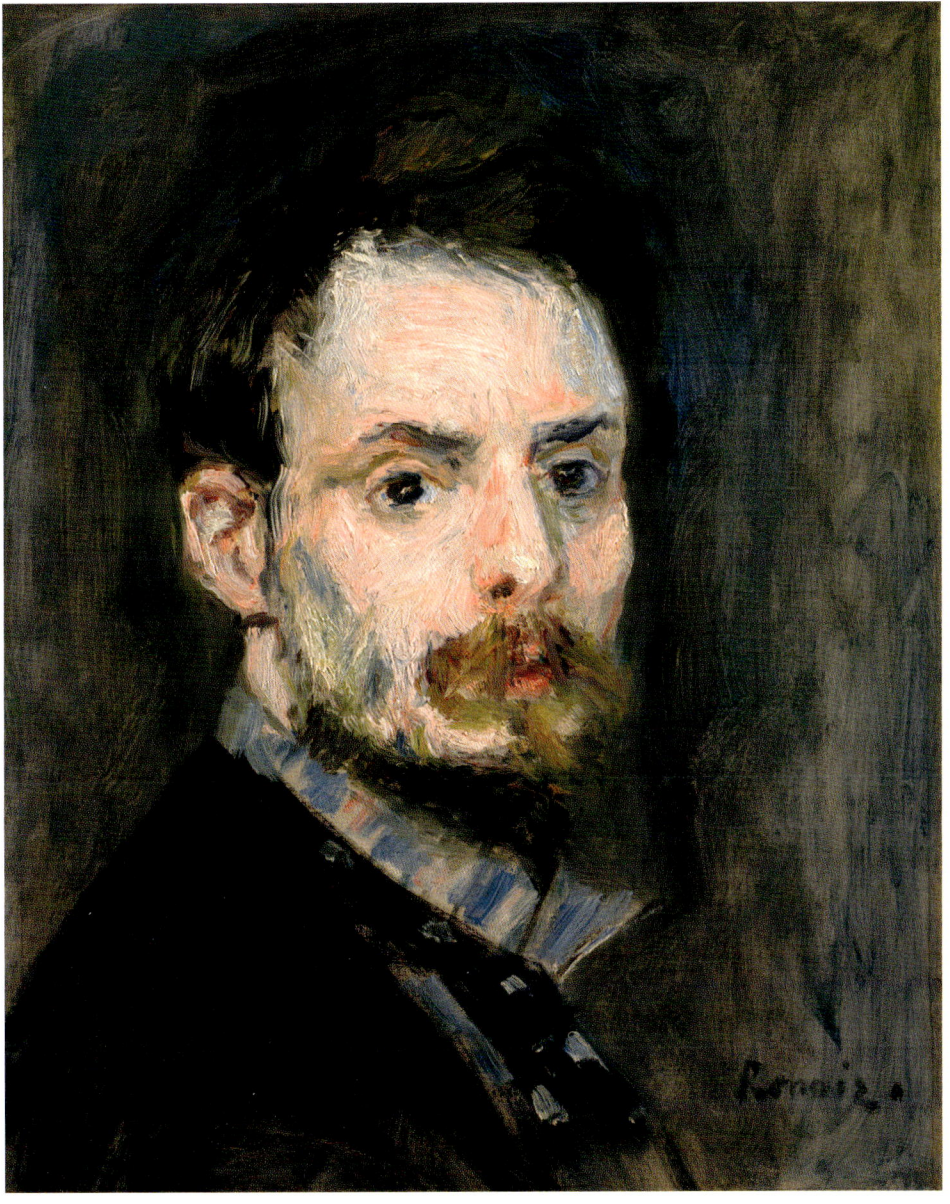

Self-portrait, 1875. *This picture shows Renoir experimenting with technique. The paint is almost transparent in some areas and applied thickly with deliberate brushstrokes in others. The artist's bohemian circumstances are signalled by his unkempt hair and beard, striped shirt, loosely knotted necktie and simple dark-coloured jacket.*

PAUL DURAND-RUEL

In 1872, a new patron emerged in the shape of Paul Durand-Ruel, an art dealer whom Monet and Pissarro had met in London during the war. He would become one of the most important figures in Impressionism, doing much to popularize and sell the new art. Following an introduction to Renoir, Durand-Ruel bought several of his paintings for a few hundred francs each, including *Le Pont des Arts, Paris* (1867, see page 34) and *Still Life with Peonies and Poppies* (1872). That same year he mounted one of the first exhibitions of Impressionist art (though the term had yet to be coined) at his gallery on London's Bond Street.

Durand-Ruel would eventually become an art dealer for most of the Barbizon and Impressionist artists apart from Cézanne whose work he considered too difficult, and he represented Renoir until the artist's death. He also helped to forge the careers of Degas, Manet, Monet, Morisot, Pissarro and Sisley, giving the artists financial as well as moral support. He took their work to New York, where his three sons ran an art gallery, and was pivotal in establishing Impressionist art in the USA.

Renoir had no doubts about his significance: 'Durand-Ruel was a missionary,' he wrote. 'It was our good fortune that his religion was painting.'

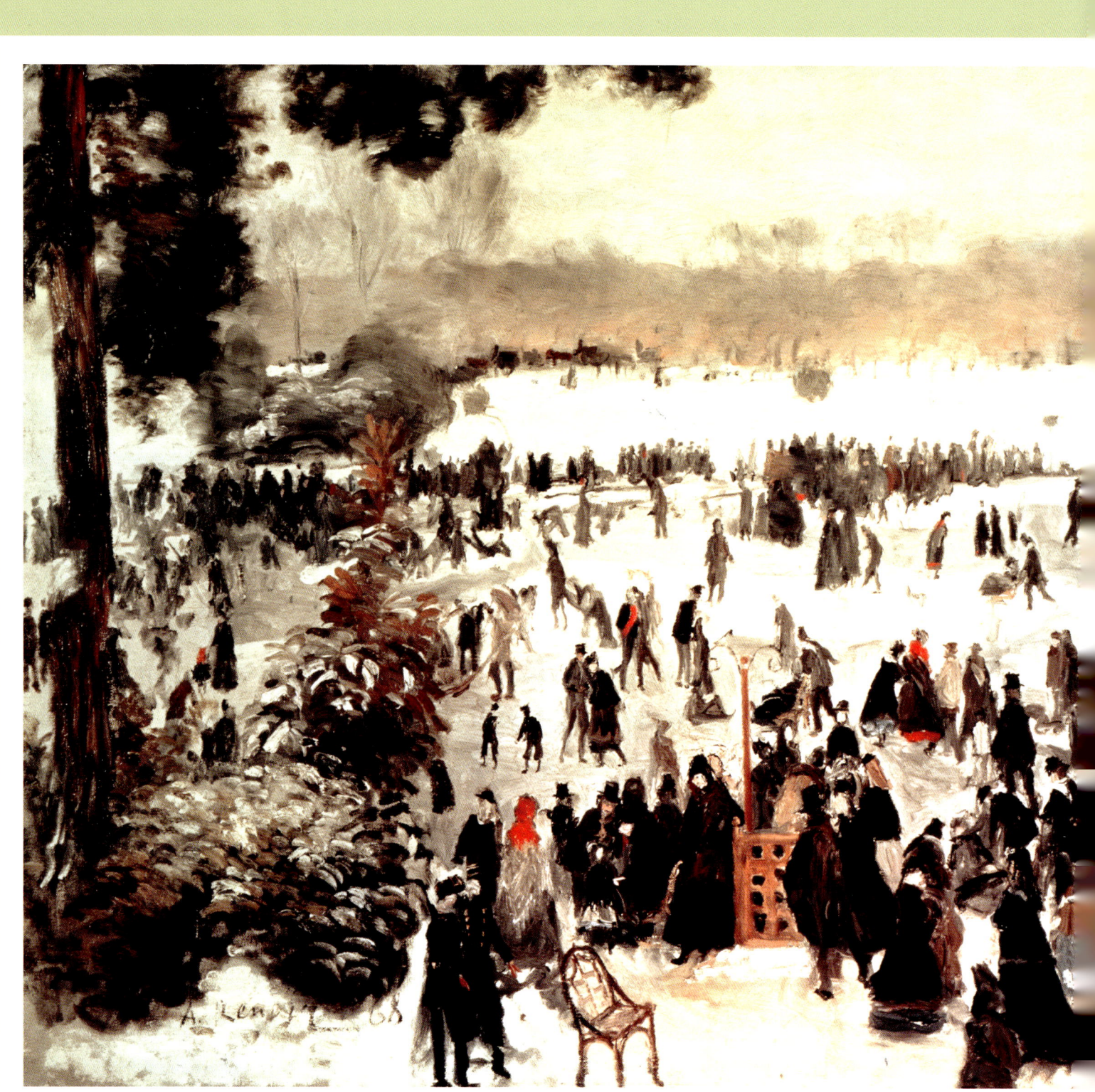

CHAPTER 2
Capturing Reality

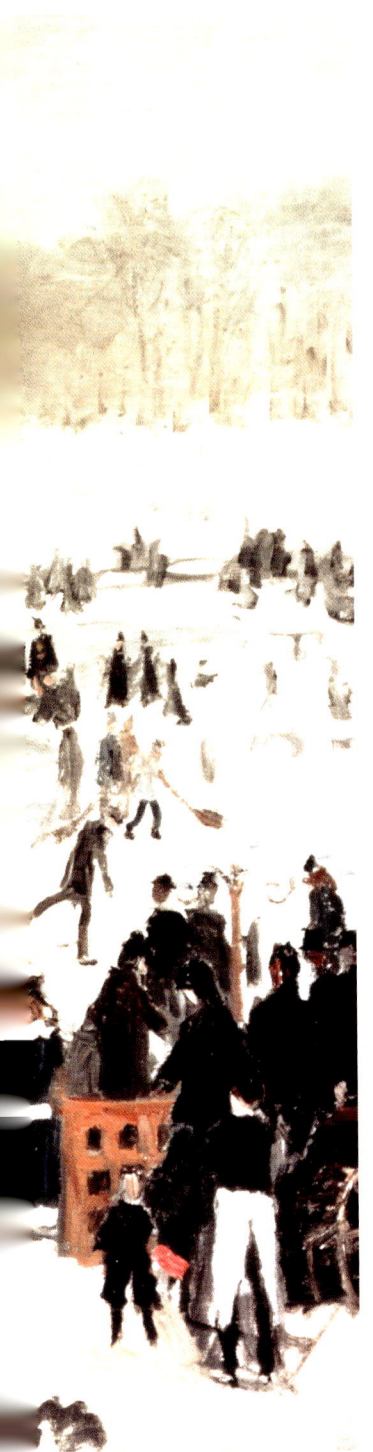

In 1873, encouraged by the support of Durand-Ruel and others and increasingly resentful of the scorn heaped upon their work by the establishment, the Impressionists made a monumental decision – to organize their own art show, separate from the Salon. Now known as the first Impressionist exhibition, it went by the title of the 'Société anonyme des artistes peintres, sculpteurs et graveurs' (Anonymous Society of Painters, Sculptors and Printmakers), and was staged between April and May 1874 at the premises of the photographer Nadar on Boulevard des Capucines, Paris.

A NEW TYPE OF ART SHOW

Crucially there was no restriction on entry. The invited artists could display whatever they liked, without the approval of an official board. There were 165 pieces on show, representing the work of thirty artists including Renoir, Pissarro, Monet, Sisley, Degas, Cézanne and Morisot. The only major omission was Manet, who chose not to exhibit. Despite the risks he was willing to take with his art and the outrage his paintings sometimes elicited, Manet had ambitions of bourgeois success and believed that the best way to progress was by continuing to exhibit officially, at the Salon.

Skaters in the Bois de Boulogne, 1868. *The January weather in 1868 was cold enough for the Seine to freeze over. Renoir's painting, made* en plein air, *shows people skating on a lake in the Bois de Boulogne, a public park that had only been completed ten years earlier. The scene is painted from a high viewpoint, with bold brushwork.*

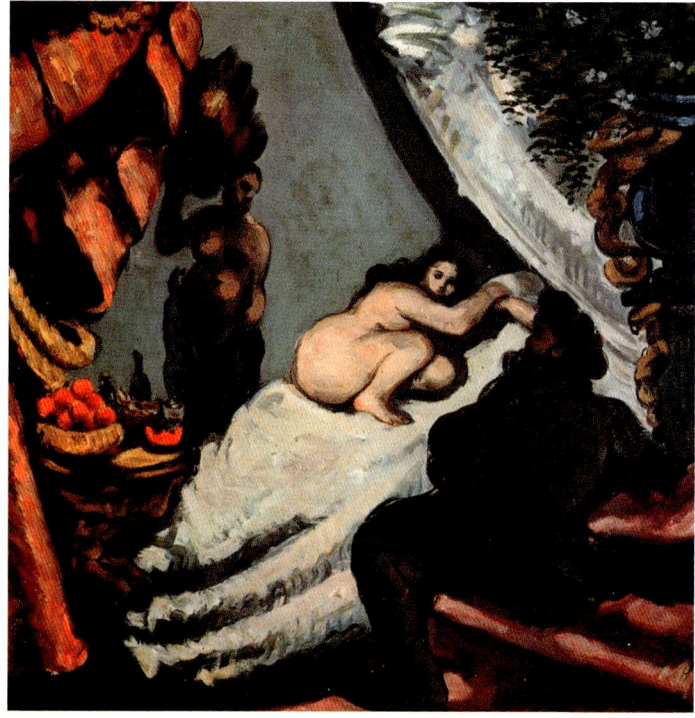

A Modern Olympia, *Paul Cézanne, 1870. A naked goddess reclining with a servant in attendance is a classical subject in art, but in 1863 Édouard Manet caused a scandal when he painted the goddess as a prostitute. Cézanne's painting, made seven years later, references Manet's original, including the presence of a dark-skinned attendant. It also features a male spectator with his back to the viewer.*

'ART IS ABOUT EMOTION; IF ART NEEDS TO BE EXPLAINED, IT IS NO LONGER ART.'

Pierre-Auguste Renoir

The show was derided by the critics. In particular, Cézanne's *A Modern Olympia* (1874) was singled out for scorn – the weekly illustrated review *L'Artiste* described it as leaving 'even the most courageous gasping for breath'. The same reviewer also said that Cézanne gave 'the impression of being a sort of madman, painting in a state of delirium tremens'. The author of an article in *La Presse* supported the notion of intellectual freedom in principle, but went on to state with withering sarcasm: 'Smear a panel with grey, plonk some black and yellow lines across it, and the enlightened few, the visionaries, exclaim: Isn't that a perfect impression of the bois de Meudon?' However, a critic in *Le Siecle* was more generous, saying: '. . . there is talent here, even much talent.'

Amid the barrage of insults, Renoir's *La Loge* (*The Theatre Box*) won some measure of critical praise. The painting features as its subject a fashionable Parisian couple seated in a box at the theatre. Dressed in the latest finery and with her opera glasses lowered in her gloved hand, the woman meets the gaze of the viewer, while behind her the gentleman trains his glasses on the audience in the balcony. In this snapshot of bourgeois urban life, the couple are both observed and observing and Renoir invites the viewer to wonder what the relationship between the two of them might be. In the early twentieth century, *La Loge* was acquired for many thousands of pounds by the Courtauld Institute in London, where it still resides; it is now regarded as a masterpiece.

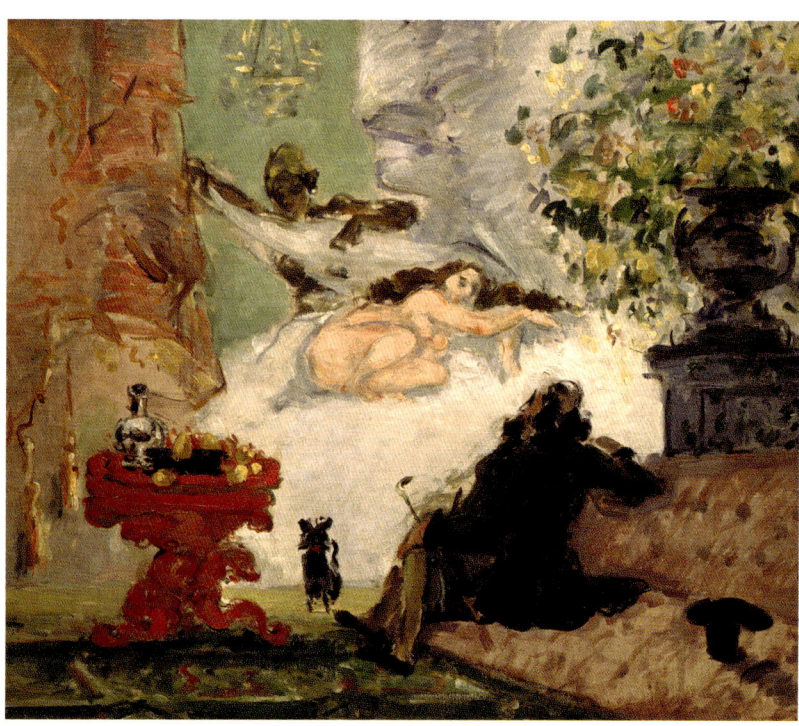

A Modern Olympia, *Paul Cézanne, 1874. Four years later, the impact of Impressionism shows in Cézanne's lighter palette and softer colours. The curtain on the left gives a theatrical effect, suggesting it may just have been pulled aside to expose Olympia to the spectator.*

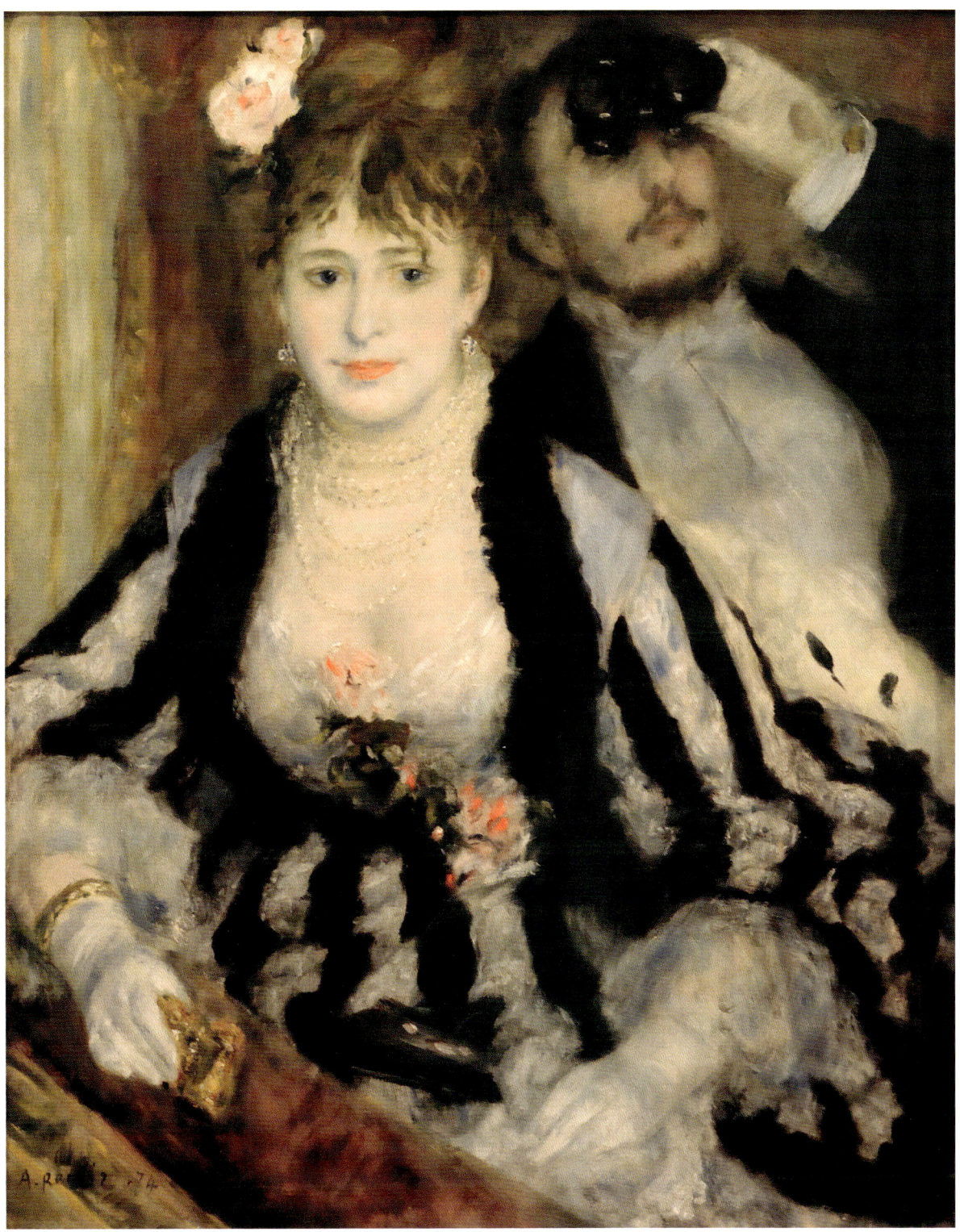

*La Loge, 1874. Included in the first Impressionist show, La Loge was
Renoir's principal exhibit. The male figure is his brother, Edmond, and
the woman is a Montmartre model named Nini Lopez. Theatre played
a huge part in the cultural life of Paris, but Renoir chooses to focus
on a couple in the audience rather than the actors on the stage.*

IMPRESSIONISM IS BORN

The exhibition occasioned the naming of this new group of artists. In an article for *Le Charivari*, the critic Louis Leroy ridiculed a now celebrated painting by Claude Monet entitled *Impression, Soleil Levant* (*Impression, Sunrise*): 'A preliminary drawing for a wallpaper pattern is more finished than this seascape,' he wrote. He called his review 'Exposition des Impressionnistes' (Exhibition of the Impressionists), a deliberate insult which he hoped would help to discredit the artists' work. But Leroy accidentally created their identity – undaunted, the young rebels took up the name 'Impressionism' as a badge of honour.

The Impressionists founded a joint-stock company to finance the exhibition, but it made a huge loss. Renoir persuaded them that they could recoup their money by staging an auction the following year. Held on 24 March 1875 and organized with the assistance of Durand-Ruel, it was a modest success, and most of the artists made sales. But the continued negative reactions of critics and public alike kept prices low. Renoir sold twenty paintings for between 50 and 300 francs each, much less than the 1,000–2,000 francs a new artist expected to fetch when selling through the Salon, and a feeble amount compared with the 10,000–20,000 francs commanded by well-known artists.

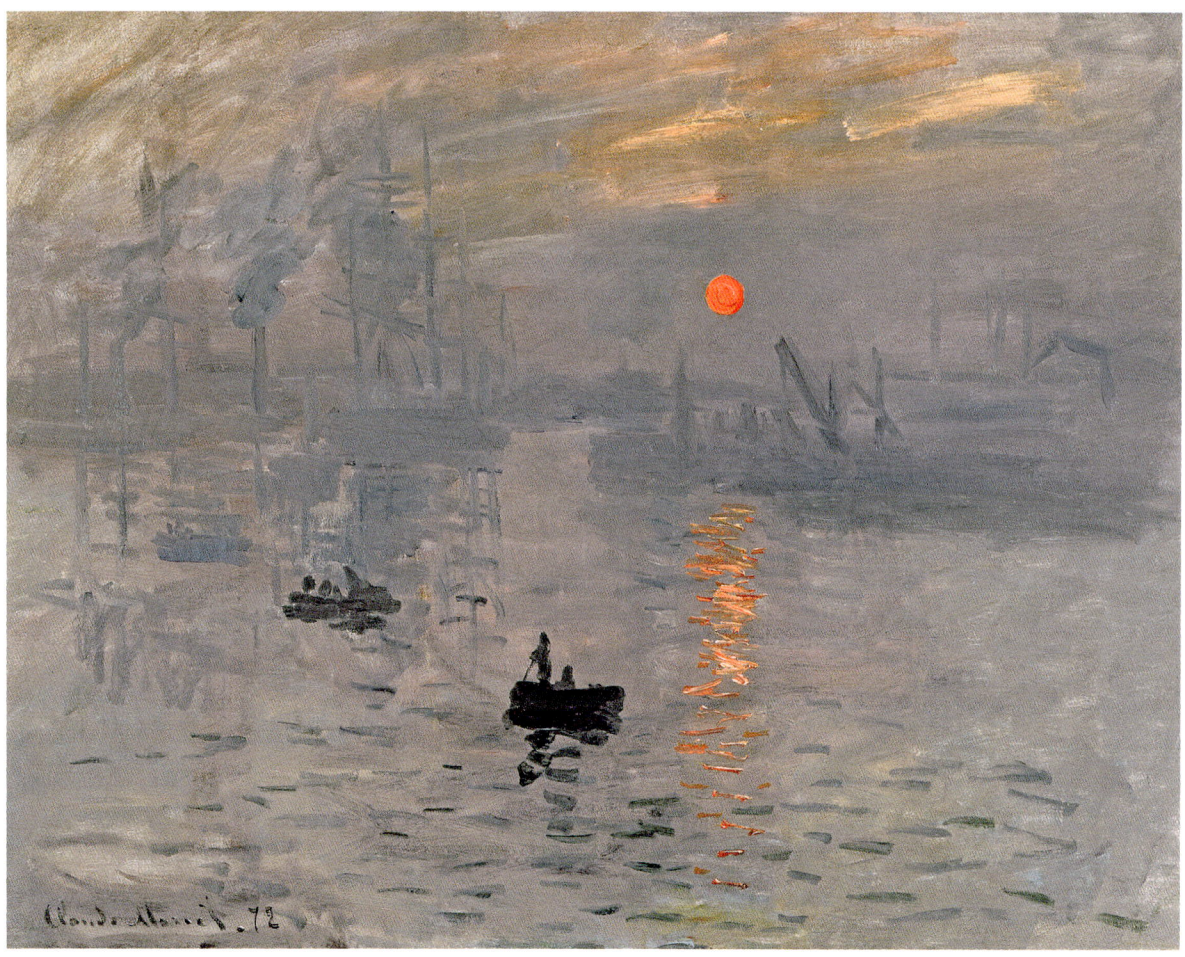

Impression, Sunrise, *Claude Monet, 1872. The cool blues and greys of Monet's painting of the harbour at Le Havre convey a landscape shrouded in early morning mist. The effect of sunlight on the water is portrayed in rapid brushstrokes and the composition, although simple, is dramatically effective. The act of expressing an individual's response to nature was a goal of Impressionist art.*

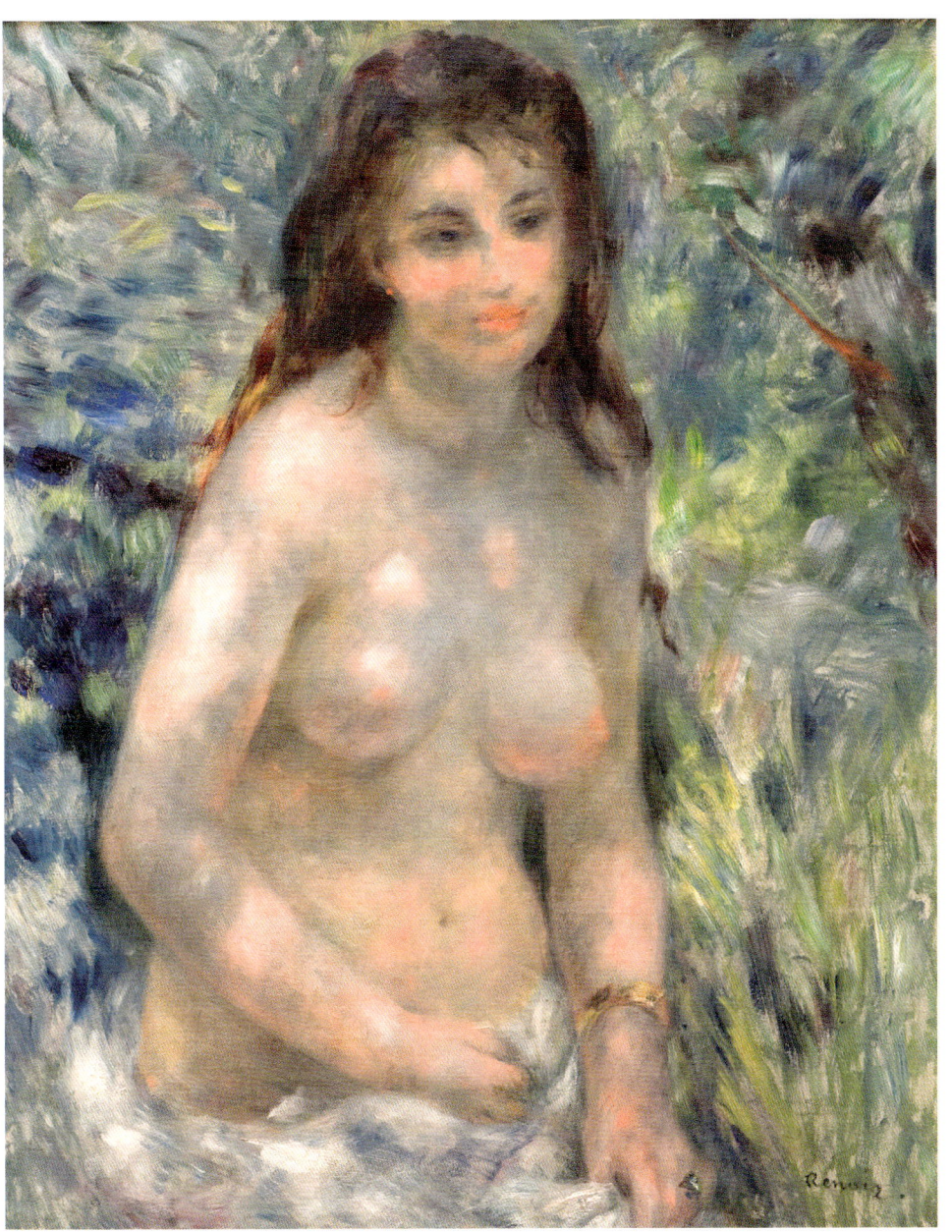

Study. Torso, Effect of Sunlight, 1875–6. Dappled light and simple strokes of colour in the background are reflected on the model's luminous skin, merging her figure into the natural world. The Impressionists' approach to the practice of en plein air *painting shocked the critics.*

THE SECOND EXHIBITION

Despite the problems of the first exhibition, the Impressionists refused to change their approach or defer to the opinion of critics or the Salon.

In April 1876 they staged a second exhibition, called 'la Deuxième Exposition de Peinture' (the Second Exhibition of Painting). This involved just twenty artists, but more artworks (252 in total) and some new faces, including the wealthy Parisian artist Gustave Caillebotte, invited by Renoir after the two men had met at the first exhibition. A trained lawyer and engineer, Caillebotte took up painting following the Franco-Prussian War. In 1874 he gave up work altogether when he inherited his father's fortune. Thereafter he focused on his art and on supporting the art of others (he bought several of Renoir's works). At the second exhibition, Caillebotte exhibited eight paintings while Renoir showed eighteen, the majority of them portraits, including his portrait of Frédéric Bazille (see page 17).

The critics were no more complimentary about the second exhibition than they had been about the first. One of Renoir's works, *Study. Torso, Effect of Sunlight*, a painting executed at the height of his Impressionist period, shows a semi-naked woman emerging from a verdant background, the sunlight shining through the leaves of the trees above her and making a dappled pattern on her skin. The painting provoked the ire of writer and art critic Albert Wolff who wrote, with an astounding lack of perception, in *Le Figaro*: 'Try to explain to M. Renoir that a woman's torso is not a mass of decomposing flesh with green and purple spots that indicate the state of total putrefaction in a corpse!' But Renoir's work also received some positive notices, among which were reviews by the Swedish playwright and novelist Auguste Strindberg and the poet and critic Stéphane Mallarmé.

EXPLAINING IMPRESSIONISM

In spite of general disapproval by the press and public, the Impressionist artists sold enough paintings at the second exhibition to stage a third in 1877, entitled 'Exposition des Impressionnistes'. Renoir, Caillebotte, Pissarro and Monet formed the hanging committee. By this point, Renoir had come to believe that hostility to Impressionist art was because the critics and public simply didn't understand it. He reasoned that if it could be explained to them clearly, they would be more appreciative, so he employed the young writer Georges Rivière to help launch a weekly newspaper to promote the exhibition. The result, entitled *L'Impressionniste: journal d'art* (*The Impressionist: Art Journal*), marked the first time the group had officially adopted the name 'Impressionists'. It included fiercely argued articles that sang the praises of Impressionist art and attacking its opponents. One article, about Cézanne, maintained that the critics were on the wrong side of history. Perhaps unsurprisingly, these impassioned arguments didn't make the unconverted any more minded to change their views.

The third exhibition, held at an apartment rented by Caillebotte, displayed a total of 230 works by eighteen artists. Renoir showed twenty-one paintings, the majority of which were portraits, but he also included two major scenes of modern Parisians at leisure – *The Swing* (see page 24) and *Dance at the Moulin de la Galette*. The exhibition was better attended than the first two had been, with visitors numbering about 500 each day, though many of them came in a spirit of derision rather than appreciation. While Rivière did his best to whip up enthusiasm and two critics wrote positive reviews, the supporters were far outnumbered by the critical voices.

When the exhibition ended, the artists arranged an auction at the Hôtel Drouot on 28 May. Renoir put forward twenty-one works and sold sixteen of them for a total price of 2,005 francs.

Dance at the Moulin de la Galette, 1876. A masterpiece of early Impressionism, Renoir's painting shows Sunday afternoon at a popular venue, an open-air dancehall and café close to his home in Montmartre. In the foreground right, his friends gather around a table; other friends and models feature in the background throng. Renoir bathes his figures in sunlight and shadow, breaking up the composition with patches of natural and artificial light. The whole effect is one of life in motion with all its gaiety and colour, yet with a touching sense of its fleeting nature. This was Renoir's most ambitious figure painting to date, a study of intimate human relationships rendered on a grand scale.

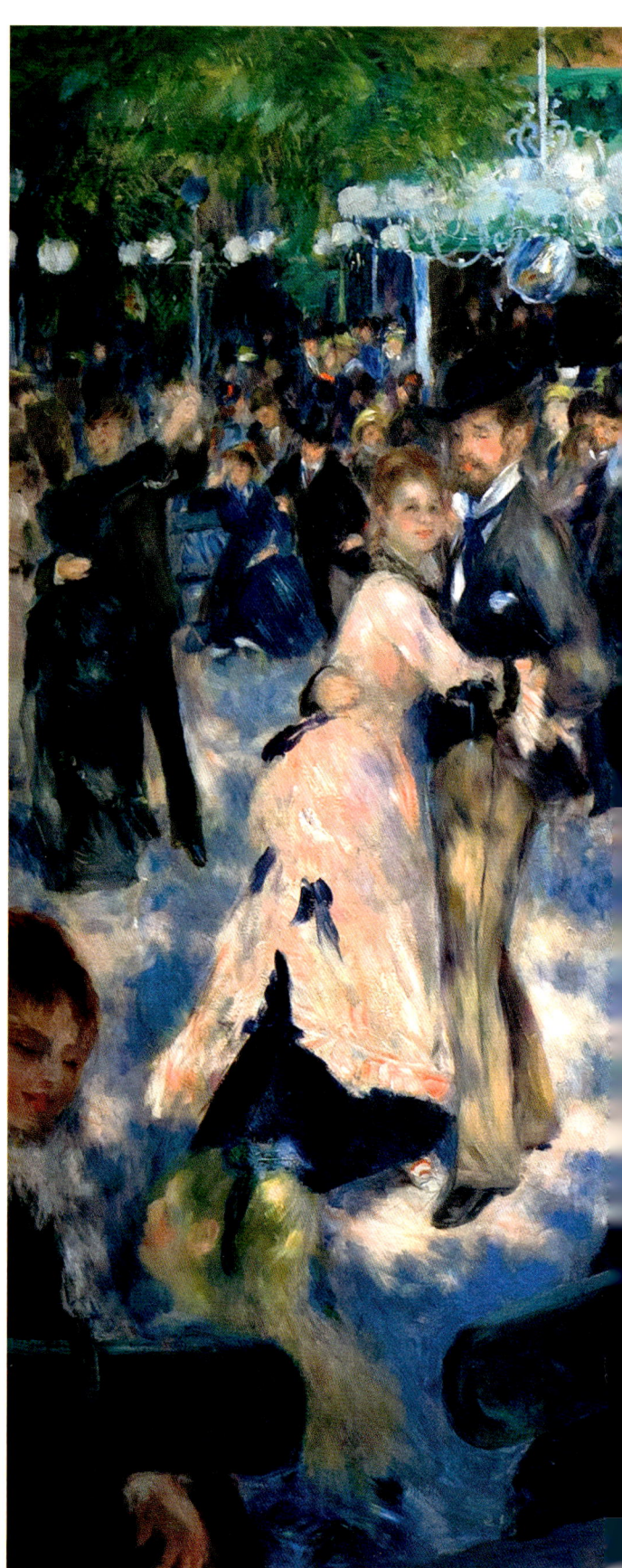

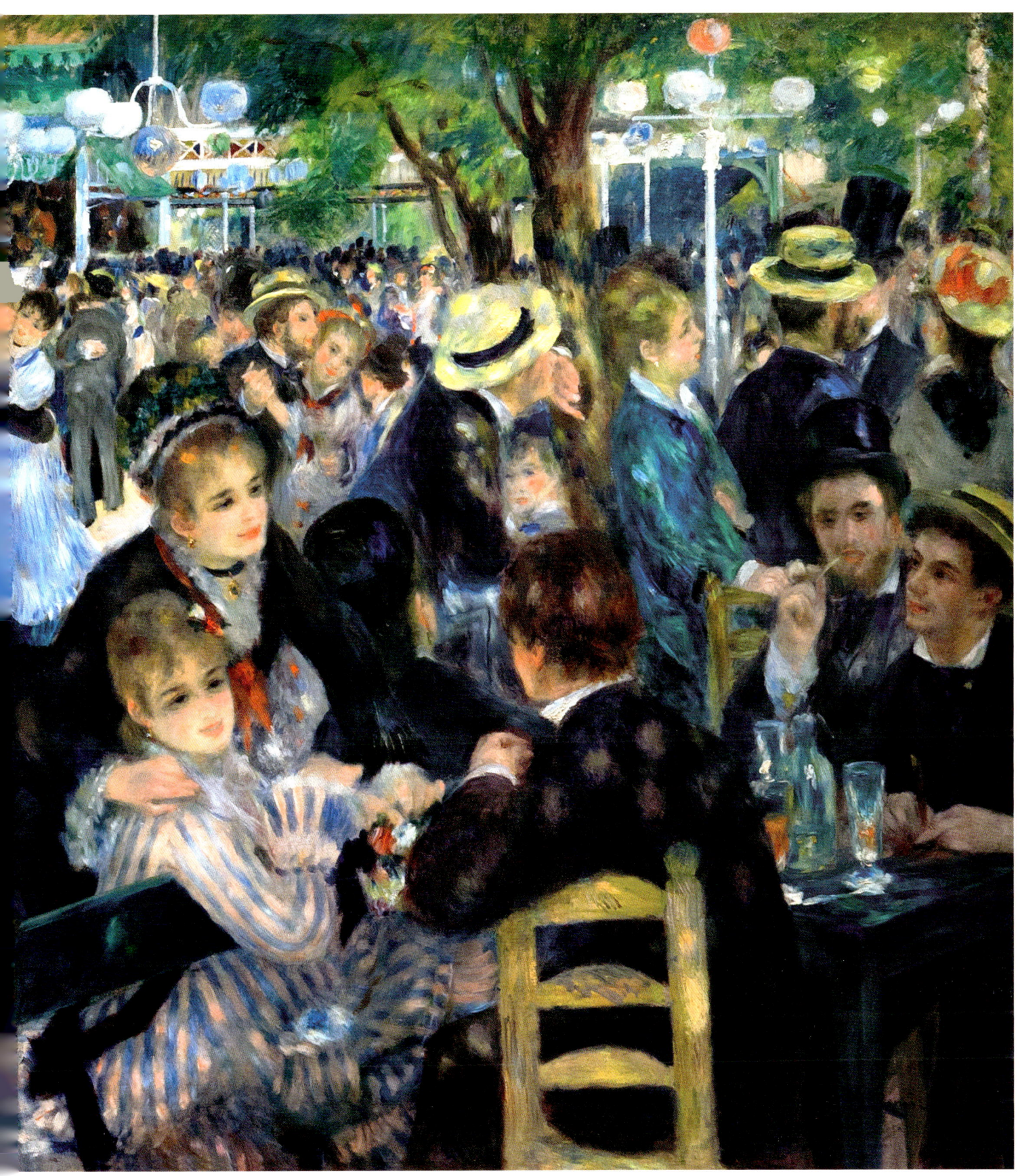

CITYSCAPES

In the 1860s, the young artists of the Impressionist movement reinvented the genre of the cityscape which had fallen out of fashion during the previous century. Their enthusiasm was prompted by a vast public works programme instigated by Emperor Napoleon III in the mid-1850s which resulted in the radical transformation of Paris. Under the guidance of Georges-Eugène Haussmann, prefect of the Seine department, acres of narrow, crooked streets dating from medieval times were replaced by the wide boulevards and sweeping vistas that still characterize Paris today. Grand buildings such as the Opéra and the Louvre stood among the new avenues and squares. Splendid public parks such as the Bois de Boulogne offered artists with innovative ideas a whole new cityscape to explore.

Renoir had spent his childhood in this city, in one of the impoverished areas scheduled for demolition. His family had been displaced twice to make room for the improvements; however, unlike a lot of other working-class Parisians, they were not relocated to the outer suburbs but found a new home at 23 Rue Argenteuil, not far from the Louvre.

Despite improvements to public health and well-being, including a more than four-fold increase in the water supply and efforts to ensure that everyone was within a ten-minute walk of a public park, Haussmann's revolution didn't win universal favour. Some people, including Renoir, believed some of the essential character of Paris had been lost.

Le Pont des Arts, 1867. As well as showing events on the quayside, Renoir's view hints at what is happening behind the artist's back, as shadows of pedestrians flit across the bottom of the painting. In the middle distance, animating the cityscape, people disembark from one of the new boats transporting visitors to the international exposition, the second world's fair, taking place at a great military parade ground along the Seine. Renoir's painting is of stop no. 8, from which visitors could also cross the bridge to the new Louvre. Tantalizingly, Renoir has chosen to omit this building from his composition.

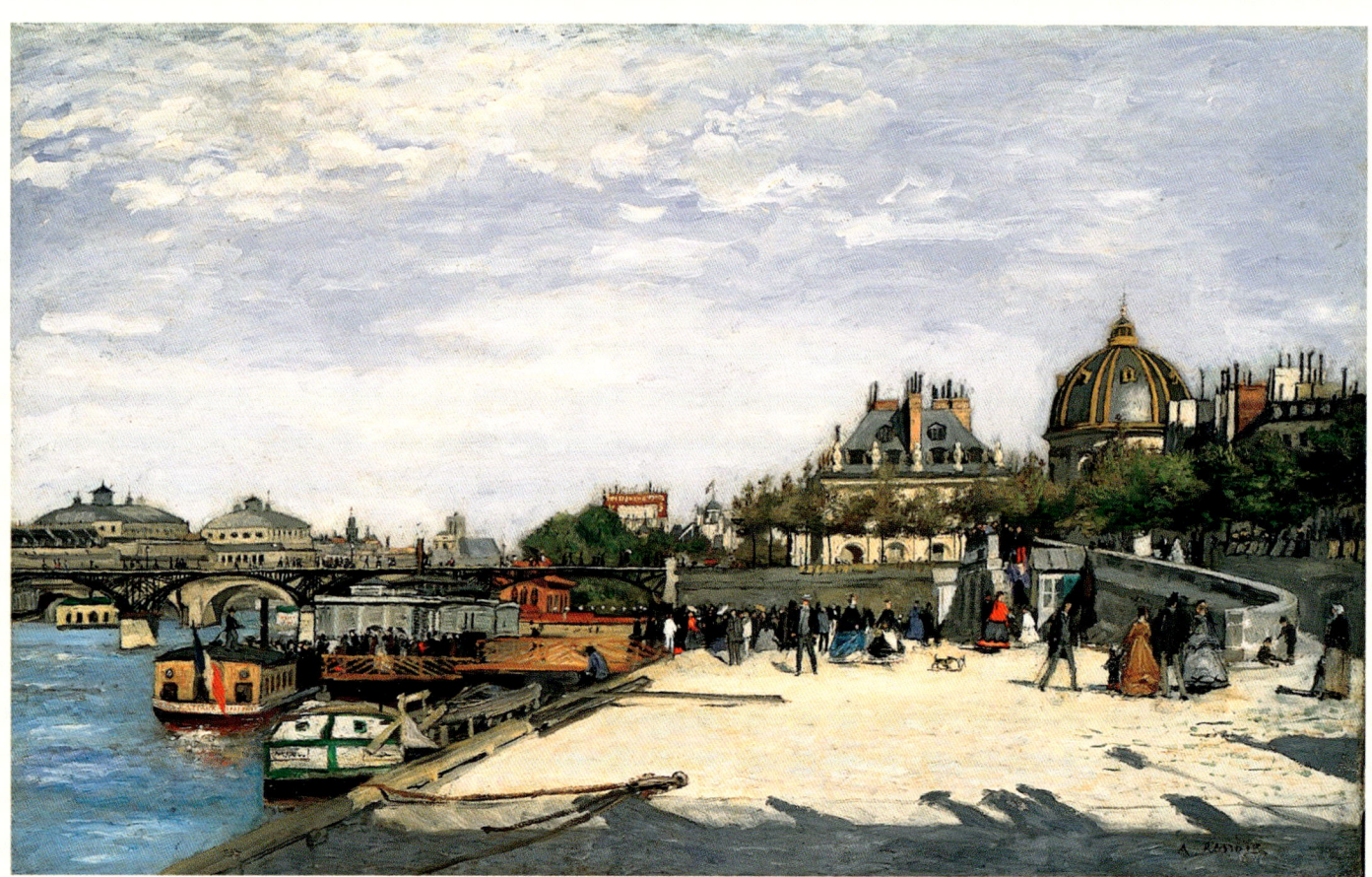

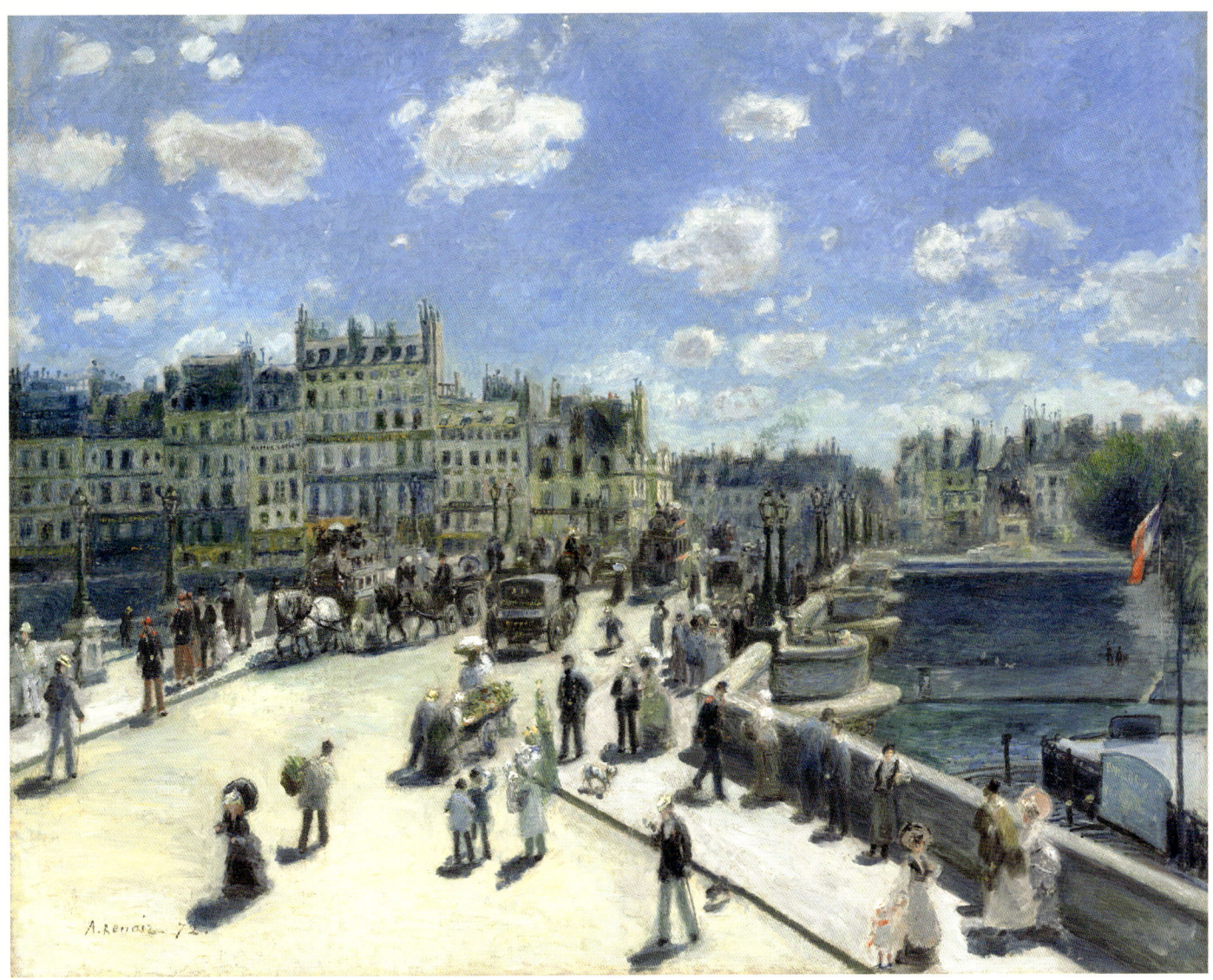

Despite this, a number of his paintings show the beauty and grandeur of the revitalized city. In 1867, Paris staged an international exposition celebrating the different cultures and achievements of forty-two nations from around the world. Monet, Manet and Renoir all painted views of the capital during that year; Renoir's works included *The Champs-Elysées during the Fair of 1867* and *Le Pont des Arts* (see facing page).

In the kind of scenes he painted with such evident enjoyment, Renoir showed ordinary Parisians experiencing their sparkling new environment under a summer sky. A later painting, *Pont Neuf, Paris*, shows people crossing the city's oldest bridge. It is executed with such depth and clarity that almost equal weight is given to the woman and child with a red sash in the foreground and to the equestrian statue of King Henry IV in the background (above them in the painting). Although alienated from the arts establishment – and the establishment in general – the Impressionists clearly found the energy of a rejuvenated city irresistible and they grasped the chance to paint it *en plein air*, almost as a heightened visual record of historical events.

Pont Neuf, Paris, 1872. *Painted a year after the end of the Franco-Prussian War,* Pont Neuf *shows pedestrians and traffic (motorized and horsedrawn) on Paris's oldest bridge across the Seine. The short shadows indicate that this is a midday scene. Renoir's brother Edmond explained that the artist had gained access to the upper floor of a café for a day to make the painting. Edmond had persuaded some of the pedestrians to stand still for a while so Renoir could paint them.*

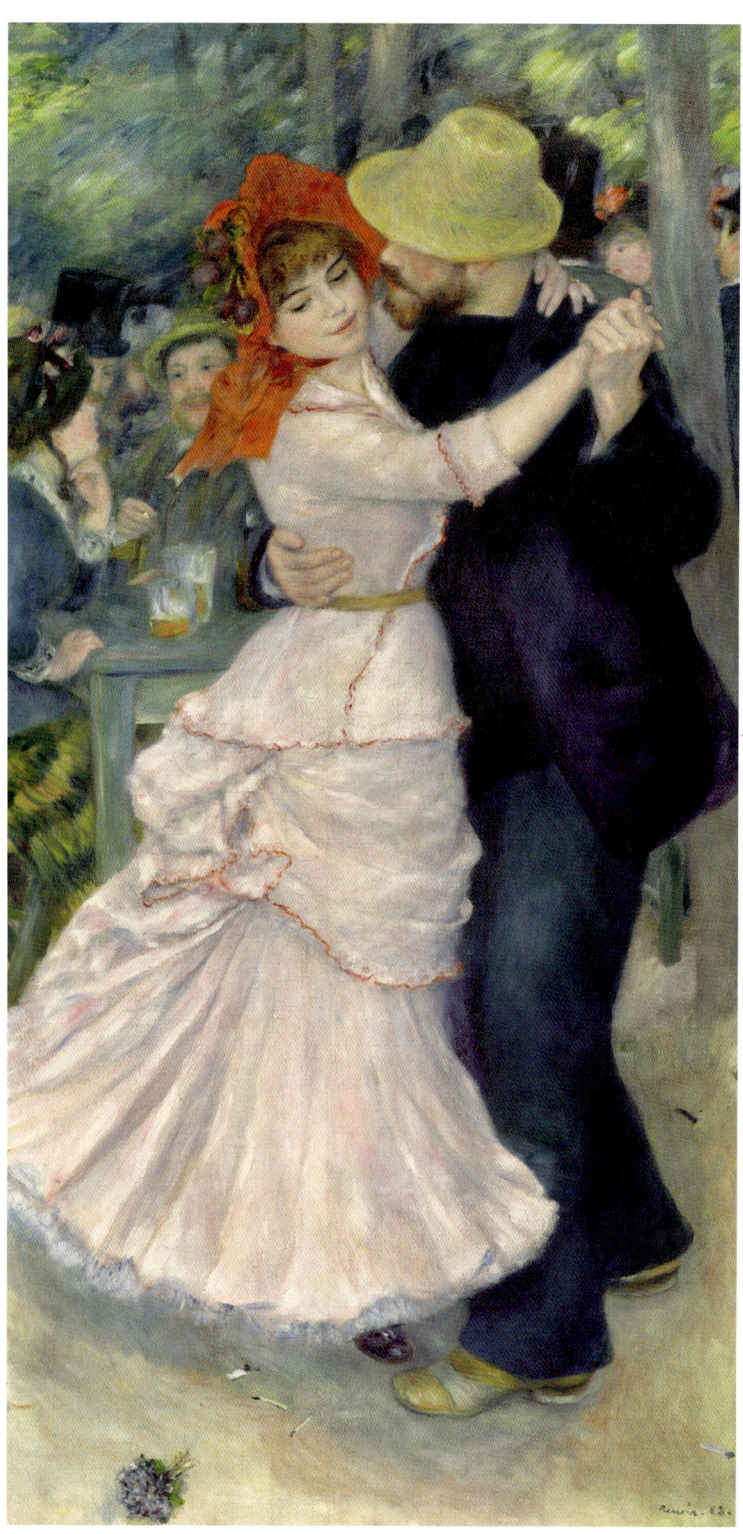

Dance at Bougival, 1883. *The open-air cafés in the village of Bougival on the Seine in the outer suburbs of Paris were favourite places for working-class Parisians to relax. The blurred background and vibrant colours that Renoir uses in this painting suggest movement and delight. The male dancer's gaze, intent on his companion, gives a sense of energy and desire.*

BACK TO THE SALON

The third Impressionist show was regarded as a disaster, so the artists decided not to mount another the following year. When a fourth exhibition was proposed for 1879, Renoir decided not to show any paintings, believing his career would be better served by a return to submitting works to the Salon. (Artists exhibiting paintings at the Salon weren't allowed to exhibit with the Impressionists at the same time.) Cézanne and Sisley followed Renoir's lead, but Degas was angered because he thought the Impressionists should remain united to their cause.

Although Renoir's work continued to be inspired by Impressionism, his return to the Salon marked a turning point in his career as he began to consider pursuing other styles of art.

NEW PORTRAIT STYLE

Between 1878 and 1884, Renoir produced what would become some of his most famous and celebrated works, including *Luncheon of the Boating Party* (1881), *Dance at Bougival* (1881) and *Dance in the City* (1883). These scenes of happy social events seemed to be the epitome of what he wanted to achieve – atmospheric, tender and colourful depictions of the people he loved. But he concluded that he could never make a living out of these Impressionistic scenes of daily life and pragmatically decided to concentrate on portraiture instead. There was a problem with this, however – most of Renoir's clients wanted exact likenesses of themselves, not blurred impressions. Competition in this field was intense, particularly as photography was becoming popular. Renoir realized that he would have to adapt his style. He began by using less visible brushstrokes and more restrained colours, while retaining the luminosity of the Impressionists' palette. This new approach succeeded and he found himself at last in receipt of a regular income. Unlike many of his contemporaries, Renoir was always a 'working' artist who needed to sell his paintings if he was to survive. Occasionally this meant having to compromise and work conscientiously to a brief.

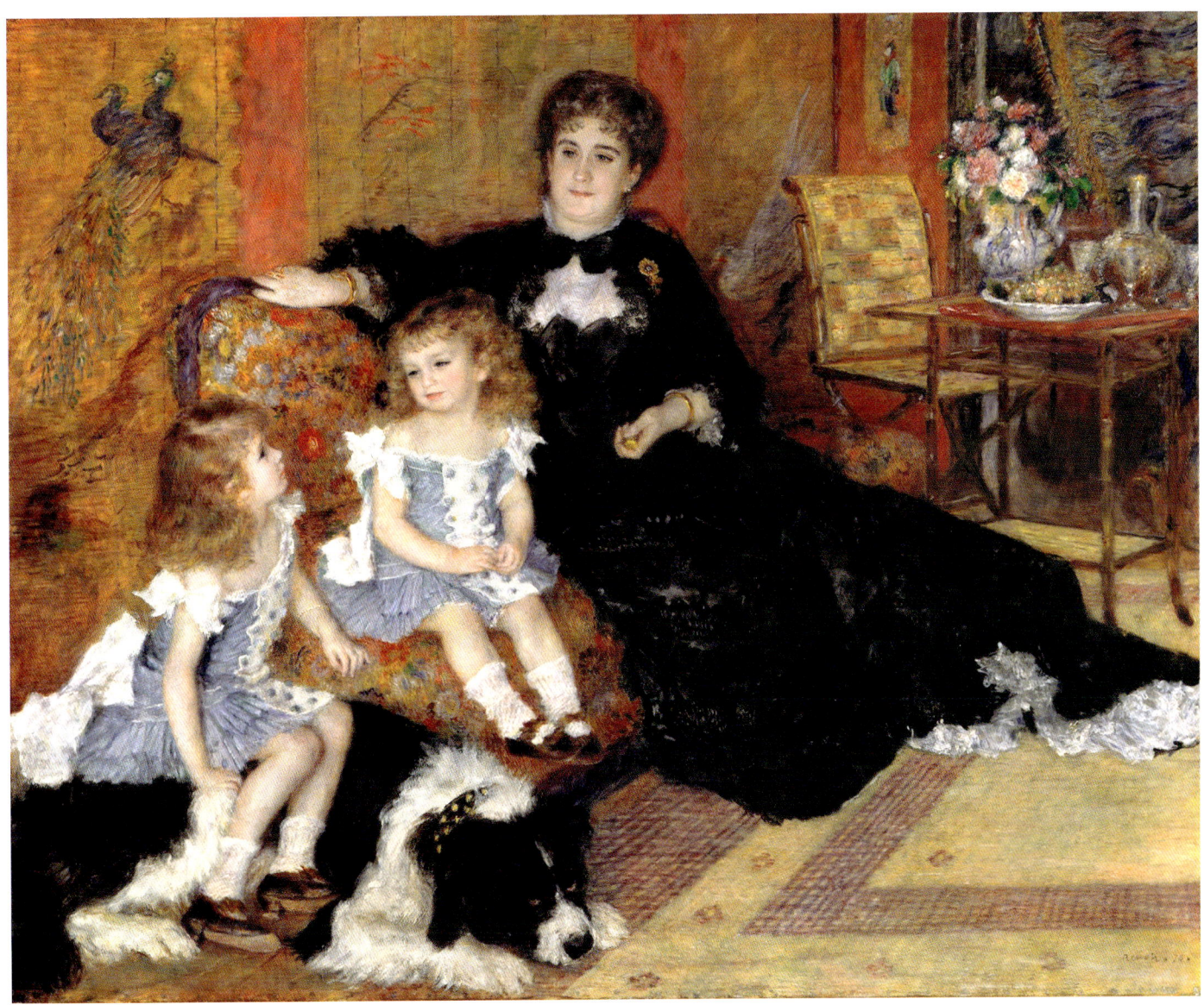

THE SUCCESS OF MADAME CHARPENTIER

One of Renoir's first portraits in his new 'Realist Impressionist' style, *Madame Charpentier and Her Children*, helped to set him on the road to success. He had met the influential book publisher, Georges Charpentier, and his wife Marguerite at the 1875 Impressionists' auction, where they had bought three of his works. Between 1876 and 1880, Charpentier commissioned Renoir to paint several portraits of his family. The first one shows Marguerite Charpentier attired in an elegant black gown, seated in their comfortable home alongside her two children. Her daughter Georgette is perched on the family dog while her son Paul sits next to his mother on the sofa. The children wear identical clothes and Paul has his hair long, as was the fashion for boys at the time. Delighted with the painting, Marguerite introduced Renoir to several of her friends, some of whom commissioned portraits from him.

Madame Charpentier and Her Children, 1878. Renoir required forty sittings to complete this work. The result is a successful fusion of Impressionist and classical portrait painting. In the Impressionist style, the relaxed, informal pose of the family describes its emotional dynamic. The figures are set against a carefully rendered and detailed background, with the trappings of bourgeois comfort handsomely painted in the classical style.

RENOIR BY THE SEA

The diplomat and banker Paul Berard was a collector of Renoir's work. He introduced the artist to similarly affluent prospective buyers and was an important patron and friend. Renoir spent time at the Berard home in Paris and at Wargemont, their country estate in Normandy; at the latter he was free to paint as he pleased and completed portraits of the Berard family as well as several seascapes.

The Berard estate was situated near the village of Berneval-sur-Mer, outside Dieppe, and encompassed part of the Normandy shoreline. Renoir loved painting the sea and the coast (from which, with traditional artist's licence, he removed evidence of unsightly buildings). He clearly felt liberated by the action of painting for pure relaxation, and this is evident in the animated scenes he produced.

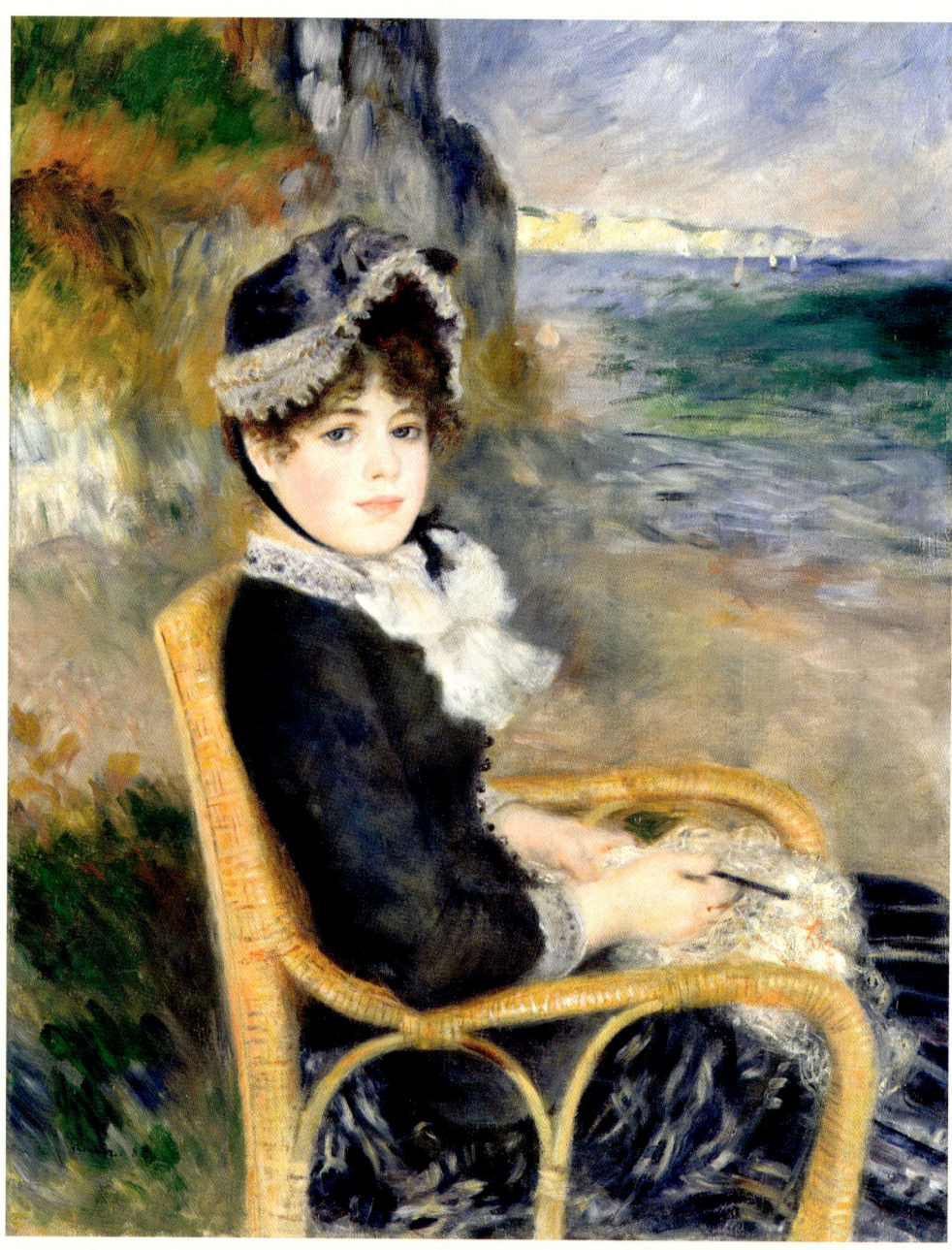

By the Seashore, 1883. It is believed that Renoir posed Aline Charigot (see page 41) in his studio for this painting, with a background that may be of the Normandy coast. The paint application on the face is in the more classical style, while the background is freely handled.

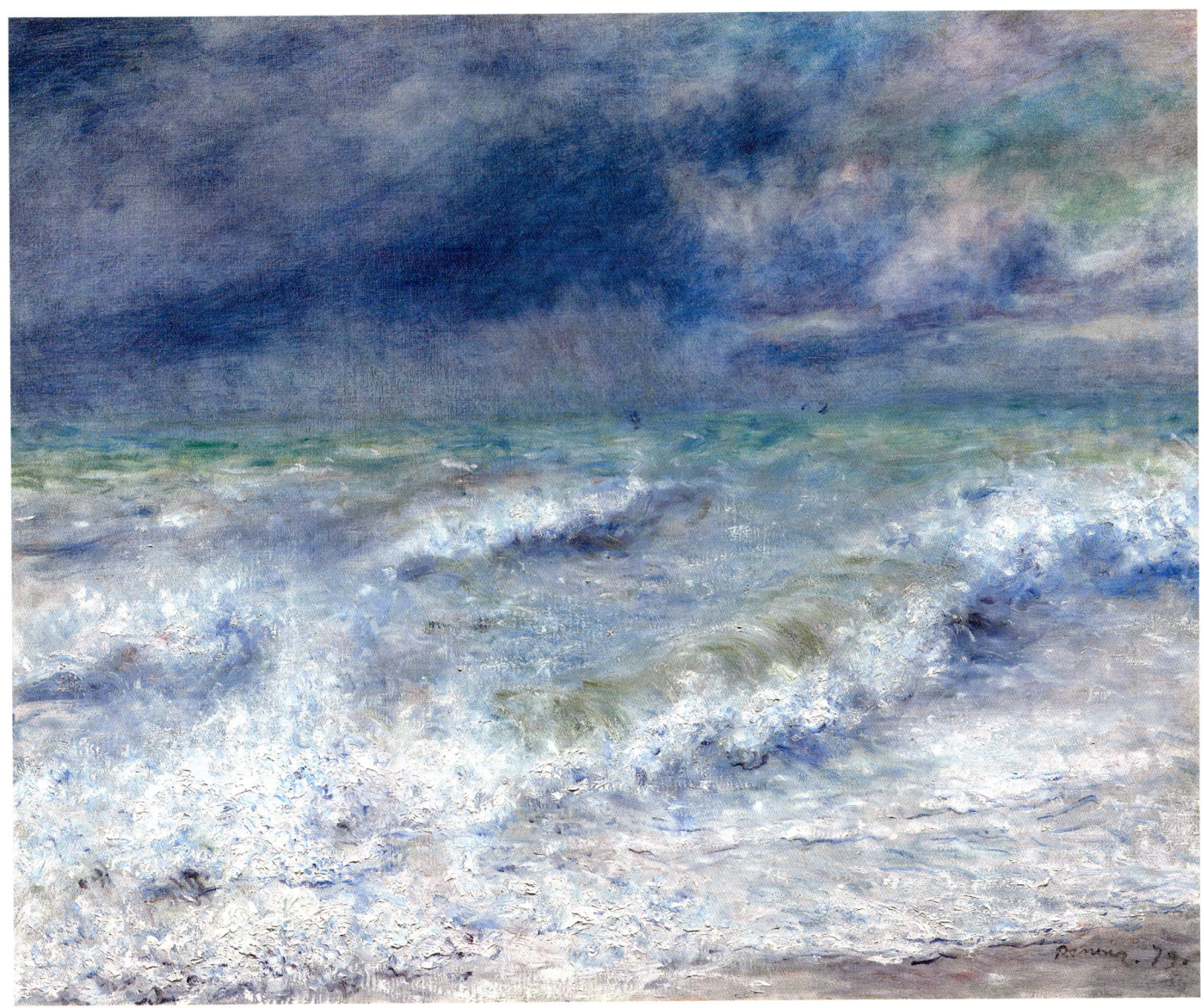

For the Impressionists, an expanse of water presented the ideal opportunity for evocations of light and its transient effects. Given its power, expanse and changeability, the sea was probably more inspirational to Renoir than the smoother waters of the River Seine which feature in many of his paintings. In some seascapes, he used fluid swirls of paint so thinned with medium that they could almost be watercolour, while in others he used opaque colours applied in lavish single brushstrokes.

In December 1883, Renoir spent nearly three weeks with Claude Monet on the Côte d'Azur. The clear, bright light of the south of France and the blue of the Mediterranean have captured the imagination of many artists. Renoir and Monet were no exception: the intensities of sunlight and colour, the rugged landscape and the exotic vegetation had a profound impact on their painting. In *Seascape (The Wave)*, Renoir painted a vision of the Mediterranean in which the cobalt blue sky is almost of a piece with the blues, greens and whites of the rolling waves.

Seascape (The Wave), 1879. *This painting approaches abstraction in its composition. For the first time, Renoir applied pigments wet on wet, blending blue and white on the canvas instead of on the palette. The white was applied straight from the tube with a vigorous hand to convey the tempestuous sea and sky.*

Not only did Renoir receive a commission of 1,500 francs for the work, he also gained a wider audience when Madame Charpentier used her contacts to get the painting accepted and displayed in a prominent position at the Salon. For the first time in his career, Renoir's art was acclaimed by press and public. The critic at *L'Artiste* described the portrait as a 'charming work'. After the show, Renoir wrote to Caillebotte about his new-found success: 'All in all, I think it's good since everyone is talking to me about it. I think I have greatly improved in my appeal to the masses.'

In 1880, Renoir once more abstained from the Impressionist group show and submitted further works to the Salon. This time, Monet joined him. But even though their works were accepted, neither artist enjoyed great success. Renoir's scenes of daily life – *Mussel Fishers at Berneval* (1879) and *Sleeping Girl with Cat* (1880) – were not prominently displayed and both were largely ignored. For the next few years he restricted his Salon submissions to portraits, which proved much more successful and gained him numerous commissions.

Madame Charpentier introduced Renoir to the banker Paul Berard (see page 38), who hired the artist to paint his eldest daughter, Marthe. Berard was so impressed with the result that he became Renoir's most devoted patron. The two men would remain firm friends until Berard's death in 1905.

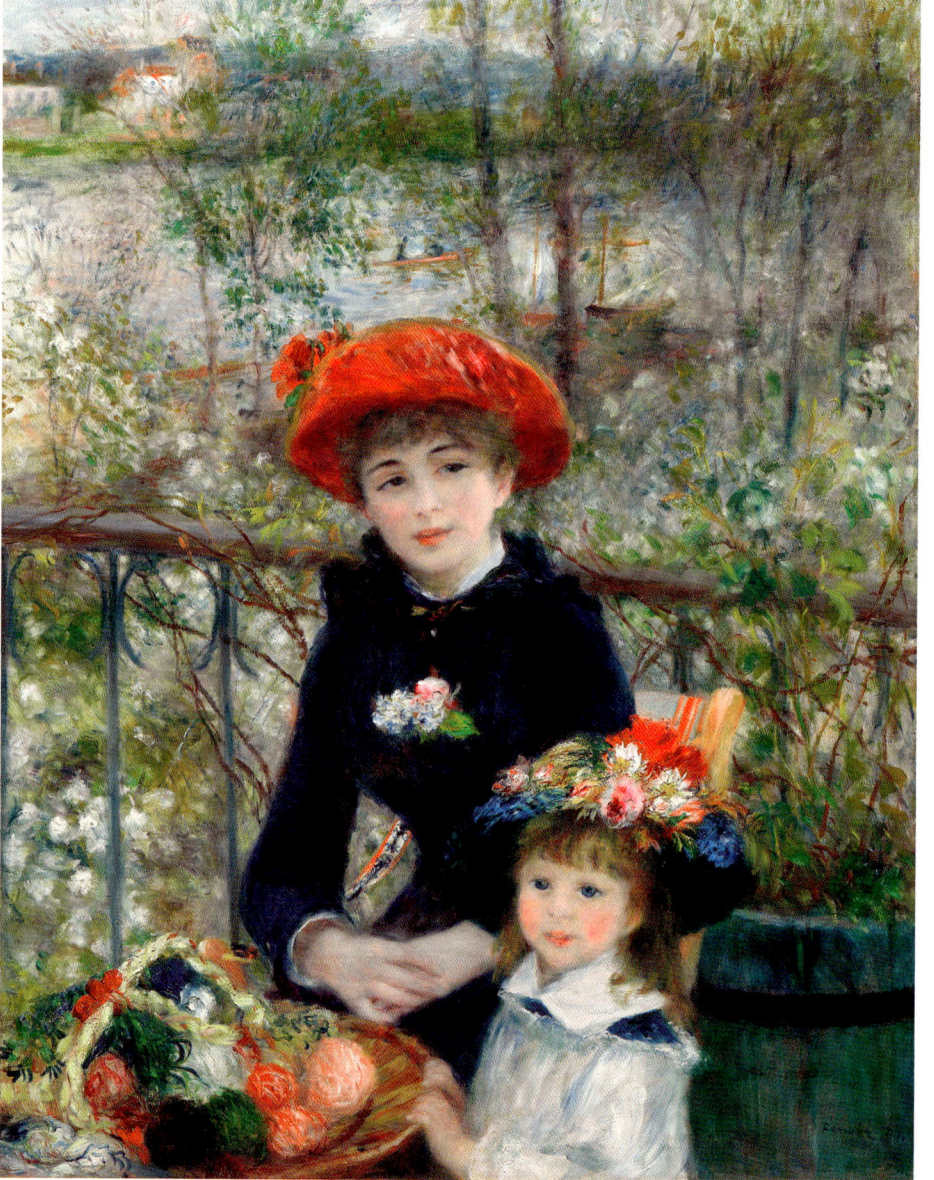

Two Sisters, 1881. The painting's title was suggested by Paul Durand-Ruel (the two girls were not, in fact, sisters). Renoir painted it on the terrace of the Restaurant Fournaise, scene of Luncheon of the Boating Party *(see page 42). The young woman seated in the deckchair wears a blue flannel dress considered* de rigueur *for boating at the time, while the little girl beside her sports a hat with trimmings that could almost have been assembled from the contents of the loaded basket. Her expectant gaze suggests she could suddenly have rushed into the the picture, not wanting to be left out. The solidly painted figures are juxtaposed with a romantic, dreamlike landscape painted in the Impressionist style. Characteristically, the mood of the painting is gentle and sunny. An anonymous reviewer once said of Renoir: 'He loves everything that is joyous, brilliant and consoling in life.'*

ALINE CHARIGOT

In late 1879, Renoir made another life-changing acquaintance when he met the nineteen-year-old Aline Charigot. She became his primary model and would go on to bear him three children and, later, become his wife. Although eighteen years younger than Renoir, she shared much in common with him. She, too, came from a working-class family – her mother was a seamstress, her father a baker. She was born in the small village of Essoyes in the Champagne region and moved to Paris with her mother at the age of fifteen following the death of her father. She met Renoir while working as a waitress in a café across the street from his studio. Letters kept by Aline show a gradual evolution of their relationship: initially Renoir was the dominant figure, constantly advising and making decisions about their lives, but later Aline increasingly made decisions regarding the family.

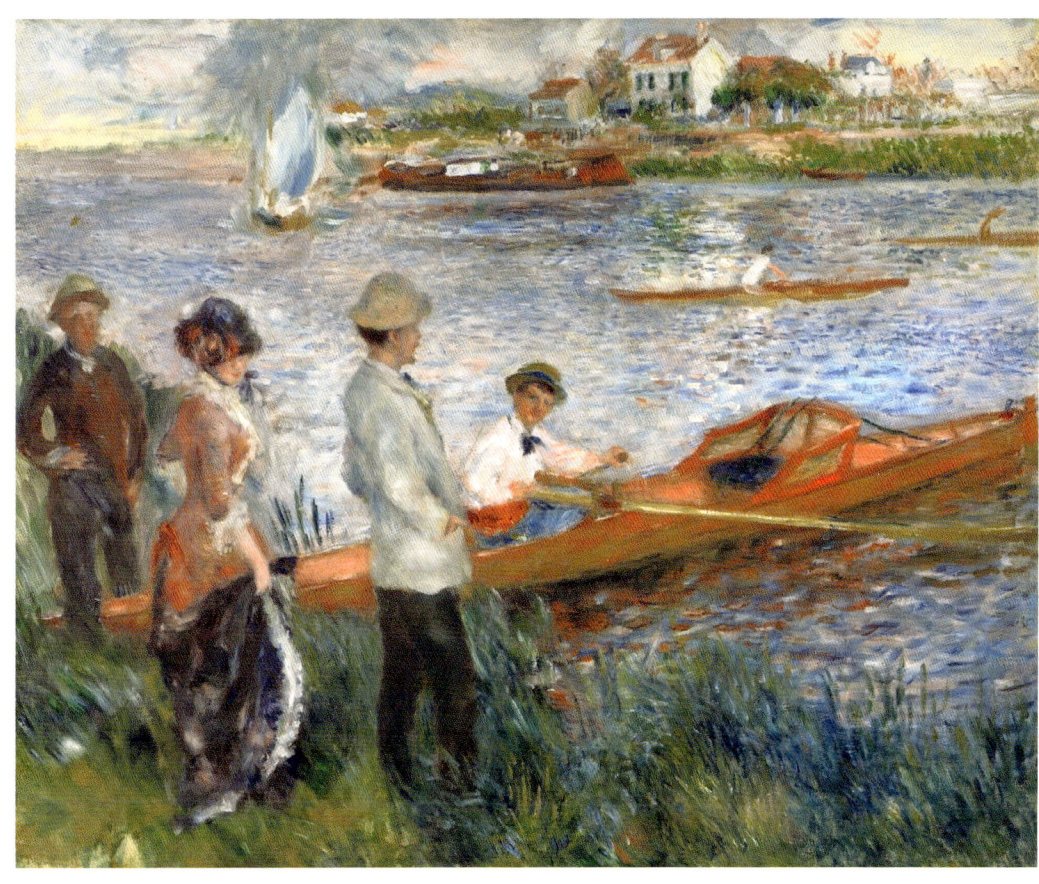

Aline's curvaceous form features in Renoir's paintings over many years. The first work in which she appears is *Oarsmen at Chatou*, a study of a group of friends on the banks of Seine at the small island of Chatou, northwest of Paris. Chatou was also the setting for *Luncheon of the Boating Party* (see page 42).

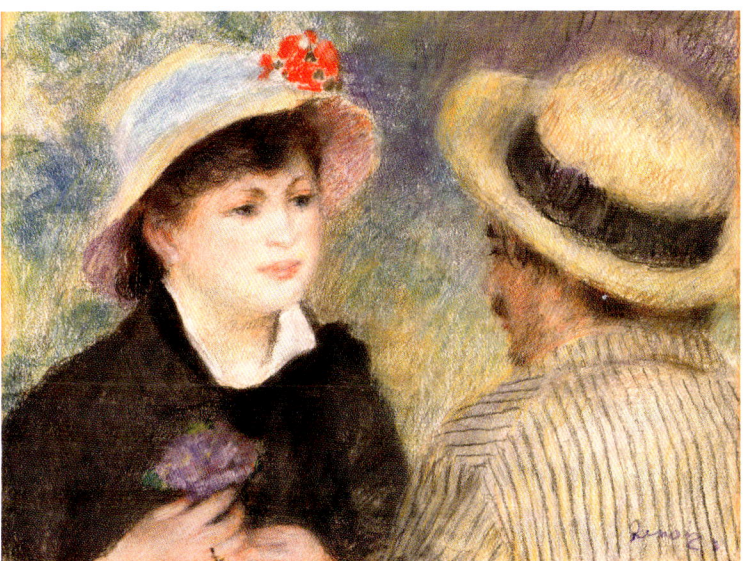

Above: Oarsmen at Chatou, 1879. *In one of Renoir's many paintings of friends relaxing at Chatou, he focuses on the wonderful spectrum of light as it floods the landscape. His brushstrokes are adjusted to capture the various textures, including the fluffy clouds in the sky, the rippling water, and the grasses blowing in the wind.*

Left: Boating Couple, 1881. *This pastel study is said to be of Renoir on the water with Aline. The smudged, indistinct background conveys the idea of a natural setting.*

LUNCHEON OF THE BOATING PARTY

Renoir made a dramatic impact when he returned to exhibiting alongside his fellow Impressionists in 1882. The seventh Impressionist exhibition, held in rented rooms at 251 Rue Saint-Honoré, Paris, was a well-organized event. Paul Durand-Ruel had taken over the running of the business side, leaving the artists to focus on their painting. The show featured one of Renoir's best-loved works, *Luncheon of the Boating Party* (1881). In this painting (below), the overlapping figures create a beautifully natural composition as they relax on the balcony of the popular Restaurant Fournaise overlooking the River Seine at Chatou. The soft, romantic style Renoir developed is particularly evident in the faces of the women, which are turned towards a young man (Italian journalist Antonio Maggiolo) who leans over the table on the right. The man leaning back against the balustrade is Alphonse Fournaise, son of the restaurant's proprietor. He is looking towards his daughter, Alphonsine, who is resting, chin on hand, on the railing. His son, Alphonse, stands behind her. Aline Charigot sits at the table in the foreground, playing with a dog, while the

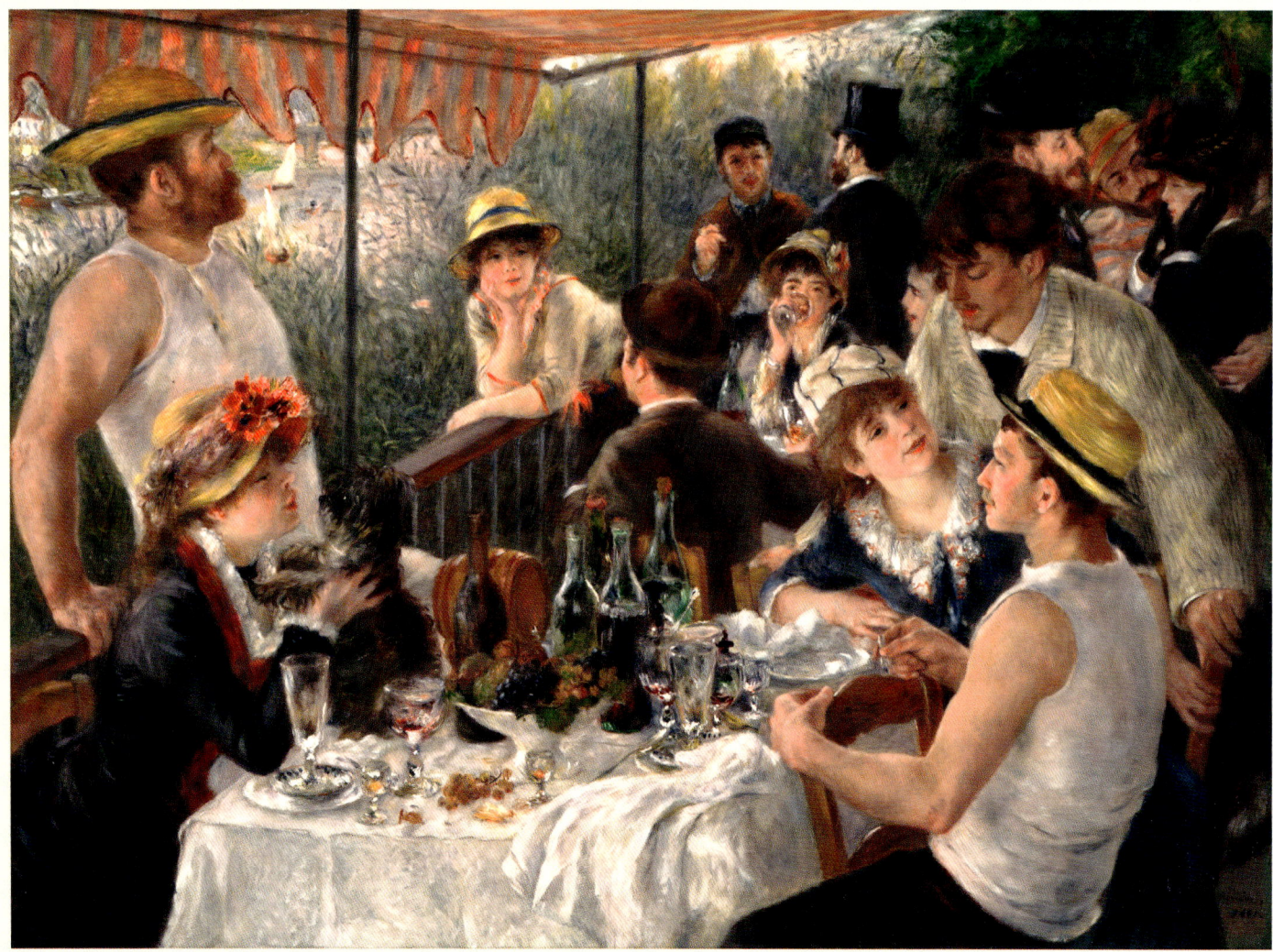

seated woman in the blue-and-white hat is Angèle Legault, model for *Sleeping Girl with Cat*. In the right foreground, wearing a straw hat, is the artist Gustave Caillebotte who was apparently a keen rower. The remaining figures include art historian Charles Ephrussi, actress Ellen Andrée, actress and model Jeanne Samary, amateur artist Paul Lhôte and civil servant Eugène-Pierre Lestringuez.

The painting is of contemporary Parisian life and shows a mix of people from all classes. The convention in art was to show people of a higher social class at a larger size, but in this cheerfully democratic scene the only hierarchical determinant is perspective. Saturated complementary colours, such as the orange-red of the flowers on Aline's hat and the Prussian blue of her dress, are reproduced in a more muted tone in the clothing of the background figures, further emphasizing the sense of depth. Beyond the group, sailing boats are glimpsed on the river, adding to the merry mood of this convivial scene.

Renoir seems to have made no sketches and only minimal underdrawing for this painting, but modern X-radiographic and infrared examinations have revealed that he revised it extensively. Analysis suggests there was originally a figure looking towards the viewer where there is now a man facing Alphonsine. It seems from Renoir's correspondence that his models came to pose in small groups or individually – and not necessarily when they were expected, to his frustration. In a letter to Paul Berard, he complained 'I no longer know where I am with it except that it is annoying me more and more.'

In spite of these difficulties, *Luncheon of the Boating Party* remains fresh and immediate and conveys the feeling of an artist casually painting while enjoying a social occasion with friends. Now one of the most famous pictures of the entire Impressionist movement, it found particular favour in the USA, where it is now held in the Phillips Collection. The American movie actor Edward G. Robinson said of it, 'For over thirty years I made periodic visits to Renoir's *Luncheon of the Boating Party* in a Washington museum, and stood before that magnificent masterpiece hour after hour, day after day . . . plotting ways to steal it.'

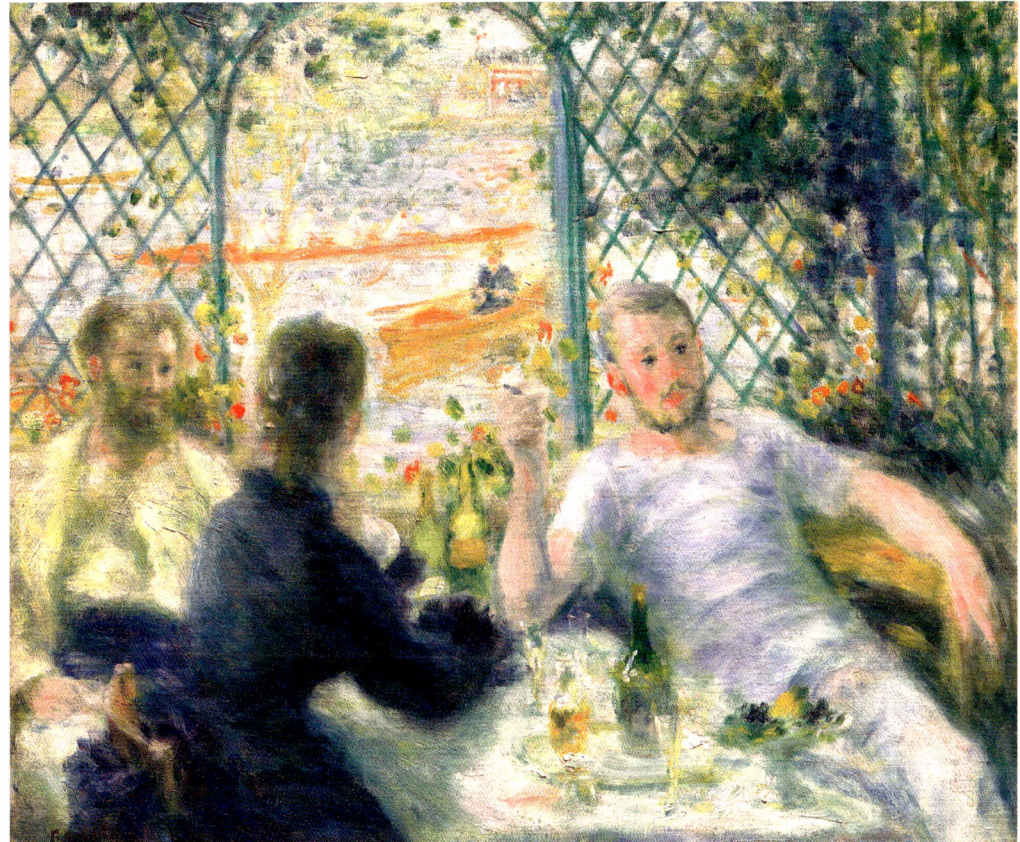

Left: Lunch at the Restaurant Fournaise, 1875. *One of Renoir's earlier paintings at Chatou, this Impressionistic scene shows a group of rowers relaxing after a meal. The palette and brushstrokes are airy and relaxed and the style contrasts strongly with the more classical treatment Renoir applied to* Luncheon of the Boating Party. *At this point in his career, he had almost entirely eliminated blacks and greys from his palette – evident from the blue shadows on the tablecloth and behind the man's chair.*

FOREIGN TRIPS AND NEW STYLES

Renoir's growing success enabled him to move out of the studio he shared with his brother and rent his own apartment with Aline in Montmartre, and his increased affluence meant he could afford to explore new locations. In February 1881, at the age of forty, he travelled to Algeria for two months to paint outdoors. He later described his visit in a letter to Madame Charpentier: 'a remarkable country . . . what beautiful scenery . . . of incredible richness.' He completed twenty-four canvases, including paintings of ancient buildings, botanical gardens with palm trees, and a scene of a bustling street festival.

At the time it was popular for wealthy young upper class men to make grand tours of Europe, visiting galleries and taking in the works of the old masters as part of their

Piazza San Marco, 1881. Renoir's study of the cathedral of San Marco in Venice shows it lit by the late autumn sun. The brushwork is sparse and areas of the canvas are left bare; the pedestrians and pigeons are indicated only with brief dabs and strokes of paint.

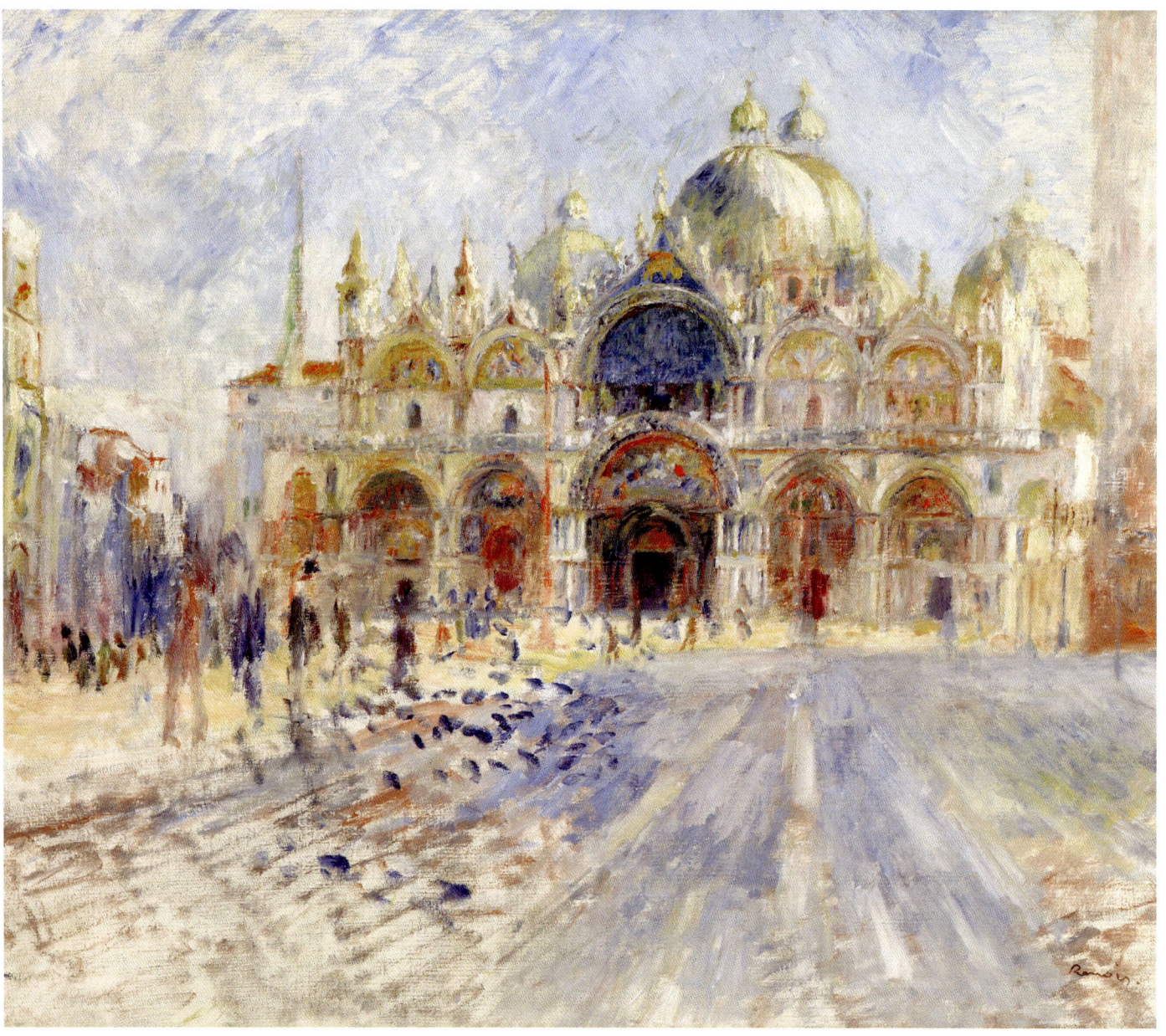

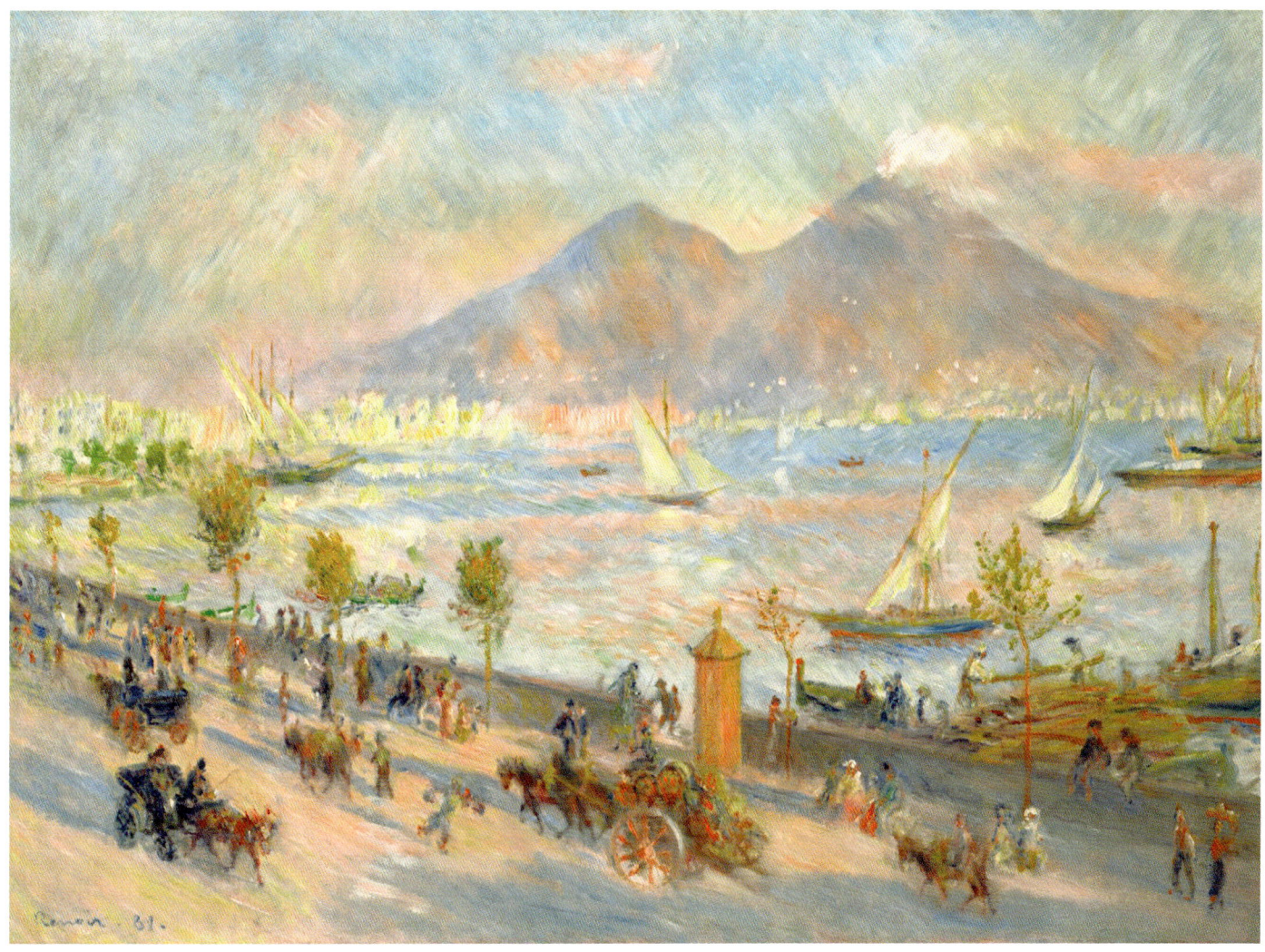

education. Degas and Manet had both travelled abroad while in their twenties, but it was something Renoir could only afford to do in middle age, after years of hard work. Later that same year, Renoir and Aline took a six-month trip to Italy, visting important artistic centres such as Venice, Florence, Rome and Naples. The art Renoir saw there, particularly Titian's masterpieces in Florence and Raphael's frescoes in Rome, had a profound effect on him and he began to re-evaluate his whole approach to painting. He later said, 'I had wrung Impressionism dry and I finally came to the conclusion that I knew neither how to paint nor how to draw. In a word, Impressionism was a blind alley as far as I was concerned.'

Over the next few years, his style would change to become more linear and classical in the spirit of Italian art of the fourteenth, fifteenth and early sixteenth centuries. But the paintings he produced on his Italian trip consisted mainly of landscapes still in the Impressionistic style, including views of the Doge's Palace and Piazza San Marco in Venice, as well as the Calabrian landscape and Mount Vesuvius (painted both morning and evening). He also completed some portraits, including *Italian Girl with Tambourine* and a sketch of the German composer Richard Wagner at his home in Palermo, Sicily.

Bay of Naples, Evening, 1881. Renoir's painting of the Bay of Naples shows the city harbour in all its energy and colour. In the background, Mount Vesuvius is bathed in sunlight with smoke rising from its peak. The paint is laid on in parallel brushstrokes, using complementary colours of blue, purple, yellow and orange.

'PEOPLE DO NOT LIKE
IT [ART] TO STINK OF
POLITICS.'

Pierre-Auguste Renoir

Renoir was deeply moved by what he described as the 'simplicity and grandeur' of the works of Raphael (1483–1520). 'I went to see the Raphaels in Rome,' he wrote to Durand-Ruel. 'They are very beautiful and I should have seen them sooner. They are full of knowledge and wisdom.' He had already made adjustments to his portraiture methods, but now he was determined to go further, to create a new way of painting.

This would be a synthesis between modern Impressionistic techniques and the classical style of his forebears, exemplified by early nineteenth-century French Neoclassical painter Jean-Auguste-Dominique Ingres. The beginnings of Renoir's new approach can be seen in a painting of Aline entitled *Blonde Bather*. Although much of the brushwork is still hazy, the outline of the figure and the careful rendering of the skin are more distinct and precise than in his previous work.

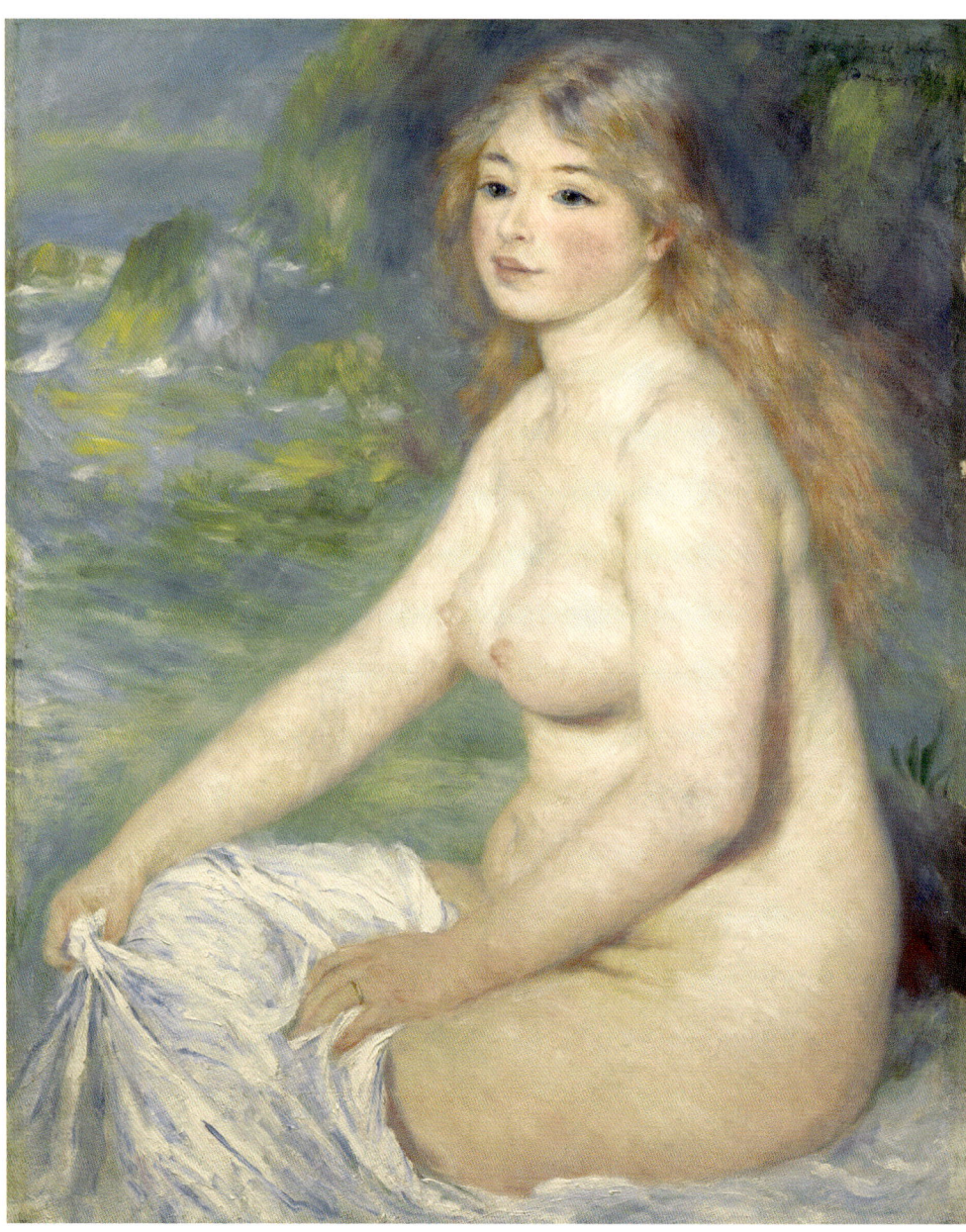

Blond Bather, 1881. *Painted in Italy, Renoir's portrait of Aline shows the influence of Renaissance art in its solidity of form. Particularly impressed by Titian and Raphael, Renoir reported that the Italian art he had seen was representative of 'eternal beauty'.*

ARTISTIC DIFFERENCES

In January 1882, Renoir travelled to Cézanne's house at L'Estaque in the south of France, planning to stay there and paint for two weeks. But after producing a few canvases, he was suddenly struck down with flu. Caillebotte contacted Renoir on his sick bed to ask him to take part in the next Impressionist show. Opening on 1 March 1882, the seventh exposition (see page 42) was to be titled the 'Exposition des Artistes Indépendants' (Exhibition of Independent Artists). Renoir disliked the new name because of its revolutionary connotations and told Caillebotte he believed it would alienate many of his prosperous clients.

In early February the same year, a major stock market crash sent the French economy into recession and severely depressed the art market. Durand-Ruel found himself in a precarious financial position and believed that a new exposition might be the answer to his problems. As he already owned a number of works by Monet and Renoir, he contacted the artists for permission to use them and asked if they would like to paint some new pictures as well.

Renoir said he couldn't prevent Durand-Ruel from showing the paintings he had already bought from him. But he petitioned for an exhibition based on talent and urged the inclusion of works by Degas, Monet, Morisot and Sisley. (Renoir disapproved of the anarchist tendencies of Gauguin and Pissarro.) In the end, Durand-Ruel exhibited twenty-five Renoir paintings, which the critics praised for their figurative work. His landscapes were largely ignored.

Later that year, Renoir submitted two works to the Salon: a small portrait of Yvonne Grimpel, the daughter of one of his patrons, completed in 1880, and the *Blond Bather*, which was rejected. Over the next few years, Renoir persisted with his new approach. He painted five portraits of Durand-Ruel's children and one of Madame Léon Clapisson, the wife of a stockbroker. In 1882, Léon Clapisson had bought three of Renoir's Algerian canvases and asked him to paint a portrait of his wife. Renoir's first version showed Madame Clapisson seated on a bench in her garden, surrounded by brightly coloured flowers. The Clapissons did not care for it, finding it too audacious. A letter from Renoir to Paul Berard reveals: 'I am not doing well at the moment. I have to start over Madame Clapisson's portrait . . . I failed completely. Also I don't think that Durand is very happy about his family's portraits . . . I must be careful if I don't want to lose the public's esteem.'

Renoir made a new portrait of Madame Clapisson, repainting it in a more sombre setting. The striking fusion of Neoclassical portraiture with a colourist palette is evident in this clear, delicate study of its subject against a free, Impressionistic background. The Clapisson family was finally satisfied and paid Renoir 3,000 francs for the painting, which was also accepted by the Salon in 1883.

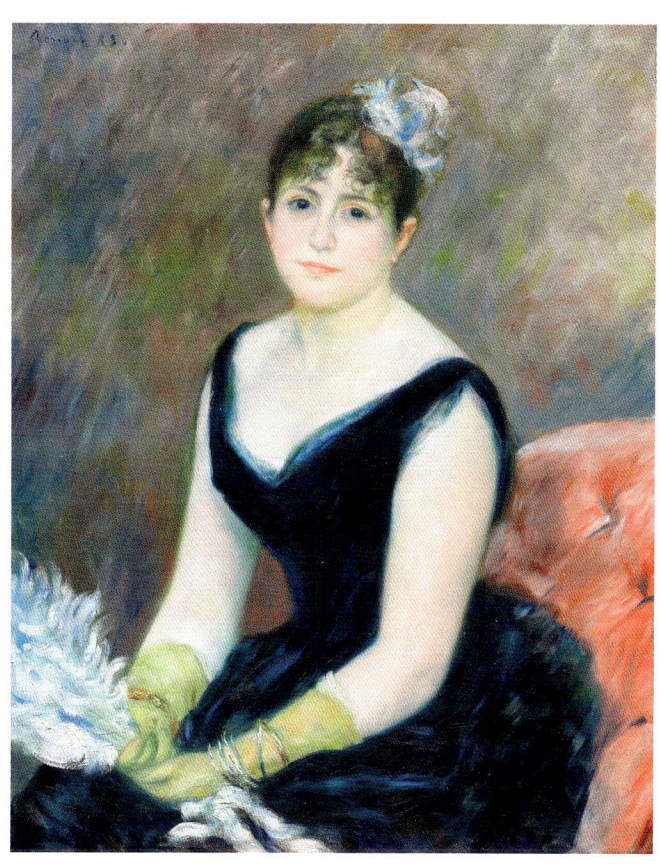

Madame Léon Clapisson, 1883. The Clapisson family was pleased with this final version. Recent scientific analysis shows that the portrait once had a rich red background painted with carmine lake, which was already known at the time to be a fugitive (impermanent) pigment. Artists continued to favour this shade even though more stable reds were available to them.

'THE WORK OF ART MUST SEIZE UPON YOU, WRAP YOU UP IN ITSELF AND CARRY YOU AWAY. IT IS THE MEANS BY WHICH THE ARTIST CONVEYS HIS PASSION. IT IS THE CURRENT HE PUTS FORTH WHICH SWEEPS YOU ALONG IN HIS PASSION.'

Pierre-Auguste Renoir

THREE DANCES

So Renoir continued to balance his artistic ambitions with the expectations of his patrons. Persisting with his classical-Impressionist style, he began an ambitious three-picture series of dancers.

The first of these paintings, *Dance at Bougival* (see page 36), is a romantic, informal scene showing a man and woman dancing outdoors. The clarity with which the two figures are painted places the focus on the intensity of their relationship, while the Impressionistic background suggests a convivial, relaxed environment in which spontaneous encounters such as this can happen. *Dance in the Country* is similar, showing a couple engaged in a happy, sensual dance in the open air next to a disorderly table. The man's hat has fallen to the ground, suggesting he has this moment leapt up for an impromptu spin.

The third painting, *Dance in the City* (see facing page), was intended to be shown alongside *Dance in the Country*. It is a more formal portrait of a couple in evening dress; in this instance, the background is Impressionistic in style but classical in content. The artist Paul Lhôte was the model in all three pictures and Aline posed for *Dance at Bougival* and *Dance in the Country*. Suzanne Valadon was the model for *Dance in the City*; she later became an artist in her own right and was the mother of the painter Maurice Utrillo.

Dance in the Country, 1883. *In this painting the figures occupy almost the entire frame. The bohemian atmosphere and warm colours contrast with the elegant restraint and cool colours of the painting on the facing page.*

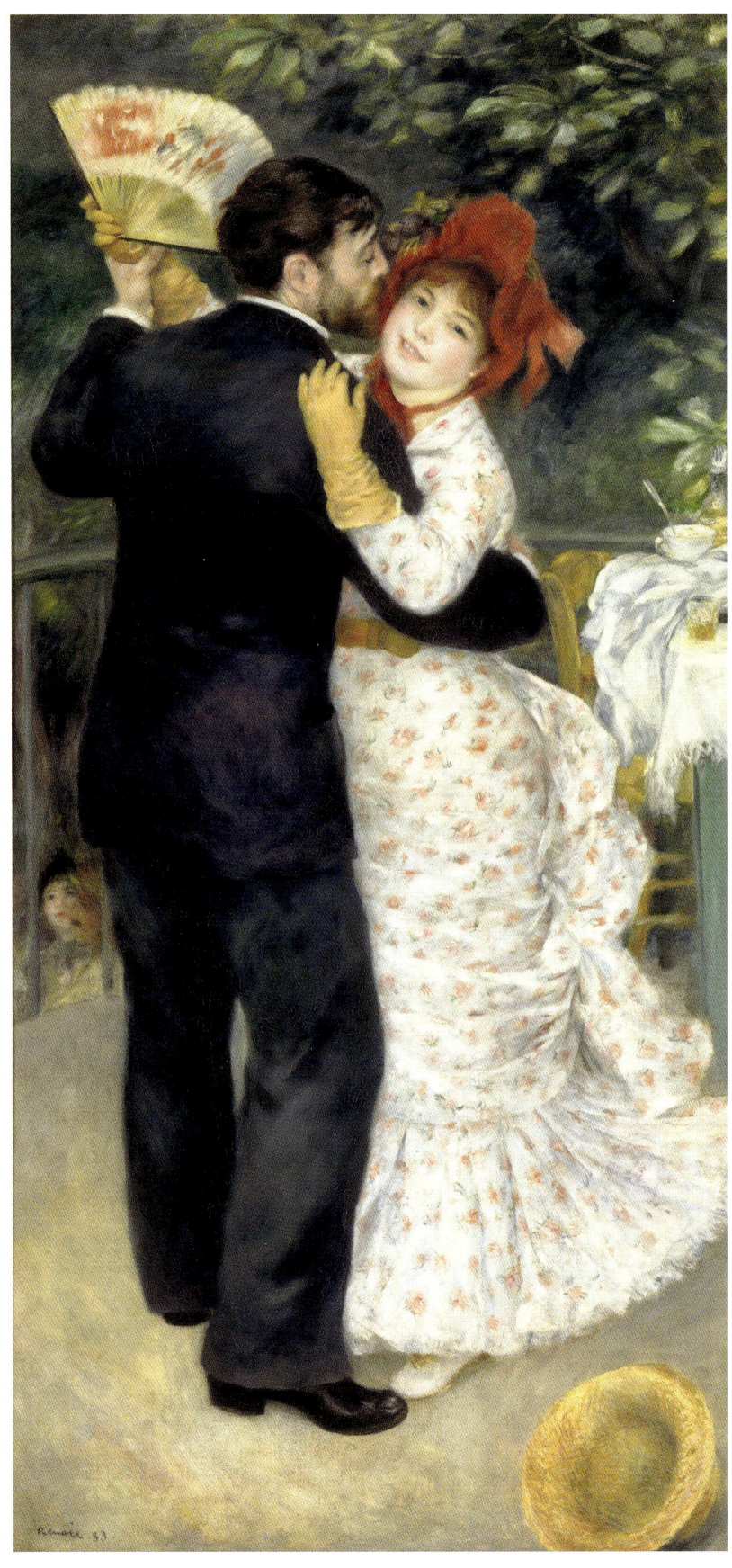

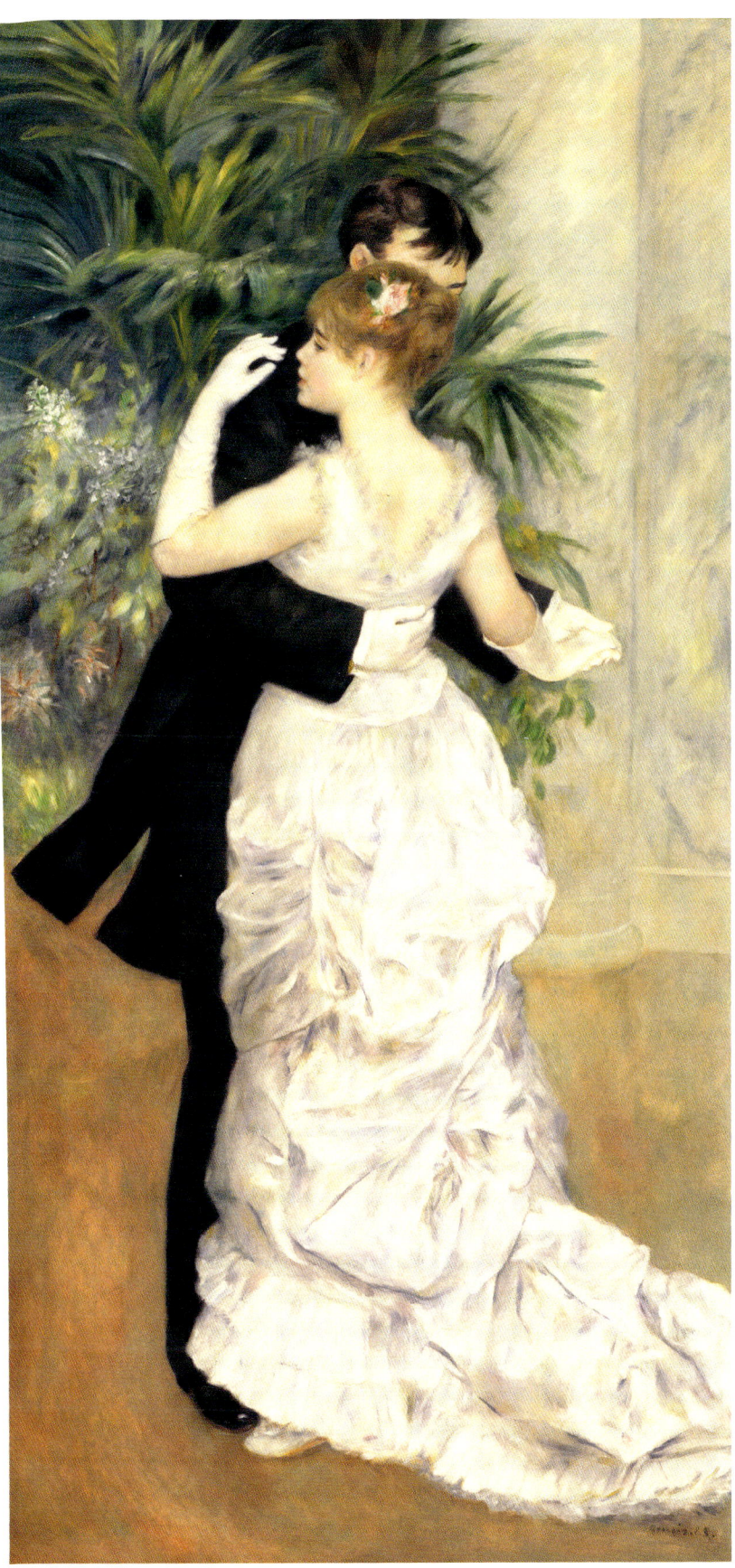

SOCIETY OF IRREGULARISTS

In 1884, Renoir attempted unsuccessfully to establish a collective of artists and artisans called the Society of Irregularists. He composed a manifesto which promised: 'to organize as soon as possible exhibitions of all artists, painters, decorators, architects, goldsmiths, embroiderers etc., who have irregularity as their guiding principle. . . ' It went on to say: 'At this time when our French art, still at the beginning of this century so full of penetrating charm and exquisite fantasy, is perishing because of regularity, dryness, and the mania of false perfection that now tends to make the unadorned cleanliness of the engineer into the ideal, we think it is useful to react promptly against the mortal doctrines which threaten to annihilate it.'

Renoir's efforts to elide the bohemian and commercial aspects of his life would continue throughout his career. But at this point a distraction occurred in his domestic life. In June 1884, Aline became pregnant and on 21 March 1885 the couple's first child, Pierre, was born.

'IF I WAS ACCUSED OF NEGLECTING MY ART OR SACRIFICING MY IDEAS FOR THE SAKE OF STUPID AMBITION, THEN I WOULD UNDERSTAND THE CRITICS; BUT AS THAT ISN'T THE CASE, THERE IS NOTHING TO BE SAID.'

Pierre-Auguste Renoir

Dance in the City, *1883. Using a similar composition to* Dance in the Country, *the precise drawing in this painting reflects Renoir's developing interest in classical art.*

RENOIR AND MONET

Two of the most famous names in Impressionism, Renoir and Monet, first met at art school in 1862. The men grew to be close friends, sharing their early struggles, lodging together and painting side by side – often until their paint ran out. In 1869 they created what are now considered to be two of the defining paintings of Impressionism: near-identical views of La Grenouillère, a popular boating and bathing resort on the Seine near where Monet lived. These sketchy, rapidly painted scenes of groups of young people in the midst of nature focus on the play of shadows on the water and exemplify one of the many terms coined by

Monet – *enveloppe* – describing the way in which a scene is surrounded by light.

Both are painted from almost exactly the same perspective and demonstrate the different preoccupations of the artists. Renoir's closer view focuses on the people standing on the circular platform at the centre of the painting (and on two dogs, absent from Monet's version). The soft, silvery tone lends a sensual quality to the work. Renoir delineates his

La Grenouillère, *Pierre-Auguste Renoir, 1869. Renoir's painting depicts a relaxed gathering of men and women in a setting of trees and water. The 'frog pond' was a popular meeting place for young working-class Parisians.*

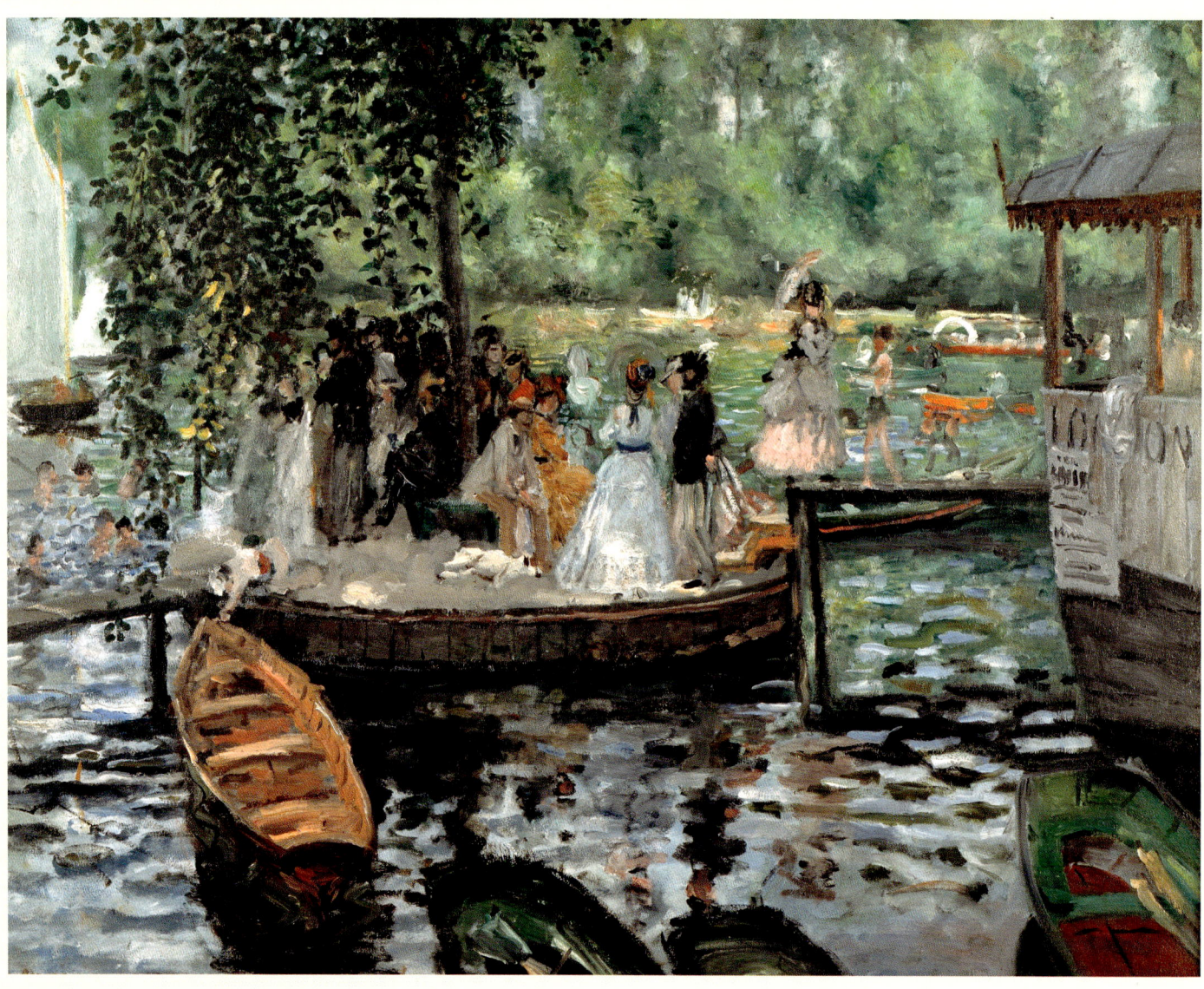

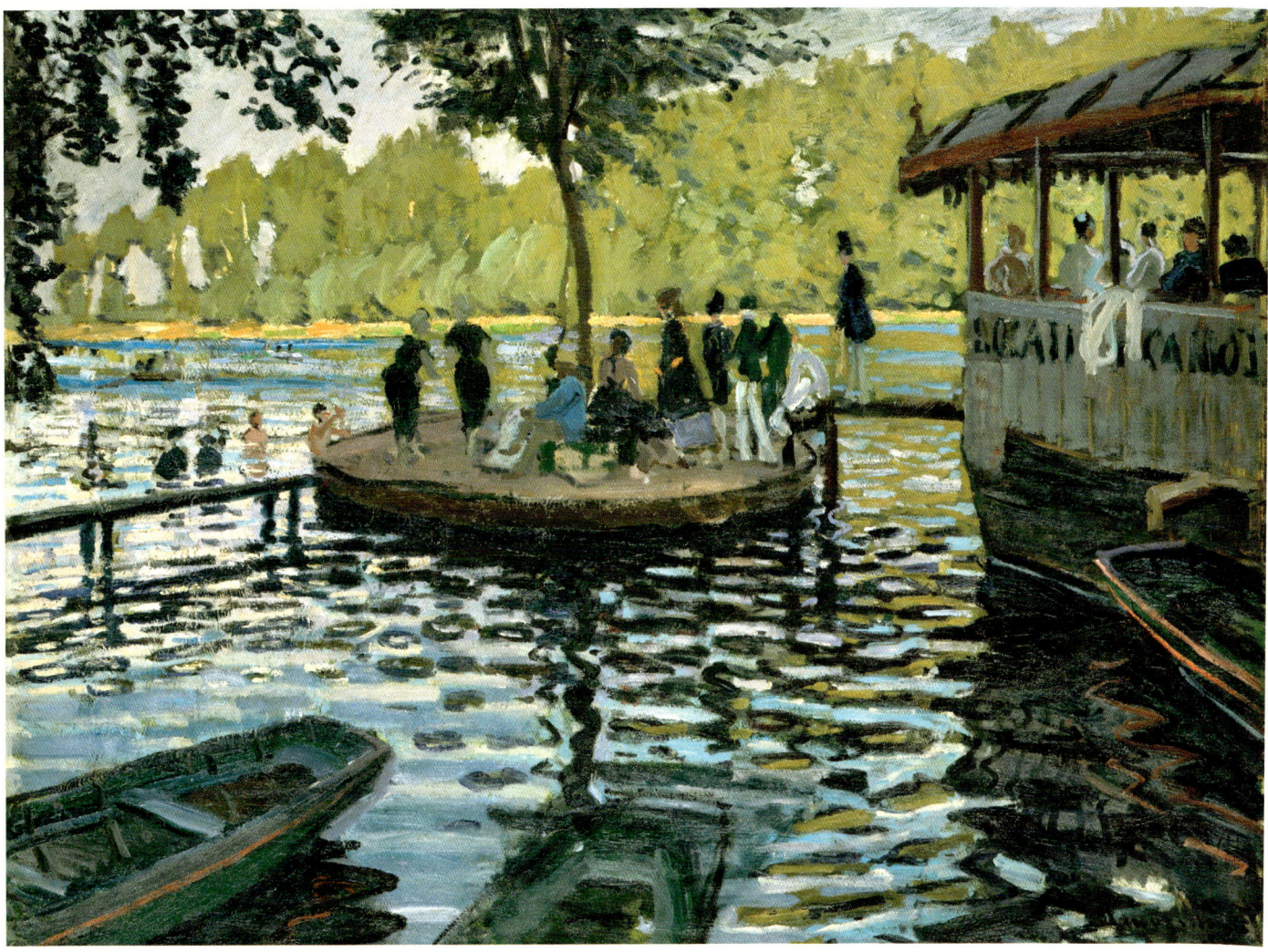

figures clearly to produce a painting full of human activity and romantic possibilities.
By contrast, Monet's painting has the immediate, 'thrown-down' feel which came to
represent one of the main tenets of Impressionism. He wanted to show a single instant
of light and to evoke emotions about the power of nature.

Monet's passion was for landscape in its own right. Although, unlike Renoir, he shows
two bathers in the water chatting to the people on the floating platform, the figures are
included to lend a human element to a painting that is essentially about light, wind and
water. He uses large brushstrokes and thick paint, which sits on the surface of the canvas
to produce a direct, dramatic impact. Both artists used the Impressionist style of bold
brushstrokes and avoided the blending of colour in order to depict light catching the
ripples of water. The truncated hulls of boats suggest passing movement and emphasize
the notion of a brief moment in time.

Renoir and Monet remained close until the former's death in 1919. At the time of his
friend's passing, Monet wrote to art critic Félix Fénéon: 'You can guess what a pain it
is for me, the disappearance of Renoir: he took with himself a part of my life. I haven't
stopped thinking of our youth filled with struggle and hope.'

Bain à la Grenouillère, *Claude Monet, 1869. Monet's figures occupy less of the space than Renoir's and are subordinate to the effects of sunlight pouring into the background of the painting and shadows playing on the water in the foreground.*

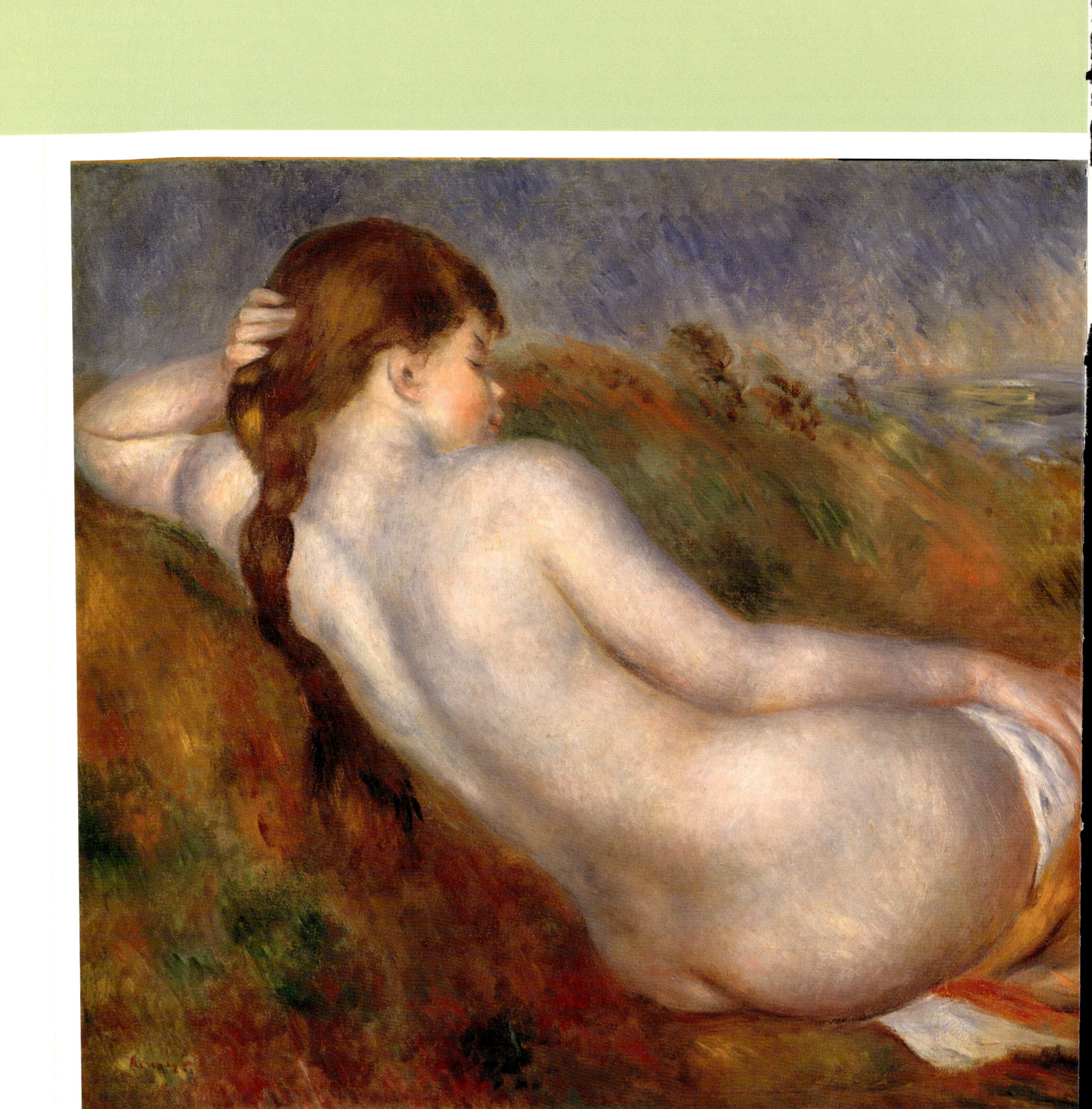

CHAPTER 3
The Classical Period

In the mid to late 1880s, Renoir moved his young family out of Paris and rented a succession of homes – in Essoyes (Aline's home town), at Aix-en-Provence (at a house owned by Cézanne), and at Petit Gennevilliers (Caillebotte's home). If ever he missed the social and intellectual stimulation of Parisian life, he would arrange trips there to paint and meet with friends. He also invited guests to visit him. In 1885, Cézanne stayed and painted alongside Renoir at a house in La Roche-Guyon.

The years of struggle appeared to be over; Renoir was by this point acclaimed as a pioneer of Impressionism and his work was well respected and collected by connoisseurs. But now, true to his independent spirit, he changed direction and entered what is sometimes referred to as his 'Ingres' period. His art took on a more linear style, reflecting his admiration for the work of the great Neoclassical artist. The influence of Ingres is particularly evident in Renoir's perfectly finished, carefully drawn nudes with their firm contours and smooth, translucent skin. He also applied this method to portraiture – the series of drawings and oil paintings he made of Aline and their infant son Pierre are early examples of the start of this, Renoir's classical period.

Reclining Nude, 1883. *Renoir's move towards a new style is evident in this painting of a female nude. However, while the pose and skin tones are classical in nature, the figure is not a remote goddess but an approachable, pink-cheeked girl. Some have remarked that this is reminiscent of Ingres' La Grand Odalisque, painted in 1814. But while the subject of the background shows the influence of Baroque artists such as Poussin, its Impressionistic rendering with dabs of paint merely suggests, rather than shows, the nature of the surroundings.*

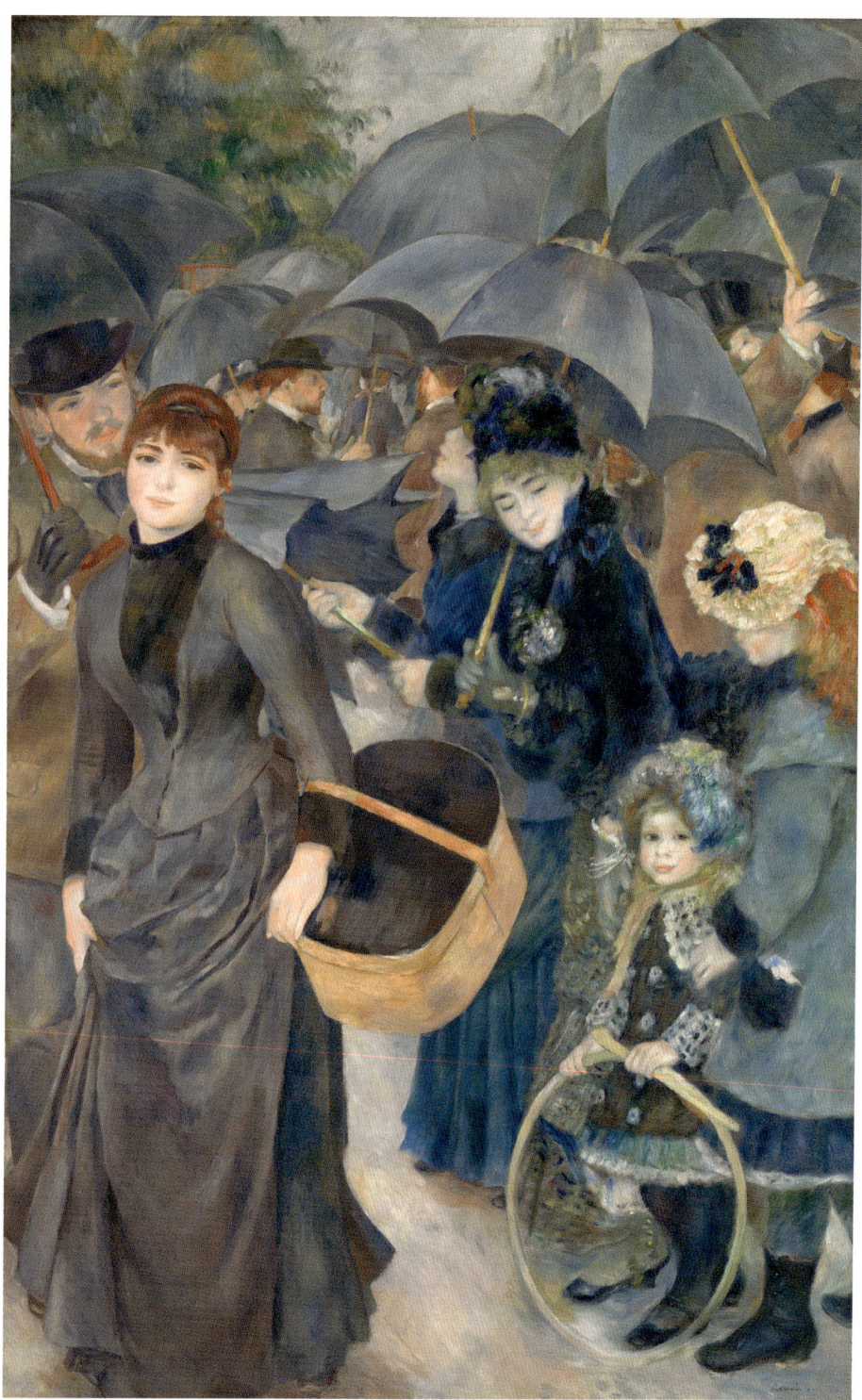

The Umbrellas, 1886. Renoir began this painting using the loose brushstrokes and bright colours of Impressionism. After his move towards classicism, he reworked it using a cool blue/grey palette.

PURITY OF LINE

Renoir grew increasingly certain that Impressionism alone was no longer sufficient for the art he wanted to paint. Inspired by Raphael and the classical artists, he strove for purity of line and the expressive power of smoothly applied paint. In a letter to Madame Charpentier, written in 1882, he said: '[I hope to acquire] some of the grandeur and simplicity of the old masters. Raphael didn't work out-of-doors, but he studied sunlight all the same – his frescoes are full of it.'

The transition was by no means painless. In 1886, Renoir produced very few works, writing: 'I scratch out, I start again and I think that the year will go by without my having finished a single painting.' Nevertheless he managed to complete his now-celebrated *The Umbrellas*, begun around 1880 in a purely Impressionistic style. X-ray analysis has revealed that the figures were originally painted with loose brushwork and in vivid colours, but Renoir later altered some of them, particularly the woman on the left. In case her position in the foreground doesn't make it clear, Renoir ensures that she is the main focus of the painting by rendering her with careful attention to contour and volume.

The influence of photography is visible in the monochrome and sepia palette and the casual arrangement of figures. At this point in time, posed photographs tended to be stiff, formal affairs. Renoir has taken full advantage of the freedom afforded to him by the medium of art and painted something akin to a still image from a film, with its random captured movements and figures at the sides partially out of frame. Only the woman with the basket and little girl with the hoop seem to be aware of the artist's gaze.

The Bather, Jean-Auguste-Dominique Ingres, 1808. *Ingres painted this while a student at the French Academy in Rome. Decades passed before it was recognized as a masterpiece. The Goncourt brothers, illustrious literary siblings, wrote in 1855 that 'Rembrandt himself would have envied the amber colour of this pale torso'. Ingres' rendition of different surfaces and gradations of light were an influence on many artists, including Renoir.*

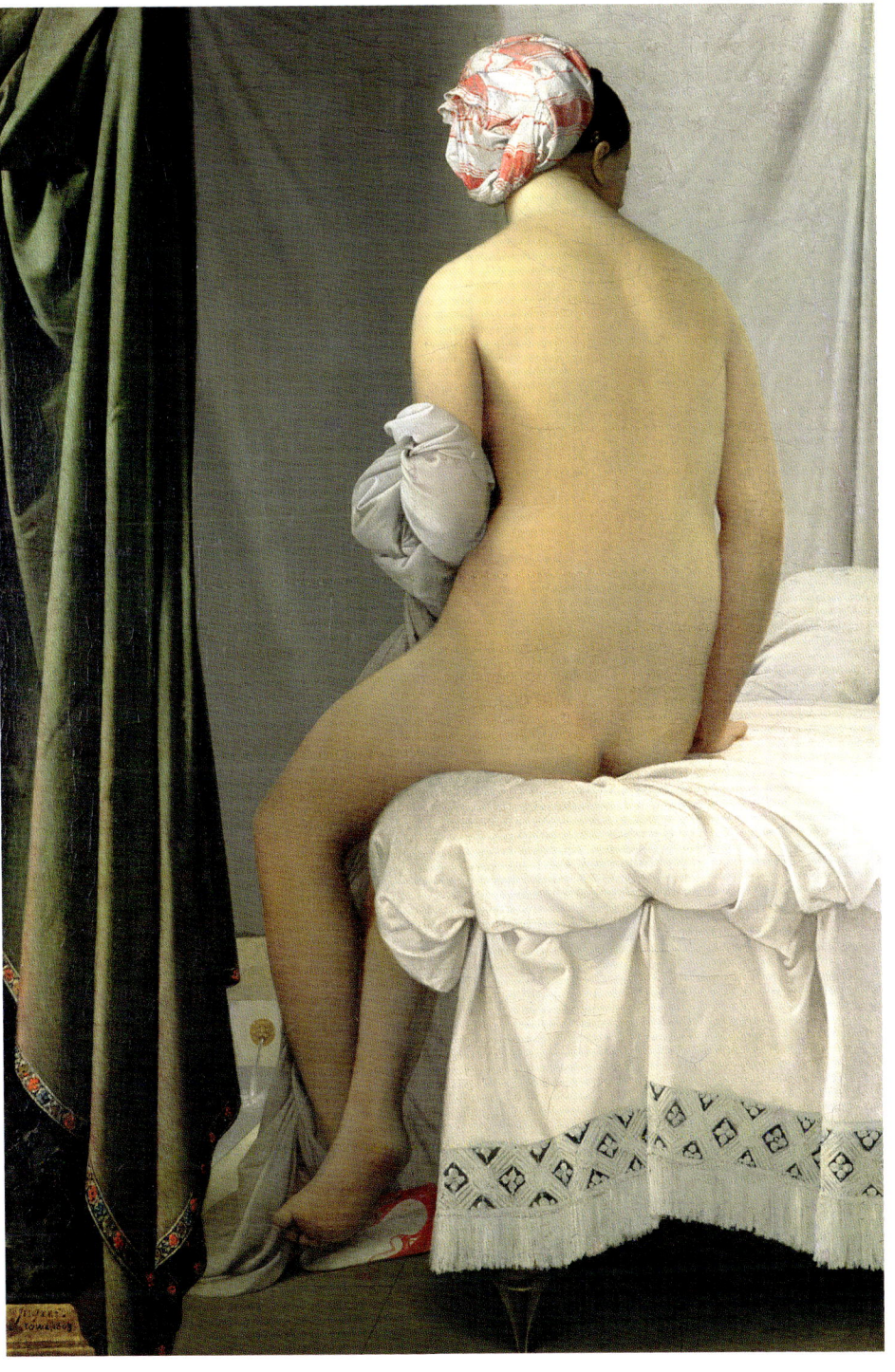

Renoir was not alone in his wish to move on artistically. The final Impressionist exhibition, held in 1886, reunited many of the artists who had come and gone over the years. It was no little irony that while these artists had once been regarded as potentially dangerous revolutionaries, their work was now receiving public acceptance and support. By the early 1890s, some of the less controversial Impressionist works had even been accepted by the Salon.

While Renoir was struggling with his process, he was still searching for new ways to publicize his art. He exhibited in Brussels with a group of modern artists known as Les Vingt and at exhibitions in Paris, some of which were mounted by Georges Petit, who was Durand-Ruel's main rival in the art trade. Meanwhile, Durand-Ruel was finding new opportunities abroad, showing Impressionist paintings in Brussels and New York, the latter with huge success, particularly for Renoir. It is interesting to note that, like most artists, Renoir's style was constantly evolving. In 1888, he had a further change of heart, writing to Durand-Ruel: 'I have taken up again, never to abandon it, my old style, soft and light of touch.' Impressionism was, it seems, a difficult habit to break.

THE LARGE BATHERS

Painted over the course of three years and completed for a summer exhibition of 1887, *The Large Bathers* (right) is the apotheosis of Renoir's classical period. The figures are rendered with an almost sculptural clarity, with little visible brushwork, while the background combines traditions of seventeenth- and eighteenth-century French painting with an Impressionistic approach. Although the scene depicts a fleeting moment, it has a timeless, monumental quality. Renoir planned it carefully, making many preparatory drawings of the individual figures and more than one full-scale drawing of the whole composition, using as his inspiration a bas-relief by François Girardon (1628–1715) in the garden at Versailles.

The artist Berthe Morisot, a close friend of Renoir's, was so delighted by the painting that she immediately commissioned him to paint a portrait of her daughter, Julie Manet. The critic Gustave Geffroy wrote, 'Here Renoir has doggedly worked towards an intellectual and pictorial idea . . . [combining] the luminous purity of the primitives and the serene draughtsmanship of Ingres.'

The painting also impressed Van Gogh: 'I think often of Renoir and that pure clean line of his,' he wrote. Monet agreed: 'Renoir made a superb painting of his bathers. Not understood by all, but by many.' But some of Renoir's contemporaries disapproved of his new direction. In Pissarro's opinion, Renoir seemed to be painting in two different styles, one on top of the other, rather than producing a single, coherent work. 'It's very good not to want to stand still,' he argued, 'But [Renoir] chooses to concentrate only on line, his figures detach themselves from one another without regard for colour; the result is something unintelligible.'

Pissarro was also changing the way he worked, moving towards a pointillist, neo-Impressionist style which Renoir disliked. This resulted in tension between the two

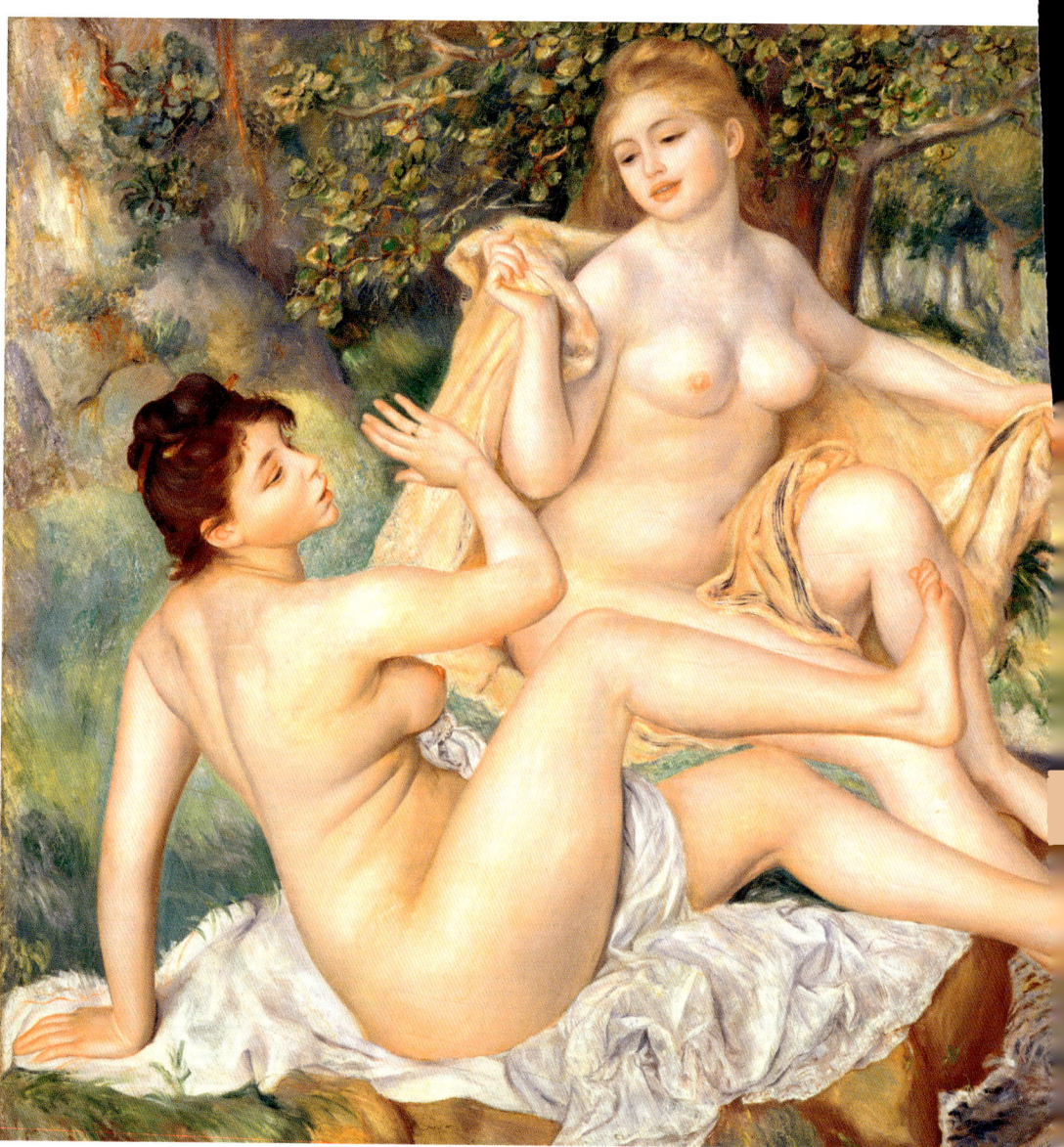

'I NEVER THINK I HAVE FINISHED A NUDE UNTIL I THINK I COULD PINCH IT.'

Pierre-Auguste Renoir

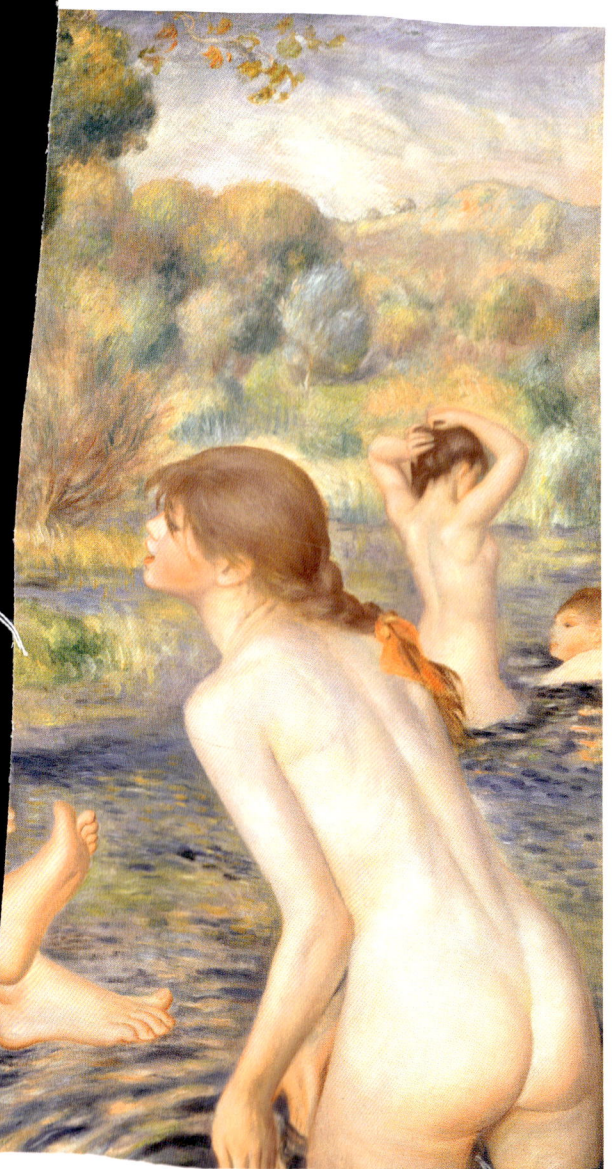

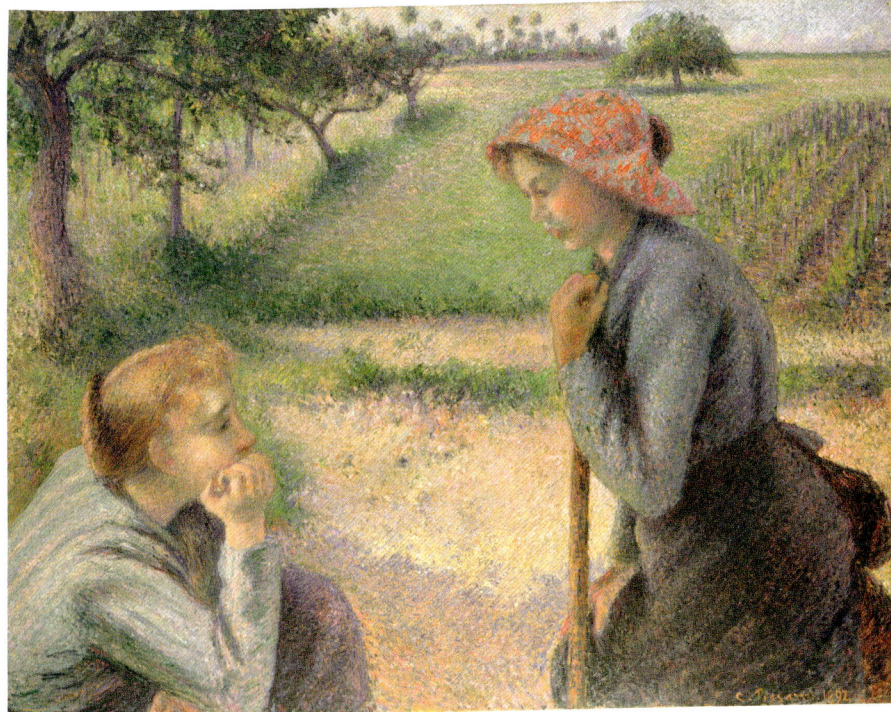

Two Young Peasant Women, *Camille Pissarro, 1891–2. Pissarro painted these farm workers in a field near his home at Éragny in Normandy, using the pointillist technique. Pointillism had grown out of Impressionism in 1886. It was based on new scientific theories which maintained that adjacent pure colours would fuse in the viewer's eye and give greater luminosity than paint mixed on the palette.*

artists. Regarding their process, Pissarro claimed he had written in a letter to Renoir: 'You wander around at random. I know what I'm doing.' In the face of such trenchant criticism, Renoir showed courage in persisting with his classical method, but he never again committed so much time and effort to a single work as he did to *The Large Bathers*.

The painting was bought for just 1,000 francs by Jacques-Émile Blanche, a young artist who had once been a pupil

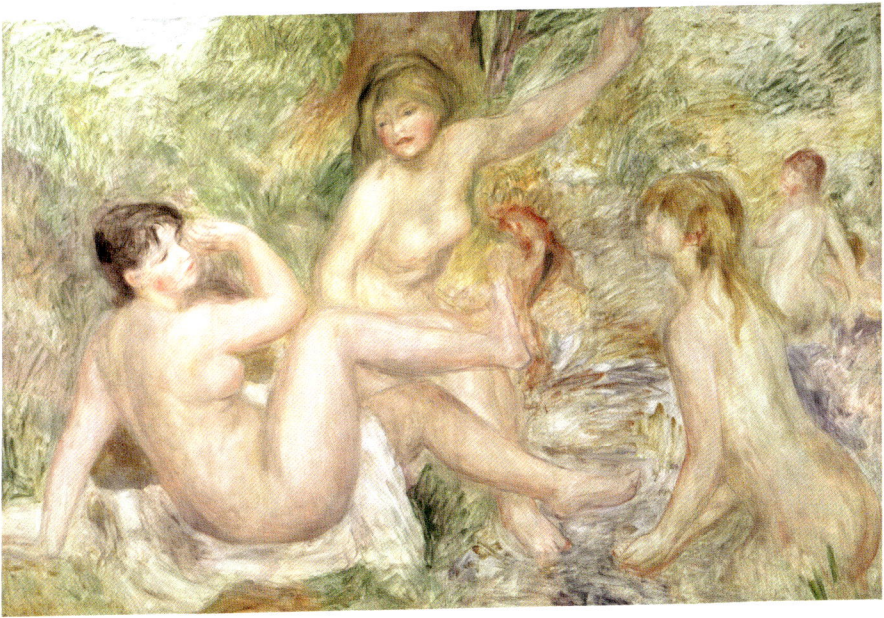

The Large Bathers – study, *1884–7. This Impressionistic early study gives an idea of the amount of artistic skill Renoir devoted to the final classical version.*

DECLINING HEALTH AND IMPROVING WEALTH

Mont Sainte-Victoire, 1889. Renoir uses warm colours and parallel brushstrokes in this landscape painting. The image is suffused with his distinctive soft, silvery light.

Renoir's commercial success coincided with the start of his health problems. In 1888 he began to suffer from neuralgic pains in his head and teeth and a facial palsy that turned out to be a warning sign of the rheumatoid arthritis which would afflict him for the rest of his life. At first he didn't know the cause and underwent a series of painful tooth extractions that made it difficult to eat. Photos

from the time show him looking frail, but by the summer of 1889 he had recovered sufficiently to spend the season in Provence at a house rented from Cézanne's brother-in-law. Here he made several paintings of Mont Sainte-Victoire, near Aix-en-Provence.

In November of that year, Renoir was invited to show once more with Les Vingt in Brussels. After some hesitation he exhibited five paintings, one of them *After the Bath* which had been lent

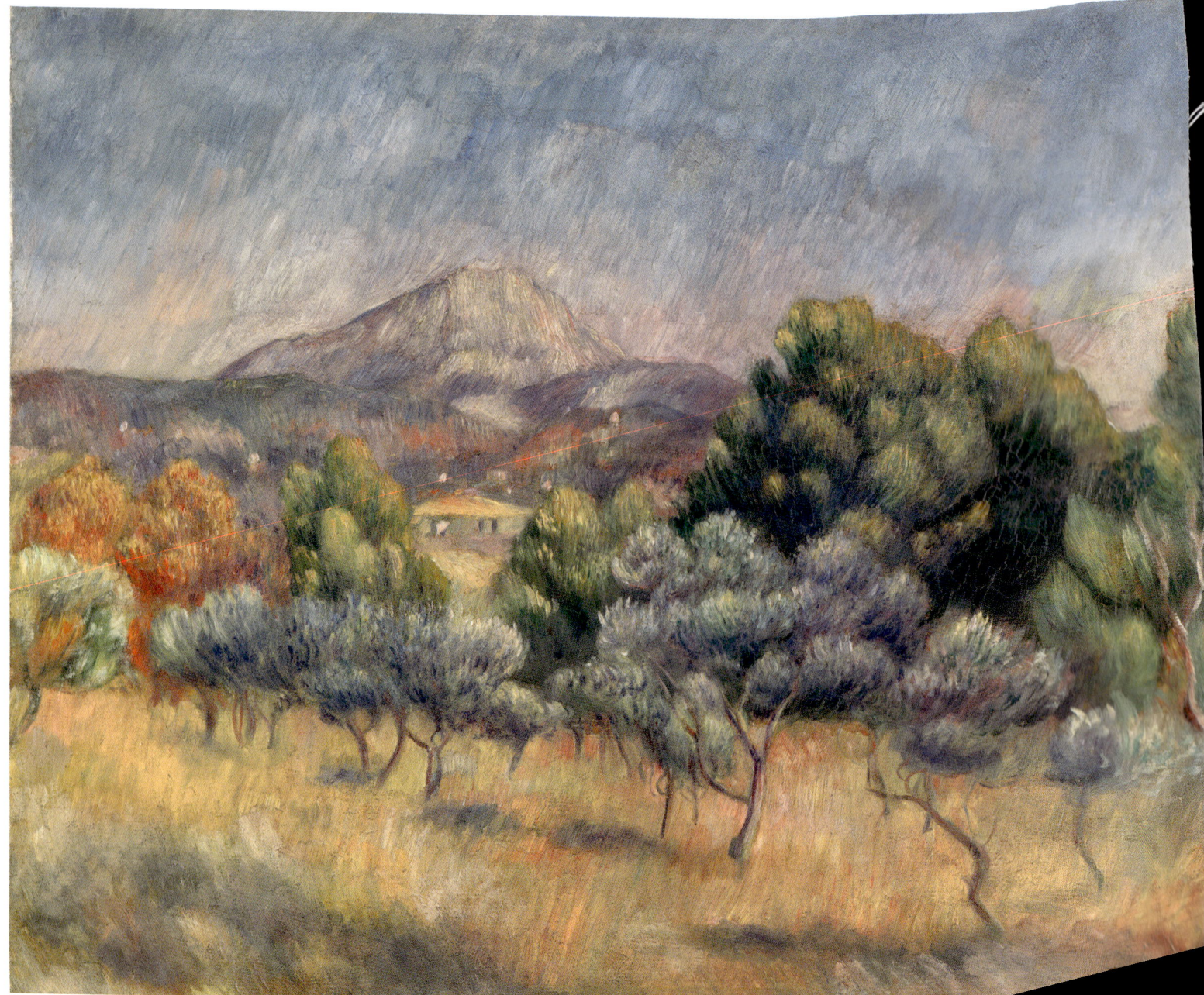

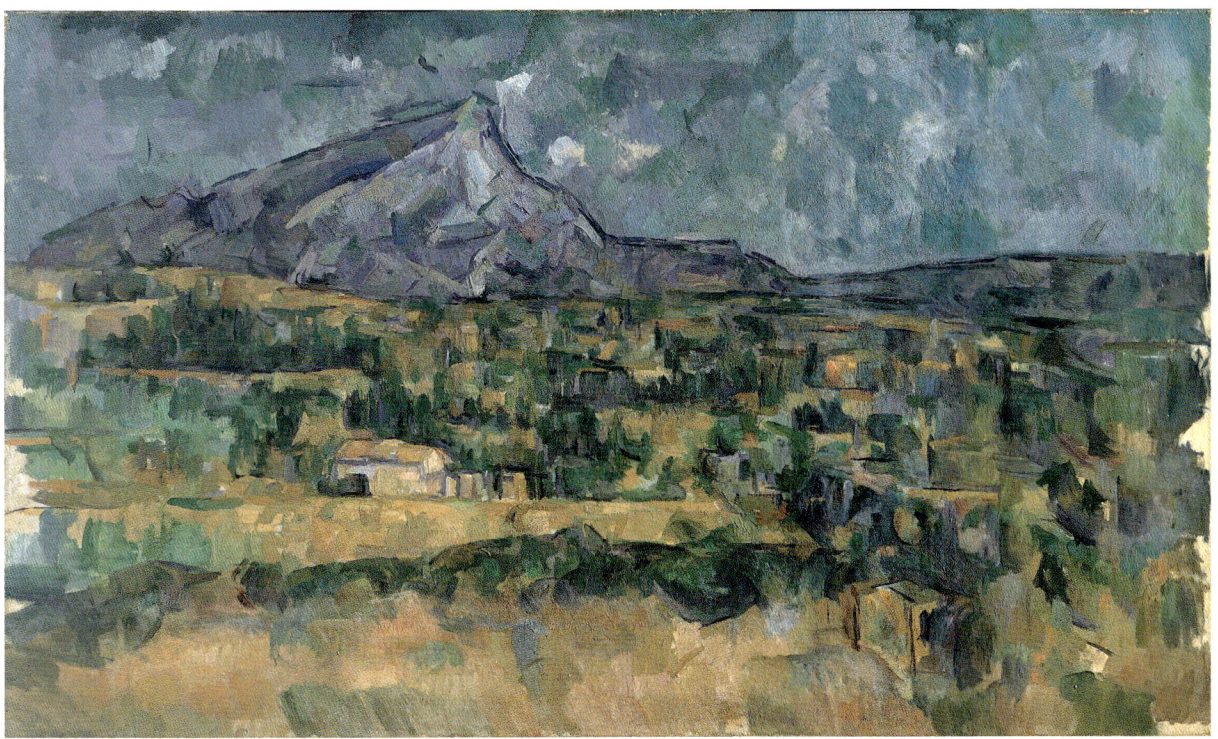

Mont Sainte-Victoire, *Paul Cézanne, 1902–6. Cézanne made a series of paintings of the same mountain and completed this one over several years. While Renoir's preoccupation was with light, Cézanne's was with form. Renoir's gentle landscape contrasts with Cézanne's geometric study, which points towards a more modernist approach.*

by writer Robert de Bonnières who had acquired it the previous year. A further change in fortune came when Durand-Ruel opened a gallery in Manhattan in 1888, and the American public started buying Impressionist art. 'Without America, I would have been lost,' Durand-Ruel later recalled. 'The Americans don't criticize – they buy.'

By 1890, many of Durand-Ruel's clients, particularly Renoir and Monet, were beginning to make serious money. The burgeoning market in the USA prompted a re-evaluation of Renoir's work in his own country. In 1892, Stéphane Mallarme and Roger Marx, a civil servant in the Beaux-Arts administration, lobbied for the inclusion of Impressionist art in French museums. As a result, the government commissioned Renoir to paint a piece for the newly opened Musée du Luxembourg in Paris; the result, *Young Girls at the Piano*, is painted in a warm palette and with delicate brushstrokes. The intimate, almost sentimental domestic scene may have been painted in Renoir's own home. For such an important commission, he painted four finished versions, including a sketch in oils and another in pastels.

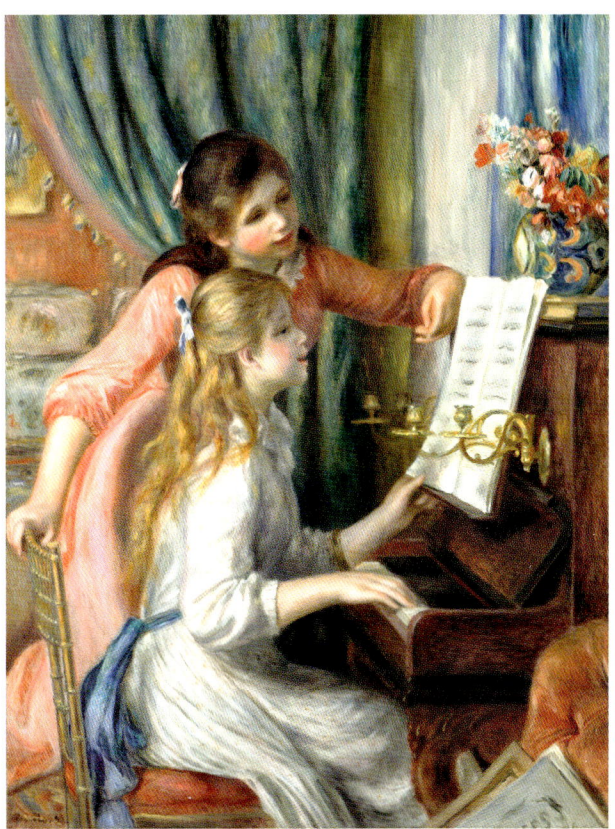

Young Girls at the Piano, 1892. *Classical artists often showed musicians in a domestic setting. In Renoir's hands, the subject was given a less formal, more intimate treatment.*

LUMINOUS LANDSCAPES

Although we tend to associate Renoir primarily with figure painting, he was also a great landscape artist whose work depicts light, humidity and texture and celebrates an innovative use of colour. His early landscapes were influenced by the Barbizon school (he once described Corot as 'the greatest artist who ever lived'), which advocated a naturalistic approach through direct observation of the living world. Many of the Barbizon artists painted pure landscapes in which figures are absent, and Renoir initially followed their example, working *en plein air* to capture as authentic a representation as possible. He painted fields, forests, mountains, coastal scenes and gardens, but as his style developed he concentrated on the luminous effects of light and colour favoured by the Impressionists. He also introduced figures as a focal point and used rough unblended brushstrokes to evoke atmospheric and weather conditions.

In *Springtime (in Chatou)*, silvery brushstrokes depict the hazy light of a quiet spring day. The painting is almost entirely an Impressionist blur, with a single male figure seen from the back, receding into the distance. Sunlight floods into the painting from the right, striking the man's back as he moves towards the shade of the forest.

Renoir's *Path Leading Through Tall Grass* is regarded as one of the greatest Impressionist landscape paintings. It shows a woman and girl descending a hill, the woman shading herself with a scarlet parasol that would figure in many Renoir paintings. The pair are engulfed by exuberant vegetation. Made in quick brushstrokes and suffused with golden light, the painting combines a narrative strand with the precise naturalistic depiction of atmosphere. The heat and humidity hanging in the air are rendered through the careful handling of tone and colour.

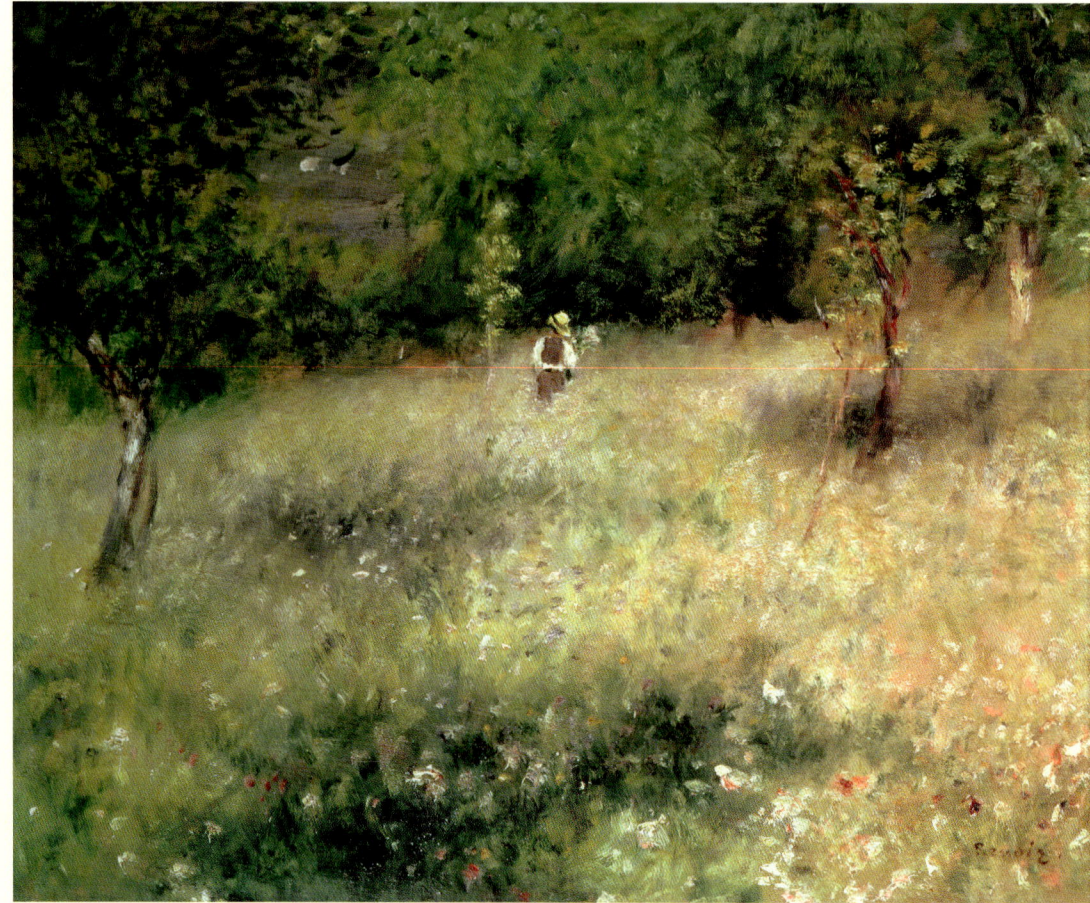

Springtime (in Chatou), c.1875. Although no sky is seen, this painting is suffused with hazy light. The trees and bushes cast long shadows across the grass. The man's lack of a jacket tells the viewer that the spring day is already warm. A narrative element is added by the bunch of flowers he is carrying, picked from the meadow.

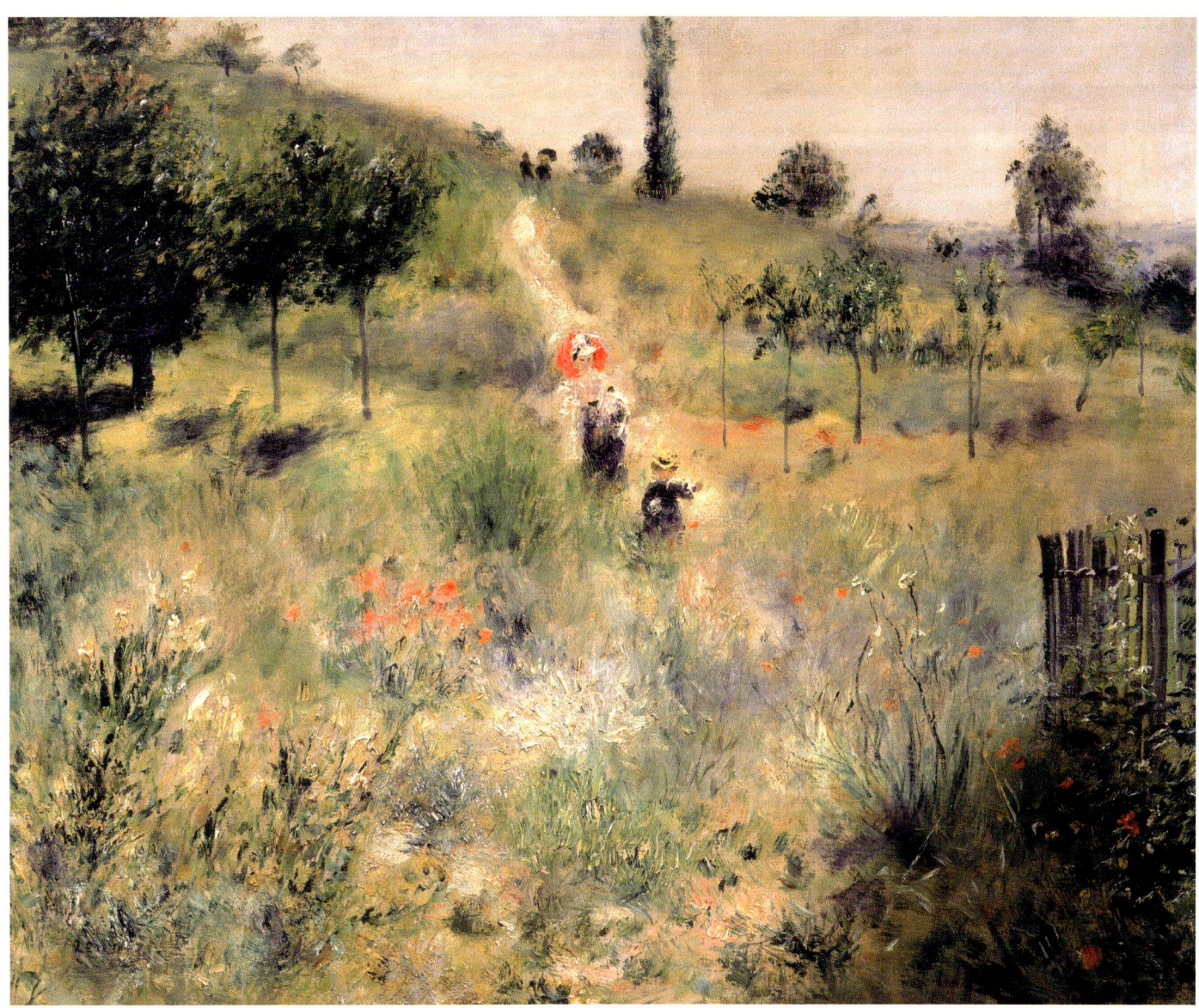

Renoir's travels abroad gave him very different landscape subjects to paint and further opportunities to experiment with light and form (or the lack of it). In a riot of urgent brushstrokes, his *Ravine of the Wild Woman* (1881), painted in Algiers, shows the artist's response to an unfamiliar North African terrain with its unusual plants and colours.

Renoir arrived in Venice in November 1881 and remained there for several weeks, capturing various aspects of the city in its limpid winter light (see page 44). He then travelled down to Naples where, according to art historian and author Christopher Riopelle, he was 'struck by the gradations of the light and by the city's imposing location on a sweeping bay overlooking the Mediterranean.' His *A Garden at Sorrento* shares the luminosity of his Venetian paintings; but its subject matter, a pastoral idyll, and its traditional perspective leading to a vanishing point on the distant horizon show the influence of classical artists such as Nicolas Poussin.

Path Leading Through Tall Grass, 1877. Renoir was more interested in the human figure than were many of the other Impressionists. Here, although only painted in an economical way, the woman and girl on the path are crucial to the composition. The red of the parasol echoes that of the poppies and adds to an evocation of languorous heat.

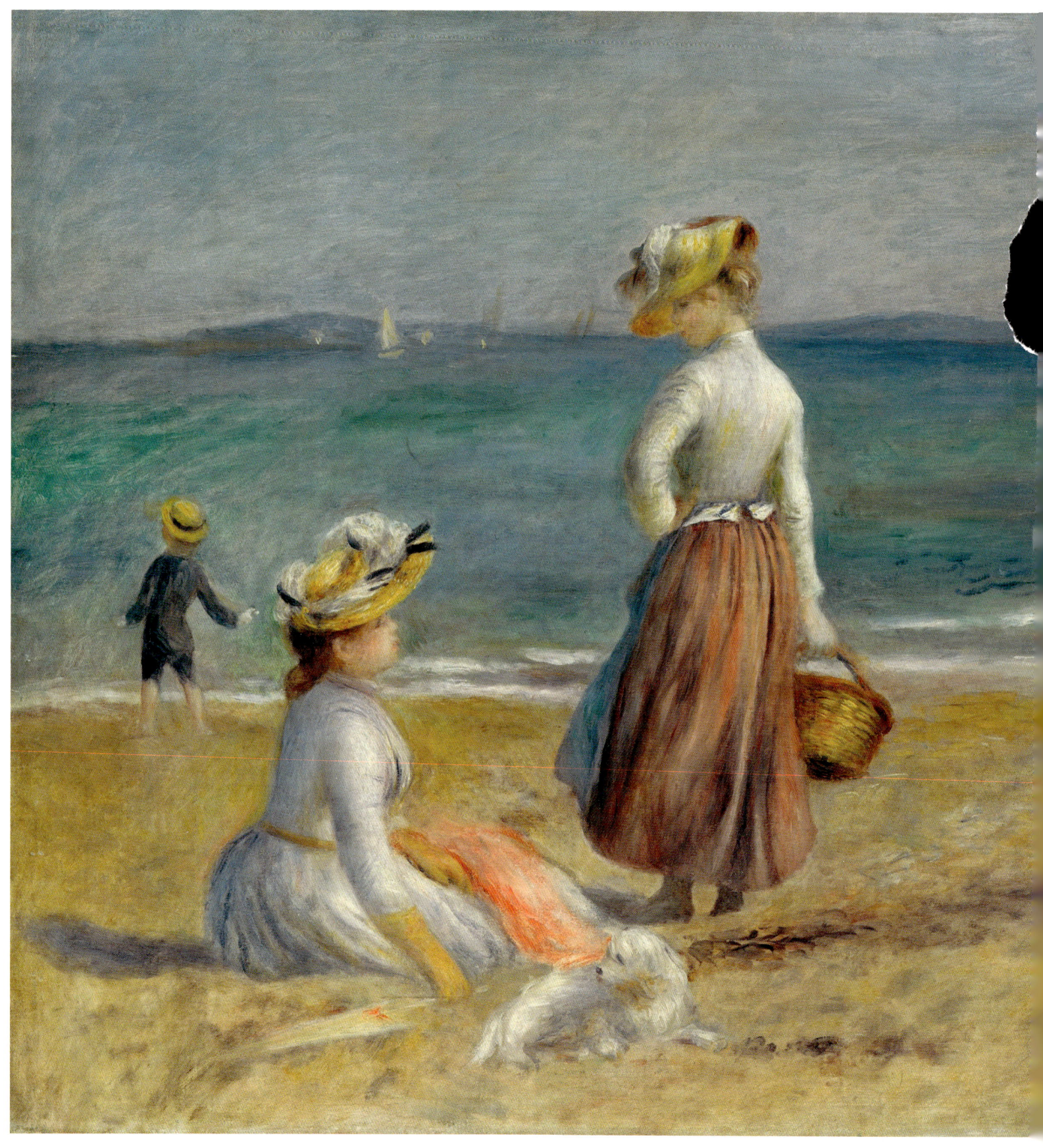

GROWING RECOGNITION

In 1890, Renoir and Aline married and in the autumn moved to a house in Rue Girardon, near the Moulin de la Galette in Paris. Renoir kept a separate studio in Boulevard de Clichy, but the attic of his new home also served the purpose when he wasn't well enough to venture out. He still travelled frequently, leaving the city for long periods in both winter and summer, but his arthritis was becoming increasingly acute and he began to consider moving to a warmer climate for the sake of his health.

In the summer of 1891, Renoir visited Berthe Morisot at her home in Mézy-sur-Seine, where he painted portraits of her daughter. Herself a gifted artist, Morisot's social circle included some of Impressionism's most famous names. She and Renoir influenced each other and he referred to their relationship as 'one of the most solid of my life'. In his book *Renoir, My Father*, his film director son Jean wrote that Morisot 'acted like a special kind of magnet on people, attracting only the genuine.'

The following year, Durand-Ruel mounted a show of Renoir's work in Paris, exhibiting 110 paintings created over twenty years. It was a huge success. Reconciling his *plein air* work with that of the workshop, Renoir had arrived at a synthesis which was distinguished by its free approach to the use of colour, subject and technique. The poet Guillaume Apollinaire wrote, 'Renoir is growing continuously. His latest paintings are the most beautiful. They are also his freshest.'

This enthusiasm for Renoir's paintings was a further step towards a widespread appreciation for Impressionism as a whole. In 1893, American businesswoman, socialite and philanthropist Bertha Palmer bought eight of Renoir's paintings. She and her husband, Chicago millionaire Potter Palmer, were keen art collectors and became clients of Durand-Ruel's. They played a significant part in helping to introduce French Impressionism to the Midwest. 'To think that, had I passed away at sixty, I would have died debt-ridden and bankrupt, surrounded by a wealth of underrated treasures,' wrote Durand-Ruel. 'At last the Impressionist masters triumphed. My madness had been wisdom.'

During the summers of 1892, 1893 and 1895, Renoir visited an artists' colony at Pont-Aven on the coast of Brittany. Its members were heavily influenced by Paul Gauguin, who spent extended periods there during the 1880s and early 1890s. Predictably, now that Impressionism had reached a wide audience, some of its proponents were looking for a new direction. Gauguin's use of bold colours and Symbolist-inspired subjects pointed to the next important modern art movement: Post-Impressionism.

In 1894, Aline gave birth to a second child, Jean, and the household expanded to include Aline's cousin, sixteen-year-old Gabrielle Renard, who was employed as a nanny. Gabrielle developed a strong bond with Jean, which would last throughout their lives, and she became one of Renoir's favourite models.

Figures on the Beach, 1890. *In this Impressionist painting of a sunny beach scene, the two girls appear to be on the brink of a decision. The composition is given tension by the pose of the standing figure who seems poised to leave, travelling in the same direction as the boats offshore. Her billowing skirt suggests the breeze that fills their sails.*

FRIENDS AND CONTEMPORARIES

Several of Renoir's family members and close friends died in the 1890s, including his mother in 1896, and Paul Lhôte and Alfred Sisley in 1899. The deaths which affected him most, however, were those of Gustave Caillebotte in 1894 and Berthe Morisot one year later. Together with Durand-Ruel, Renoir helped to mount posthumous shows of the work of both artists.

As the executor of Caillebotte's will, Renoir was involved in the aftermath of his friend's death. Caillebotte had built up an important collection of Impressionist works, including several by Renoir, and his will specified that all the paintings be left to the Louvre. This caused no little controversy. Despite the recent success of the Impressionists, many French establishment figures were still deeply opposed to their art, and the minister of fine arts initially turned down the collection. Seven years later, after much argument and wrangling, the government finally accepted forty of the total of sixty paintings. They are now among France's most cherished artworks and are on display at the Musée d'Orsay in Paris.

Although not strictly speaking an Impressionist artist, Caillebotte's detached observational style was innovative in other ways. His *The Floor Planers* is said to be one

The Floor Planers, *Gustave Caillebotte, 1875. While country peasants were a popular subject of Barbizon and Impressionist artists, urban workers were largely ignored. Caillebotte combines classical tonal values and drawing with a modern subject, the semi-clothed workers apparently engaged in conversation as they toil. He was a keen collector of photographs – the rich browns and blacks of this painting suggest the quality of contemporary photographic prints. The Salon jurors rejected the painting as 'vulgar subject matter'. It now hangs in the Musée d'Orsay, Paris.*

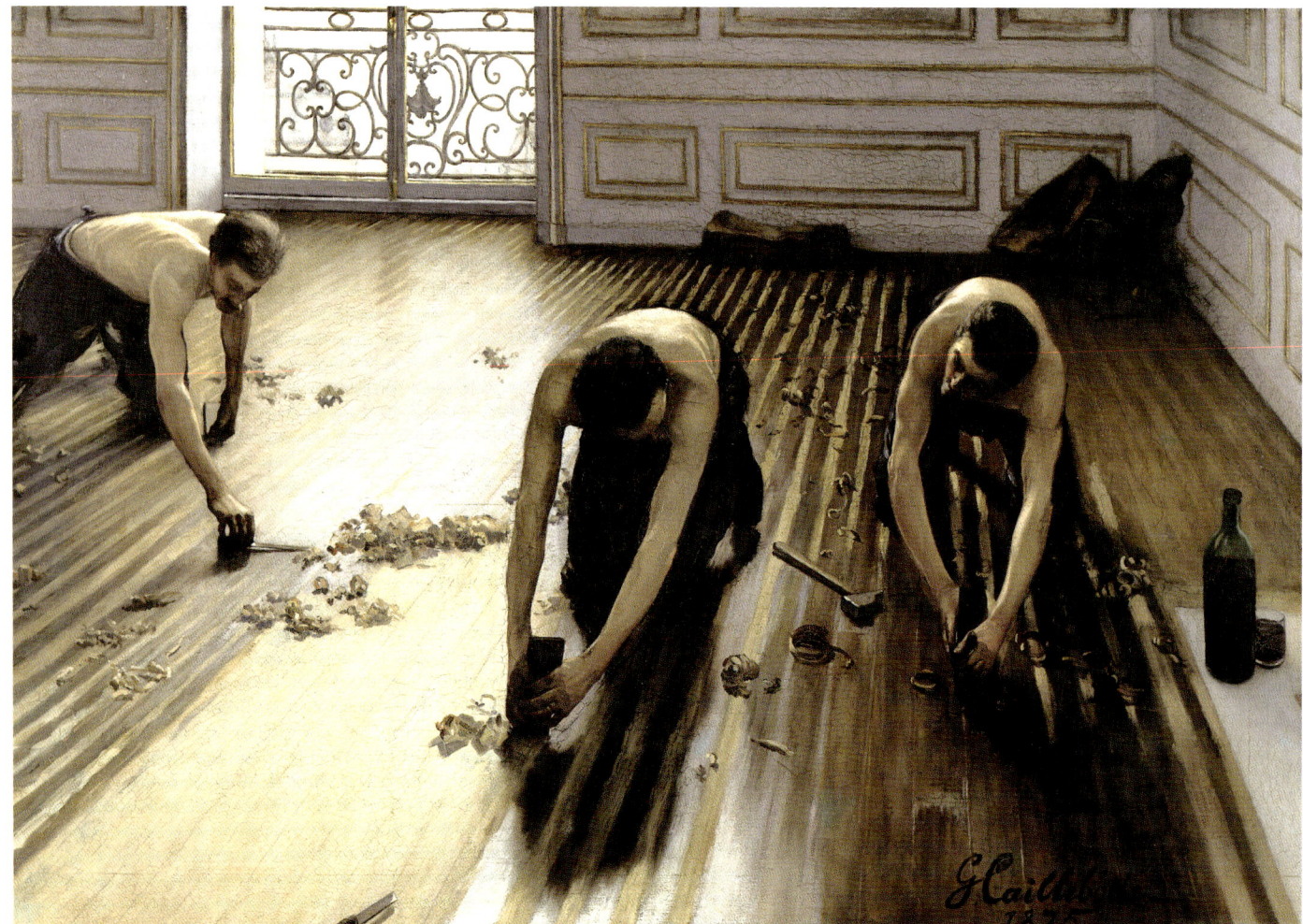

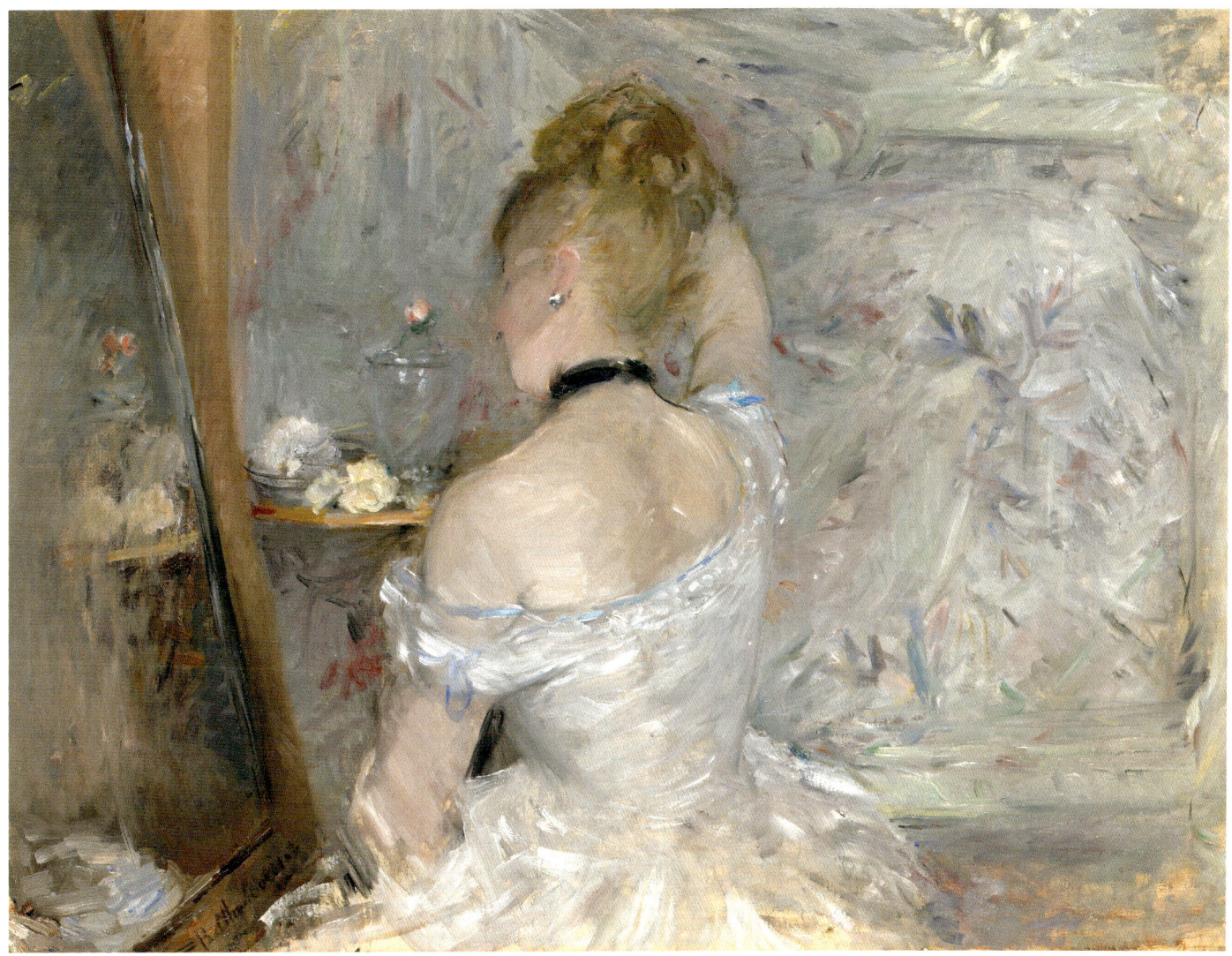

of the first depictions in art of an urban workforce. Unlike some of his contemporaries, Caillebotte didn't try to hammer home any social or political message, he simply documented the scene in a Realist manner, carefully rendering the tools and accessories necessary to the men's labour (together with the obligatory bottle of table wine).

Berthe Morisot died of pneumonia at the age of fifty-four; she had contracted the illness while tending to her sick daughter, Julie. Morisot's husband, Eugène, younger brother of Édouard Manet, had died in 1892. At the age of sixteen, Julie was left an orphan. Renoir provided her with financial and practical support and she spent the first summer following Morisot's death at the

Renoir home. For the next few years (until her marriage to the artist Ernest Rouart in 1900), she was a regular guest and accompanied the Renoir family on several holidays. One year after her mother's death, Julie undertook the emotionally and logistically difficult task of organizing a retrospective exhibition of Morisot's work. Renoir offered advice and support with the hanging of the 300 pieces of art.

Like her fellow Impressionists, Morisot had painted a wide range of subjects – still lifes, landscapes, urban and domestic scenes and portraits. Her scenes of motherhood, including one of her most famous works, *The Cradle*, depict a private world seldom shown in art at the time.

Woman at Her Toilette, *Berthe Morisot, 1875–80. In Morisot's sensitive and sensual painting, rendered with soft feathery brushstrokes, shades of grey, lavender, pink, blue and white create a visual tone poem. Morisot signed her name along the bottom of the mirror as if to emphasize this fleeting glimpse of her subject, almost a silvery reflection itself.*

THE COLOURIST TRADITION

In 1896, Durand-Ruel exhibited forty-two of Renoir's works including his three dance scenes (see pages 36 and 48–9) at the National Academy of Design in New York. The reaction was so positive that Durand-Ruel opened his own gallery in Manhattan the following year.

Back in France, the Renoir family moved home again, this time closer to the centre of Paris, and Renoir took up a position teaching painting. He instructed his students to imitate and study works of the old masters, as he had done as a young man.

His own working method shifted from linear classicism to a softer approach influenced by the colourist tradition of Rubens and Titian. *Young Girl Bathing* (1892) and *Woman Reading* (see right) are good examples of this – portraits thinly painted with soft, caressing brushstrokes.

ROCOCO INFLUENCES

Renoir also experimented with modern versions of genre scenes in the style of Fragonard, Boucher and Watteau. His enthusiasm for Rococo art and the vitality and optimism of Fragonard in particular led him to draw increasingly on eighteenth-century influences while simultaneously maintaining his own personal style. His *Young Girls at the Piano* (see page 59) nods towards Fragonard's *The Music Lesson* (1755) and even towards seventeenth-century Dutch artist Jan Steen's *The Harpsichord Lesson* (1660–9), though Renoir's painting sidesteps the salacious subtext of these earlier works. Instead it focuses innocently on the affectionate relationship between the two girls and the power of the music that brings them together.

Renoir's health progressively worsened. His arthritis attacked periodically, without warning, and he endured painful episodes during which his feet and hands became swollen, parts of his face were paralyzed and movement was painful. Then, just as

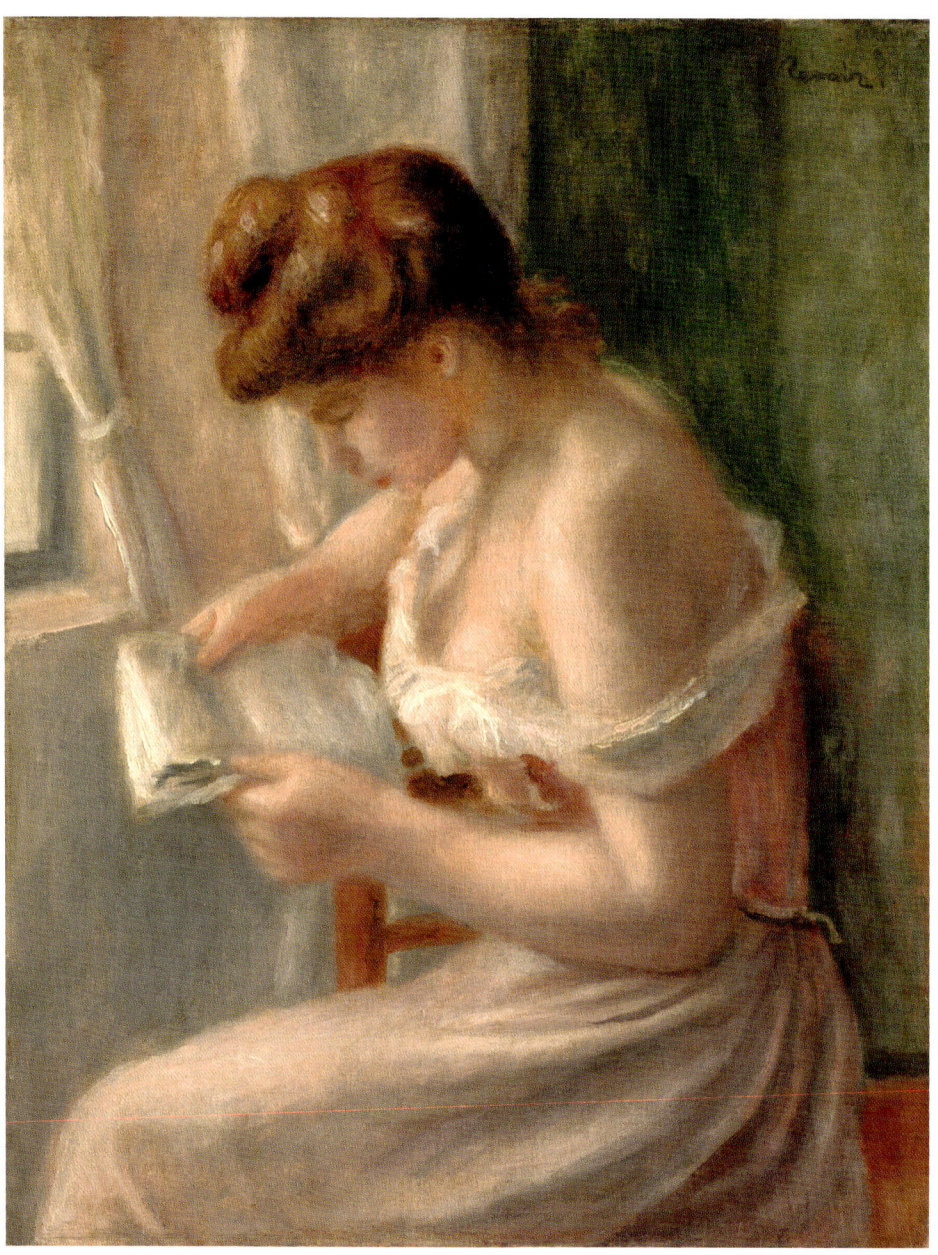

Woman Reading, c.1895. A figure engrossed in reading is a traditional subject in art. Renoir's young woman is reading what seems to be a copious letter; she is apparently oblivious to the artist's presence. Soft window light models her form and highlights the curtain, letter and chemise.

suddenly, his condition would improve and he'd return to work almost as normal. 'One day it's bad and one day better,' he wrote. 'All in all, I think I'll have to get used to living like this.' Another effect of his illness was that he found it increasingly difficult to hold a paintbrush and to master fine details. Nevertheless he continued to produce art, adapting his painting methods and tools to his condition as necessary.

In 1901, Renoir was appointed to the rank of Chevalier of the Légion d'Honneur. He wrote to Monet telling him the news, saying he hoped 'this bit of ribbon' wouldn't stand in the way of their relationship. It didn't – even though by this point Renoir's paintings were selling for more than twice the price of Monet's, they remained firm friends.

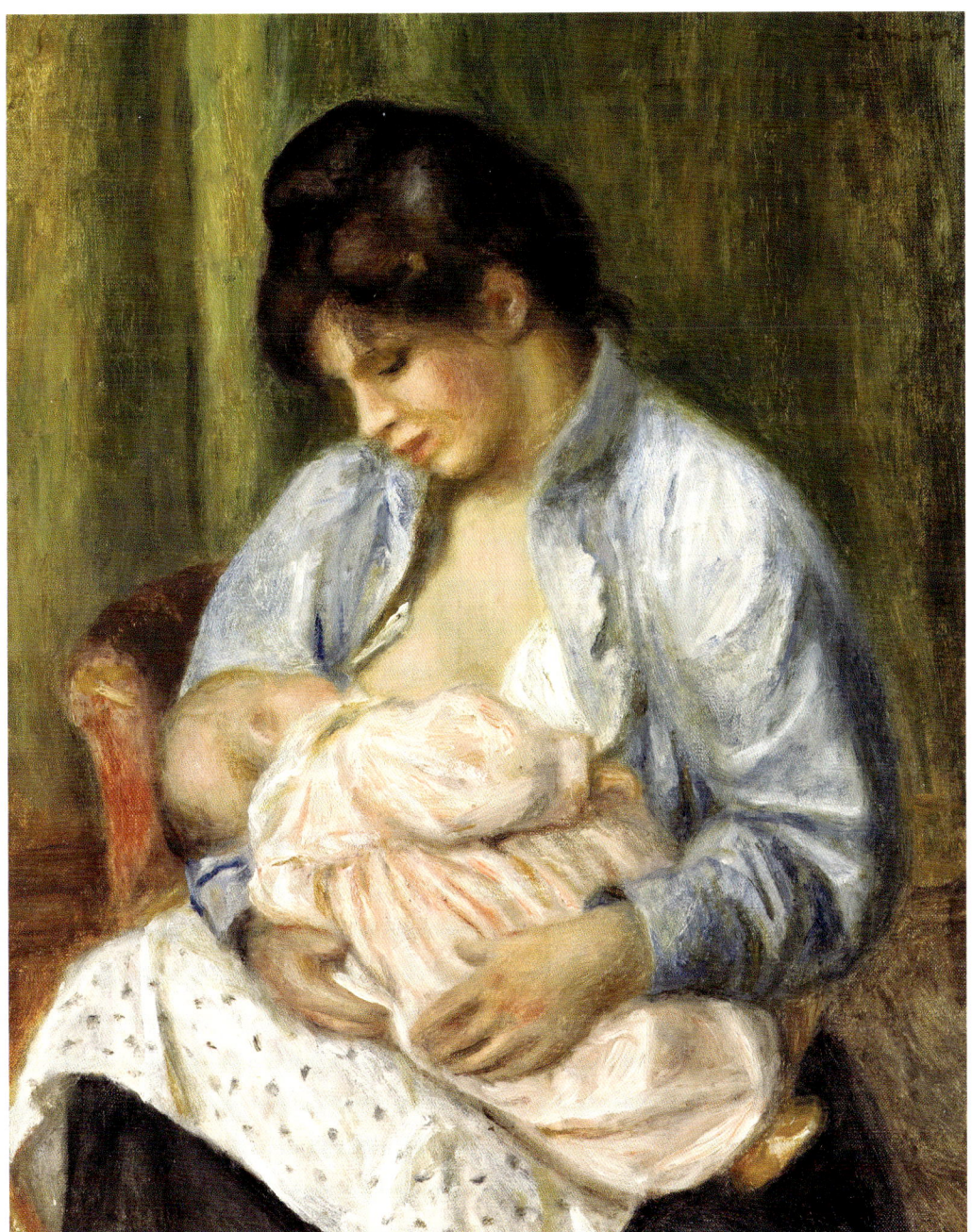

A Woman Nursing a Child, *1894. By the late nineteenth century, allegorical paintings of 'madonnas' had become a mainstay of French visual culture. Renoir's portrait breaks with tradition by showing the mother and child in a Realist setting and thereby illustrating a divine moment of connection in the everyday. He positions them close to the viewer to create a sense of intimacy.*

RENOIR'S NUDES

The nude was and often still is considered the most challenging subject of all. As a young artist with a keen interest in women, it is perhaps surprising that Renoir painted fewer nudes during his youth than in his old age. The early paintings such as *Study. Torso, Effect of Sunlight* (see page 31) are the most immediate and to some viewers the most charming, with the model delineated in the same Impressionist brushwork as the surroundings. But the most famous Renoir nudes date from his later period, after he had adopted a more classical approach and begun to experiment with techniques inspired by the old masters. Over the years he made several hundred works that celebrated the nude, using various media. His later fleshy, bucolic nudes, influenced by the works of Titian, Rubens and Boucher, have aroused the greatest controversy.

Renoir's classical approach meant that he now spent more time in the studio. In these conditions he could achieve the sculptural quality he wanted, using thin layers of paint to depict subtle gradations of skin tone, though he would often set his clearly delineated nude figure against an Impressionistic background.

Towards the end of his life he embraced the influence of the great Renaissance artists and adopted a warmer, reddish palette and an expansive sense of monumentality. Some thought these works overblown and grotesque, but others, including Pablo Picasso and Henri Matisse, admired and emulated Renoir's uncompromising, exaggerated style.

Nude in a Landscape, *c.1887. From Renoir's earlier period, this view of a female nude traces the sensuous lines of her back. Swirling Impressionist brushstrokes blend her body with the landscape.*

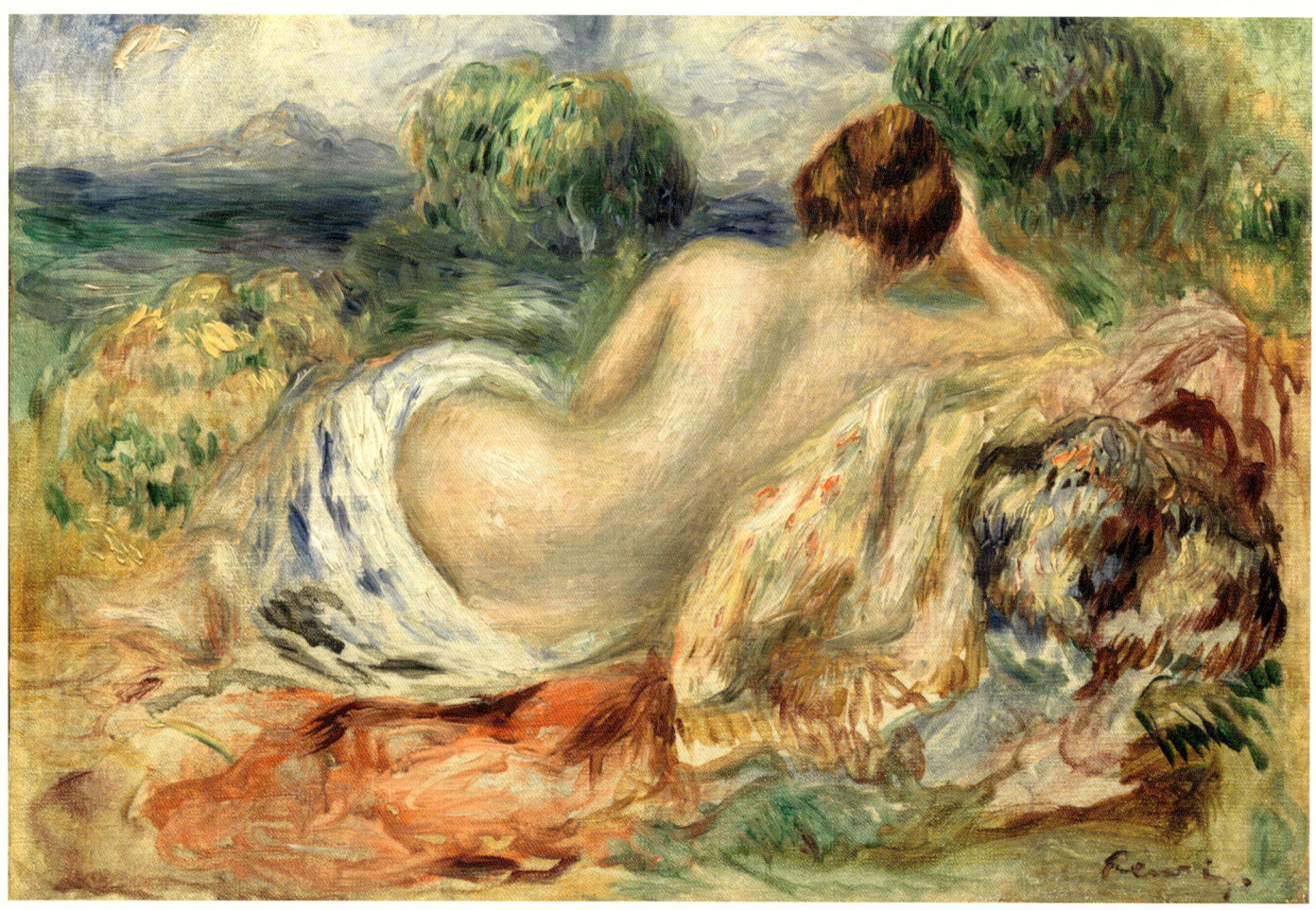

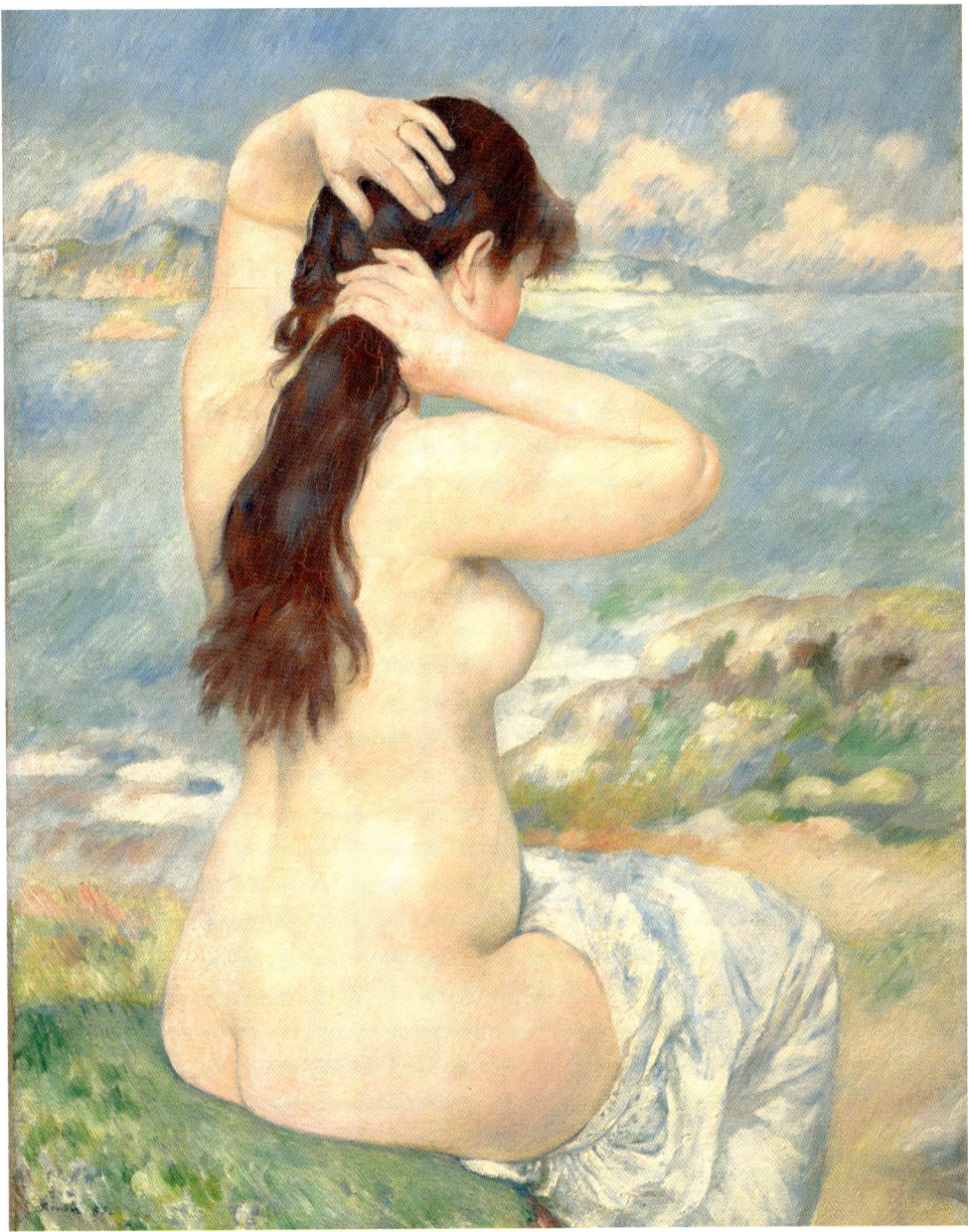

Bather Arranging Her Hair, *1885.*
Some of Renoir's works made during
his classical period appear to show a
pregnant model (Aline was pregnant
with the couple's first child in 1884–5).
The figure here is painted with Ingres-
like precision; the smooth, sculptural
modelling of the female form ensures
that it is sharply defined against the
Impressionist background.

Renoir was also influenced by classical sculpture. He first saw the works of Jean Goujon (*c.*1510–67), a Renaissance sculptor and architect, when he was a young man and never lost his admiration for them. And he learnt from Ingres that it wasn't essential to reproduce the female form as it existed in front of his gaze; he could exaggerate proportions as he wished and merge traditional classical influences with his own unique artistic vision.

The effect of the exuberant Rococo style of Watteau and Fragonard can be seen in Renoir's paintings of nudes in panoramic Neo-classical tableaux, splashing one another with water or reclining languidly in Arcadian landscapes. Henri Matisse described *The Bathers* (see page 88), completed in the year of Renoir's death, as 'one of the most beautiful pictures ever painted'.

Visiting the Louvre as a young man, Renoir had been impressed by François Boucher's *Diana Bathing*. In his old age, this painting returned to his mind and he made several works of his own which echoed the theme. His later nudes show little attempt to capture the sitter's personality – he was more interested in technique, particularly that of Rubens, of whom he said, 'There is magnificent colour, of an extraordinary richness, even though the paint is very thin.'

Elsewhere in the art world, movements such as Fauvism, Cubism and abstraction were beginning to develop. Renoir's voluminous nudes seemed to belong to a different age and therefore fell out of fashion. The American Impressionist artist Mary Cassatt described

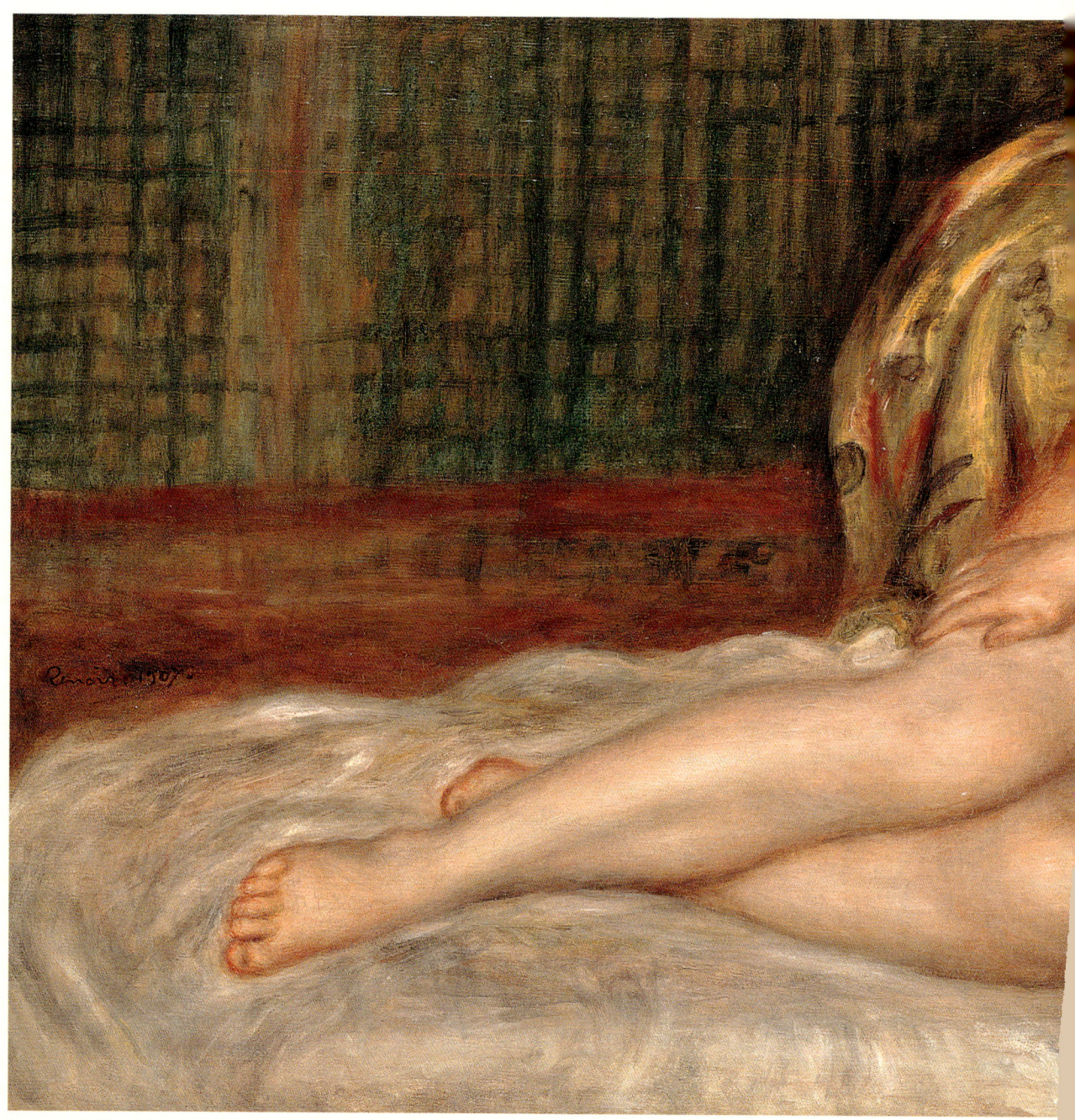

Renoir's late-period nudes as 'enormously fat red women with small heads'. And although Matisse admired *The Bathers*, elsewhere it was criticized for the 'enormousness of the legs and arms, the weakness of the flesh, and the pinkish colour of the models'.

Undaunted by criticism and by his failing health, Renoir persisted. In 1919, the year of his death, he was still painting every day, producing large canvases of unashamedly erotic nudes. In *Large Nude* (below) he restricted his palette to a harmonious assortment of subtle tones and bathed his figure in a warm, gentle light. The influence of Ingres can be detected in the elegant pose. Matisse wrote: 'Even as he was going into decline, his soul seemed to be stronger and to express itself with a more radiant facility.'

Large Nude, 1907. While the background and furnishings are described with loose brushstrokes, the interior setting and smooth modelling of the naked body in an even light are a world away from the Impressionistic style of Renoir's earlier works.

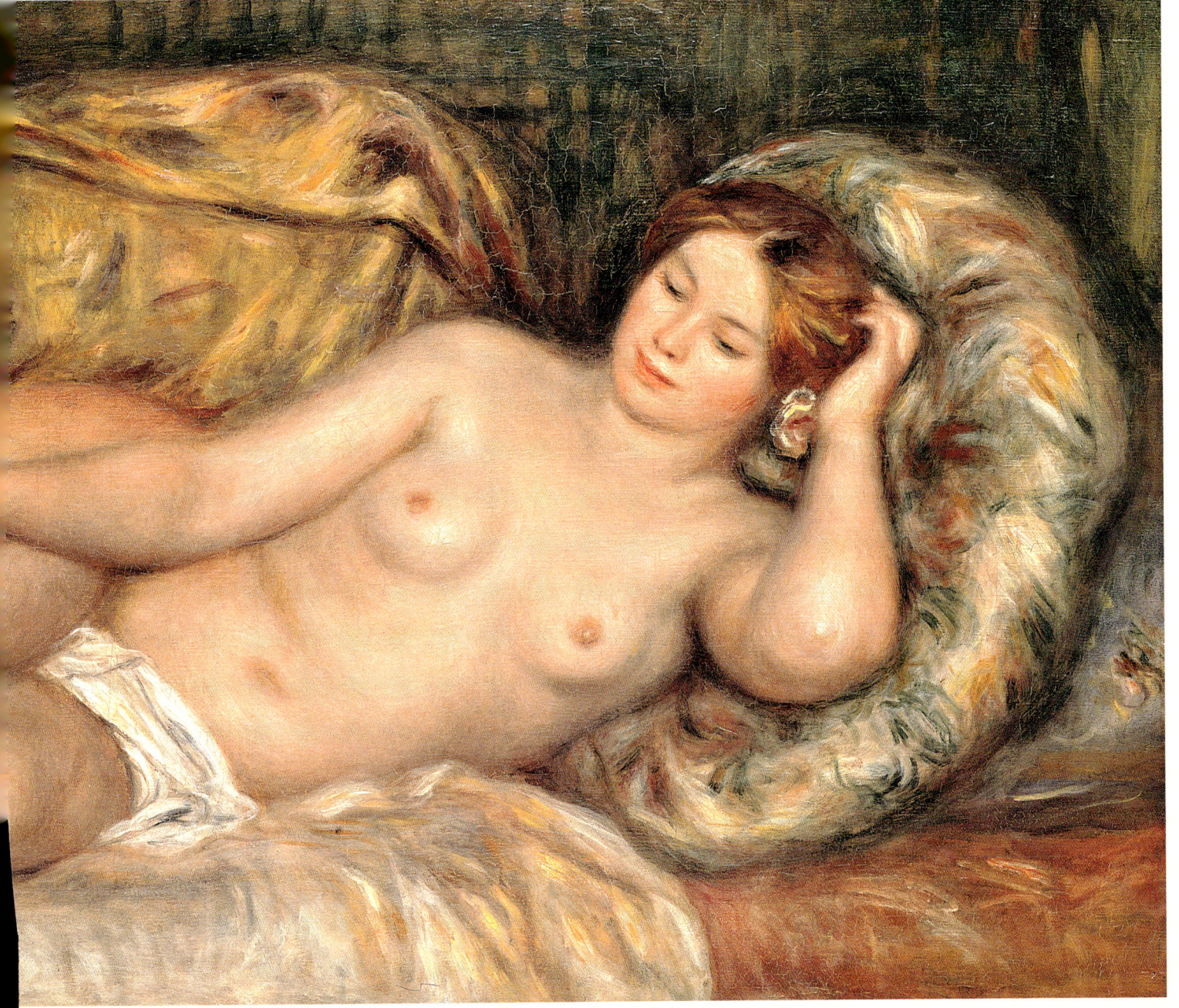

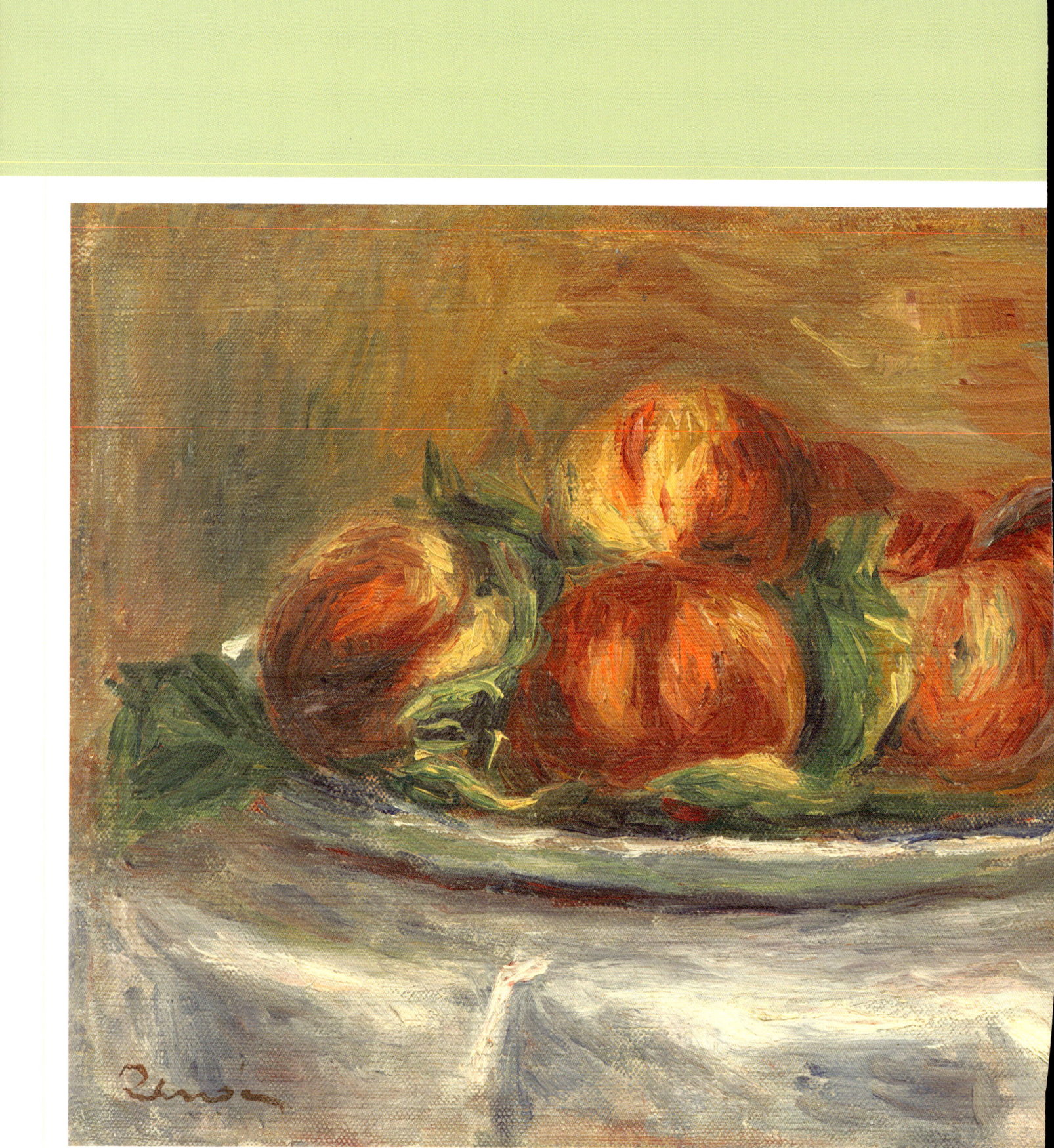

CHAPTER 4
A New Century

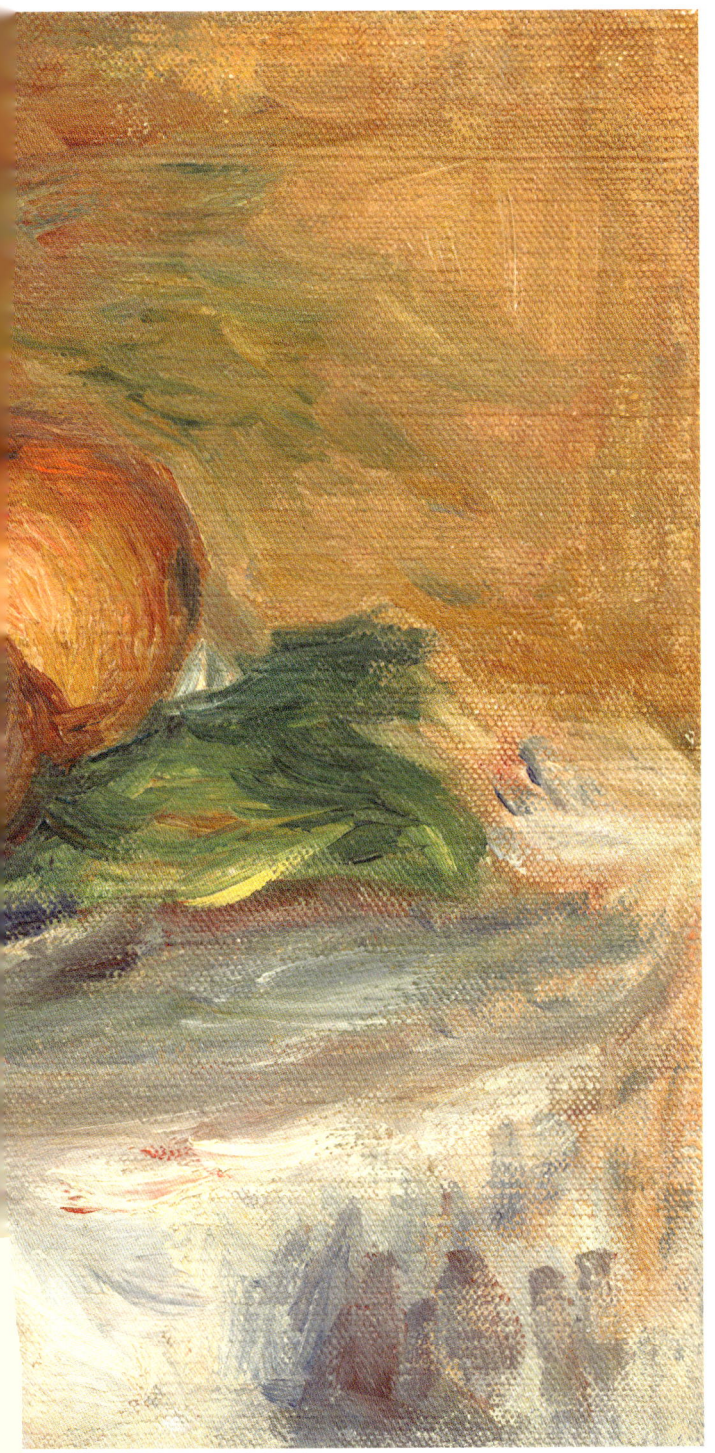

By the turn of the century, Renoir was spending much of the year in the south of France. He concentrated on painting still lifes and landscapes, and on portraits of his wife, children and Gabrielle, who posed for several of his nude works.

A third child, Claude (nicknamed Coco) was born to Renoir and Aline, then aged 60 and 41 respectively, on 4 August 1901. Renoir went on to paint his youngest child regularly; a strong bond developed between father and son and over the next few years Coco would feature in more pictures than his two brothers combined.

In spite of his infirmity, and sometimes because of it when he needed to journey for treatment, Renoir still travelled frequently. In 1901 he visited Fontainebleau to fulfil a commission for the art dealer Alexandre Bernheim, who wanted a portrait painted of his twin sons with their respective fiancées. Bernheim owned an art gallery and represented Barbizon and Impressionist artists; he organized the first significant exhibition of Vincent van Gogh paintings in Paris, also in 1901.

By this stage, Renoir's infirmity had become severe – he needed a cane to walk and his hands were distorted from the effects of arthritis. But his indomitable spirit meant his suffering was never reflected in his paintings.

Peaches on a Plate, c.1905. Art historian Meyer Schapiro described the still life form as 'a democratizing trend in art that gives a positive significance to the everyday world'. This is evident in Renoir's still lifes, which are always intensely committed to their subject, however mundane it may be. In this painting, peaches ripened in the Mediterranean sun imbue their surroundings – even the white tablecloth – with a warm orange glow.

'YES, PRETTY! LIFE
BRINGS ENOUGH
UNPLEASANTNESS –
WHY NOT APPROACH IT
FROM THE LIGHT SIDE
ONCE IN A WHILE?'

Pierre-Auguste Renoir

GLOBAL SUCCESS

In the early 1900s, Renoir was at the peak of his success. Feted around the world, his works were exhibited in the USA, France, Germany, Spain, Switzerland, Britain and elsewhere. Their price continued to rise, sometimes spectacularly so. In 1907, the Metropolitan Museum of Modern Art in New York bought his 1878 portrait *Madame Charpentier and Her Children* (see page 37) for an astonishing 92,000 francs – more than sixty times the sum (1,500 francs) he had been paid for painting it. Such was his success that the burgeoning market for Renoir forgeries caused the artist, at least on one occasion, to launch a legal complaint. In an effort to thwart the forgers, Durand-Ruel started to take the precaution of photographing every painting he bought from Renoir and getting the artist to sign the photo.

Despite his success, Renoir continued to paint with gusto as though he were a struggling artist. In 1909 he wrote to Durand-Ruel: 'I am glad to know that the collectors are less stubborn. Better late than never. But this will not keep me from continuing my daily grind, as if nothing had happened.'

Although his style of painting altered considerably over the years, he continued to concentrate on subjects that had dominated his work since the mid-1880s – landscapes,

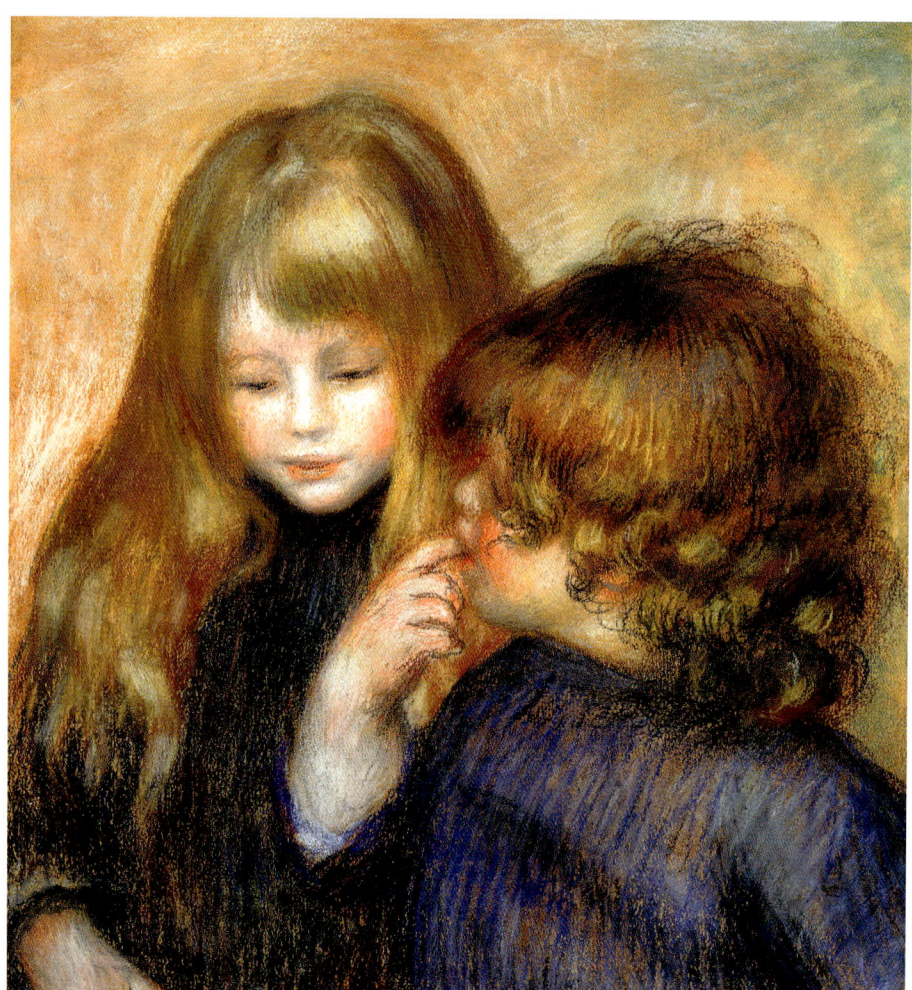

domestic intimacy, still lifes and the female form. He seemed determined to show life as intensely beautiful, even if the reality was precisely the opposite. His paintings were always joyous, sensual and accessible, a feature of his work that has led some critics to describe it as superficial and sentimental. But this assessment vastly underestimates his contribution to Impressionism and to twentieth-century art as a whole.

Once at the forefront of a radical new art movement which was scorned by the elite, in his later years Renoir was spurned by the same elite for experimenting with traditional methods and themes and adapting them to his personal vision. The cruel irony of the situation is unlikely to have escaped him.

Jean and Coco, c.1902. *This gentle picture of Renoir's youngest children is rendered in pastels with blue, purple, gold and brown predominating.*

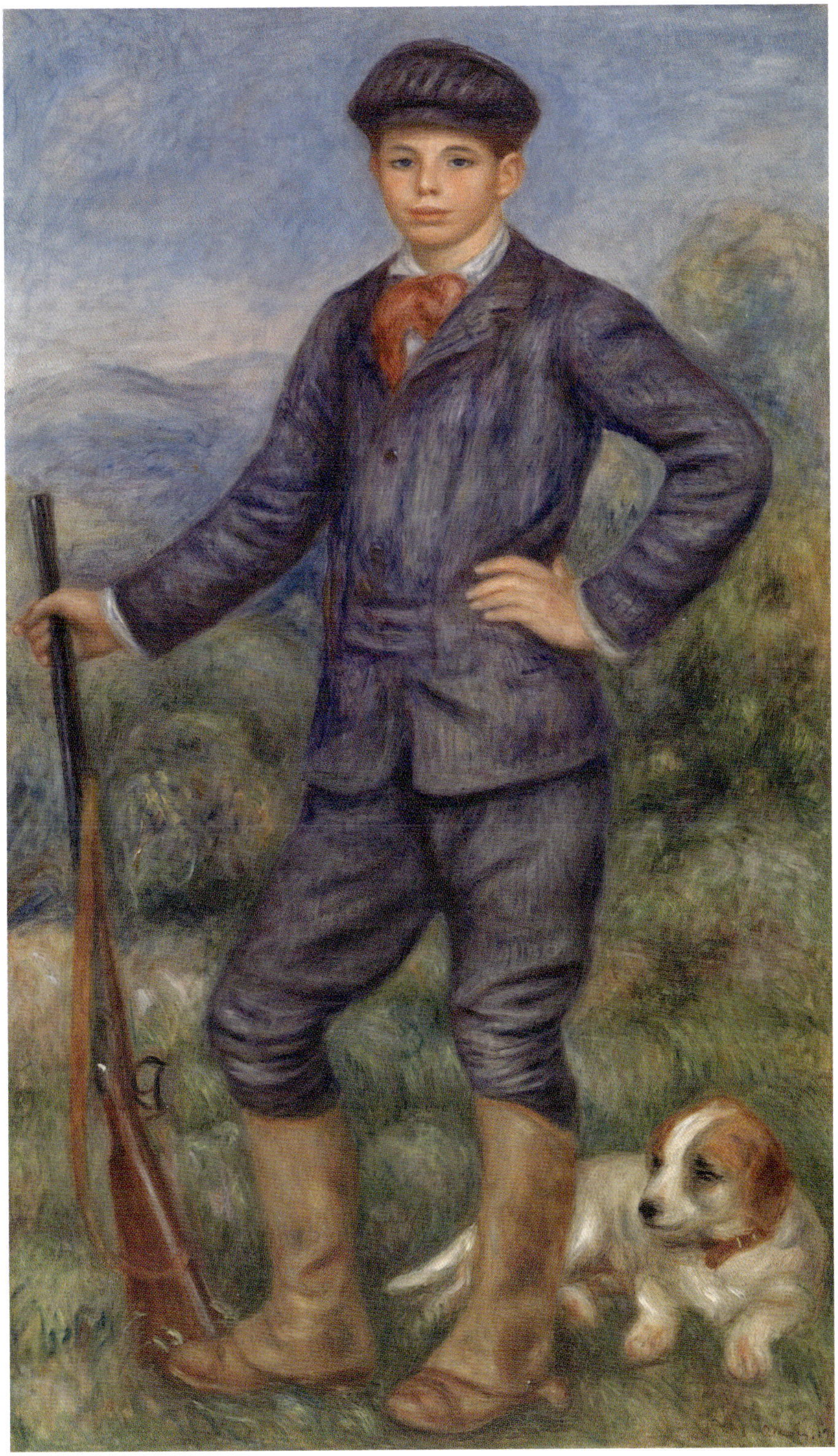

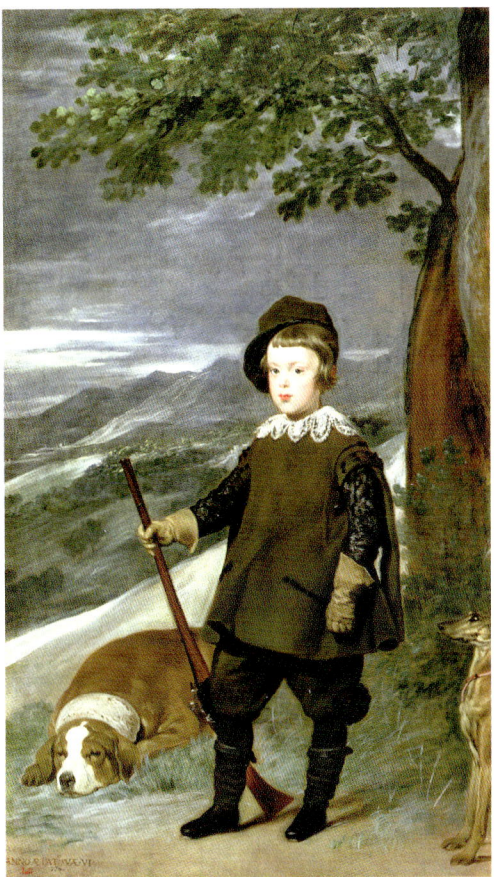

Above: Prince Baltasar Carlos in Hunting Dress
Diego Rodríguez de Silva y Velázquez, 1635–6.

Left: Jean as a Huntsman, 1910. *This portrait of
Renoir's son Jean is clearly influenced by the painting
above. Renoir takes inspiration from the formal pose
of the young Spanish prince but imbues the painting
with fresh meaning. Occupying the entire frame and
wearing a rough blue/green suit, Jean appears to
have grown out of the landscape – he belongs to it.
Instead of being lord of all he surveys, he is a man of
the people, a rebel even.*

RENOIR'S PORTRAITS

Renoir painted a huge number of portraits, including ones of his wife, family and friends and, importantly from a financial perspective, clients and business associates. In his youth, actresses and models predominated; they were often painted in their finery but sometimes as nudes. Renoir's handling of delicate fabrics such as silk and gauze and his skill at depicting the quality and glow of youthful skin would have started to develop during his teenage years spent painting intricate decorations on porcelain plates.

One of his favourite models was the actress Henriette Henriot who appeared in at least eleven of his paintings during the 1870s. In 1874, he portrayed her in a dress which neo-Impressionist painter Paul Signac described as 'a pure intense blue. . . . The interaction between the colours is captured admirably. It is simple, fresh and beautiful. It was painted twenty years ago, but you would think it had come straight from the studio.' This painting, known as *La Parisienne* (see facing page), is now one of Renoir's most famous portraits. Two years later, he painted the eighteen-year-old Henriette elegantly posing in a diaphanous white blouse, again gazing directly towards the viewer (see right).

At the Impressionist auction in 1875 at the Hôtel Drouot, Renoir came to the attention of the art collector Victor Chocquet, a senior figure in the Customs Office. Chocquet wrote to him requesting that he paint a portrait of his wife. Chocquet was a great admirer of Delacroix and

had recognized some of his influence in Renoir's work. He commissioned several portraits of himself, his wife and his daughter and became an early supporter of Renoir and other Impressionists while they were still largely unappreciated.

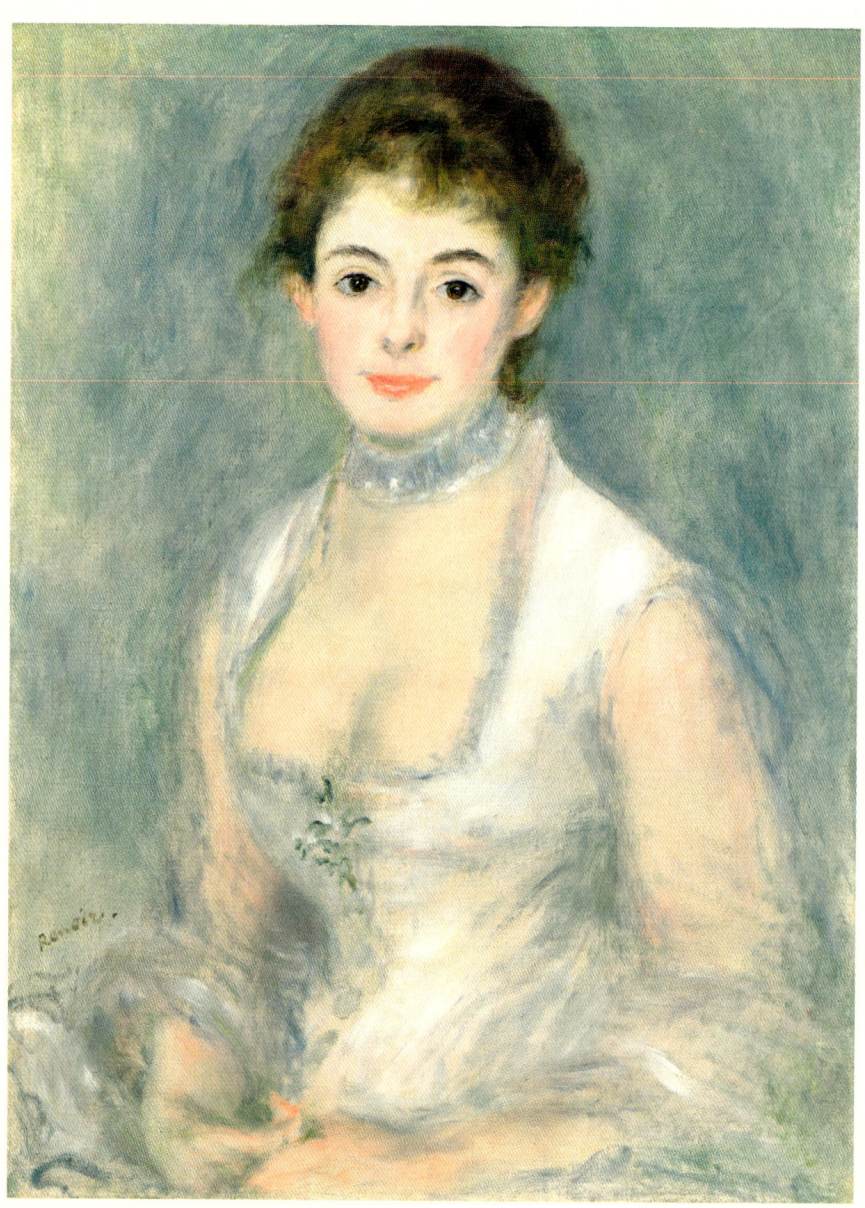

Portrait of Madame Henriot, 1876. *This portrait was a gift from the artist to his model. Most of the painting is economically worked, with the blue background colour scrubbed across the canvas. Only the face is given detailed treatment, making it the primary focus.*

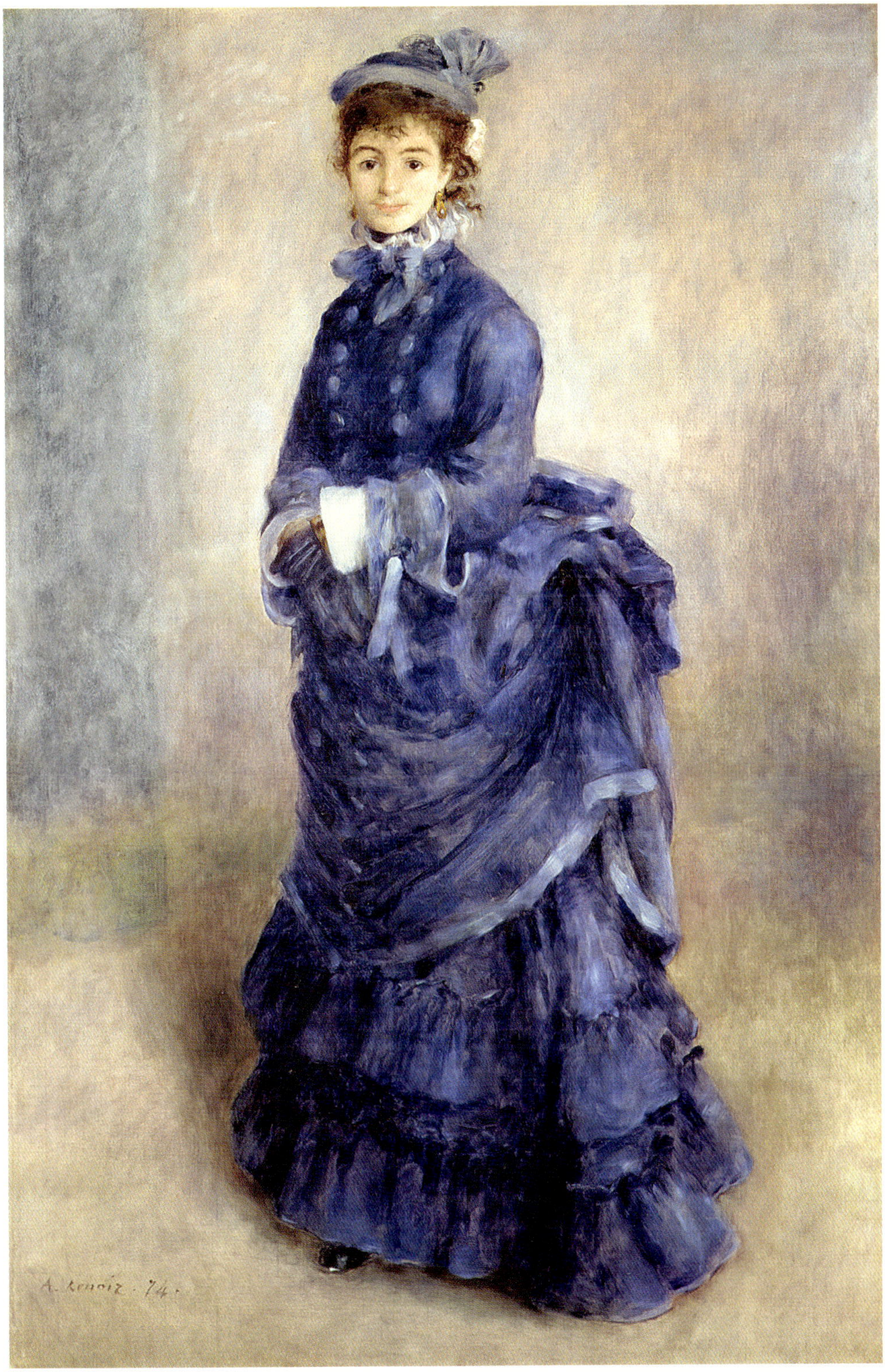

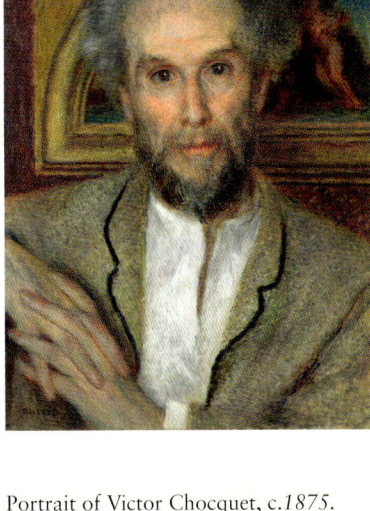

Portrait of Victor Chocquet, c.1875.
*While Renoir's portraits of men often
lacked the sense of intense engagement
he found with his female models,
this painting of his friend and patron
conveys an affectionate relationship
between artist and sitter.*

*One of Renoir's best-known portraits, La Parisienne, 1874, shows the sixteen-year-old Henriette
Henriot in a cornflower blue dress. Although at first glance an image of sobriety, it is a bewitching piece.
Contemporary critics remarked on the 'daringly coquettish' tilt of the hat and the 'little black mouse' of
a shoe peeping out beneath the hem of her dress.*

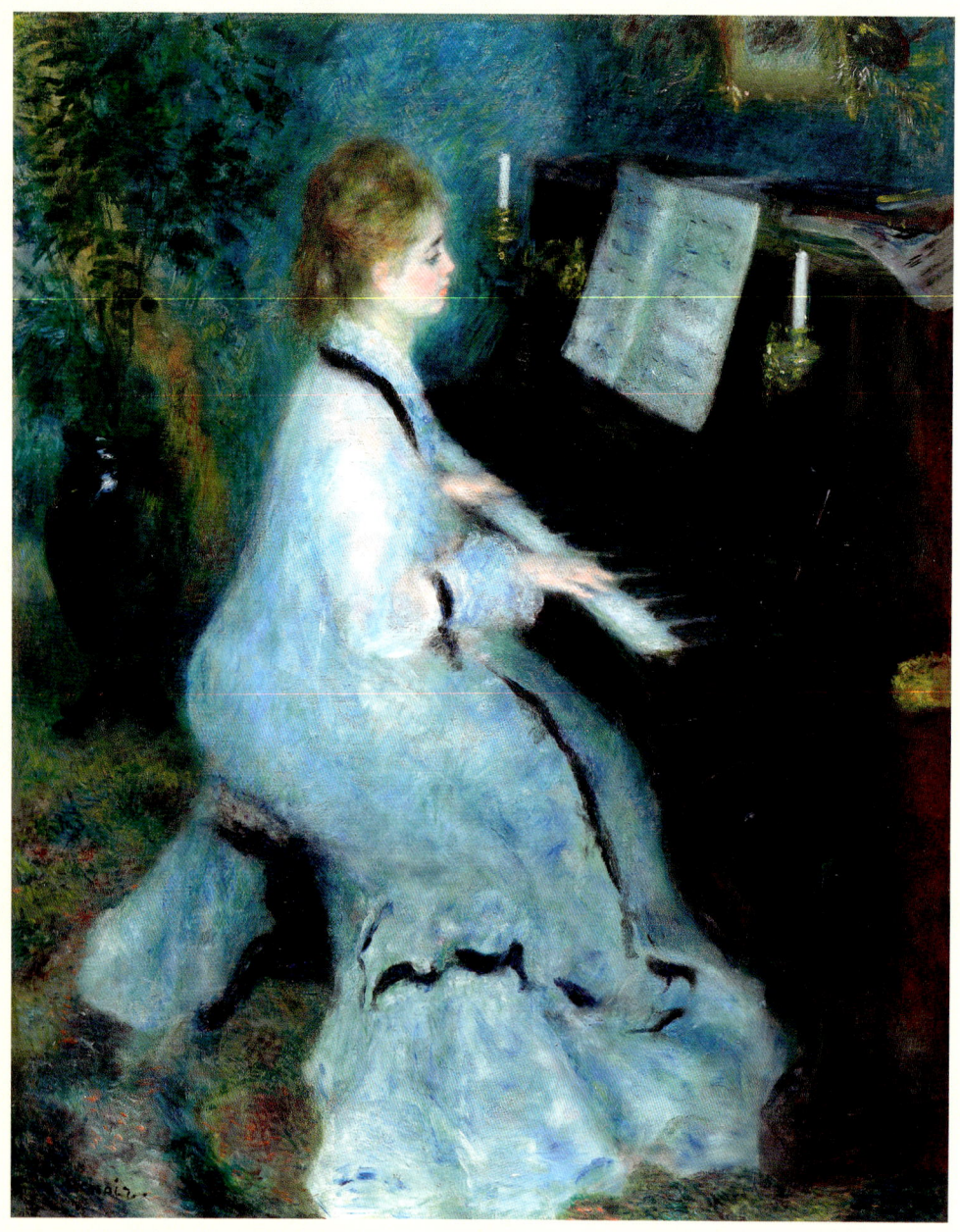

Woman at the Piano, *1875–6.*
This painting of a young woman emphasizes her delicate beauty as her luminous hands pick out a tune on the piano keys. The skin of her arm is faintly visible through the diaphanous fabric of her white gown and she shimmers against the dark background. This is portrait painting at its most romantic and soulful.

Renoir was much more interested in painting figures than most of the other Impressionists. The city of Paris offered him an endless supply of models, from the young working-class girls who populated the streets and cafés of Montmartre to their polar opposite, the elegantly attired theatre-goers and wives of his wealthy clients. Then, of course, there were the actresses, including Jeanne Samary, a performer at the Comédie-Française. Fascinated by Jeanne's golden hair, beautiful complexion and captivating personality, Renoir used her in twelve of his paintings, including *Luncheon of the Boating Party*, and for several portraits, such as *La Rêverie*.

Renoir's Impressionist portrait style is perfectly illustrated by the painting on the left. The swift, broken brushstrokes and focus on artificial lighting effects are a world away from the monumentalism of *The Large Bathers* (see pages 56–7). With its dark, shadowy environment and contrasting white/blue palette for the woman's dress, this painting is reminiscent of the work of fellow artists Édouard Manet and Berthe Morisot.

After the success of *Madame Charpentier and Her Children* (see page 37), Renoir received many commissions for family portraits. For more than fifty years he explored the genre, creating charming, vivid images of bourgeois wealth, comfort and elegance that capture the spirit of Paris during the Belle Époque. Although from a working-class background, Renoir was at ease in the homes of the wealthy and treated all his sitters equally, regardless of their social standing. He particularly enjoyed painting portraits of children. The comfortable relationships he established with his clients are evident from the canvases. Over time, his portraits became more restrained and formal, although he always maintained his adventurous use of colour.

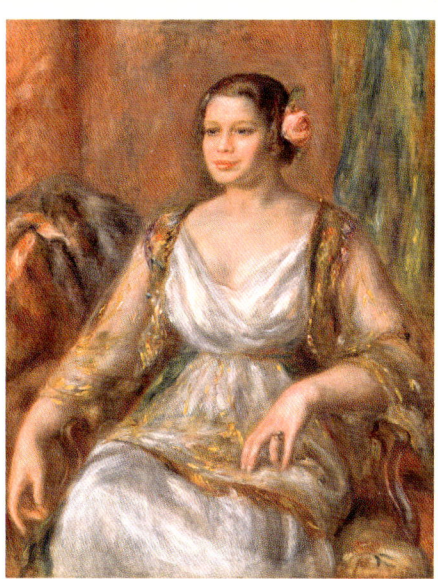

Children Playing Ball, *1900. In contrast to the formality of Renoir's commissioned portraits, this colour lithograph captures a fleeting moment in which children merrily play and squabble, oblivious to the artist who is sketching them.*

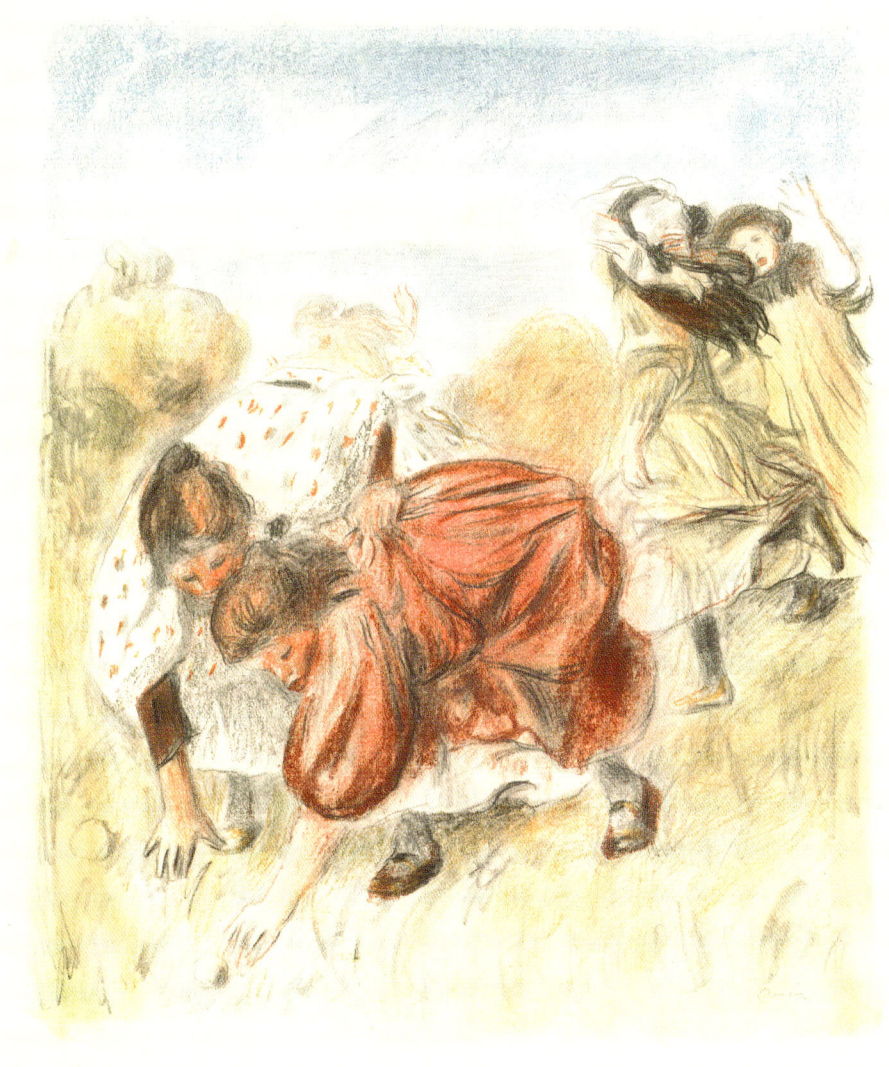

Portrait of Tilla Durieux, *1914. An Austrian movie and theatre actress, Tilla Durieux visited Paris in 1914 to have her portrait painted by Renoir. By this time the artist was in a wheelchair, brushed strapped to his hand. He painted his sitter in a statuesque pyramidal pose in the classical style.*

In his final years, Renoir's sitters were depicted in a very similar style, with voluptuous figures and pearly skin. His last commission was probably a portrait of the actress Tilla Durieux, wife of the German art dealer Paul Cassirer. In her memoirs, Tilla wrote of posing for him for two weeks. When the painting was finished, she claimed that he commented: 'I have improved, wouldn't you say?' Summing up his father's art, Jean Renoir wrote: 'His nudes . . . declared to men of this century, already deep in their task of destruction, the stability of the eternal balance of nature.'

Renoir also painted more personal scenes for his own pleasure. Full of life, they convey the impression of an artist surrounded by loving friends and family, and include freely expressed observational images of his children and others playing in the wilderness around Cagnes.

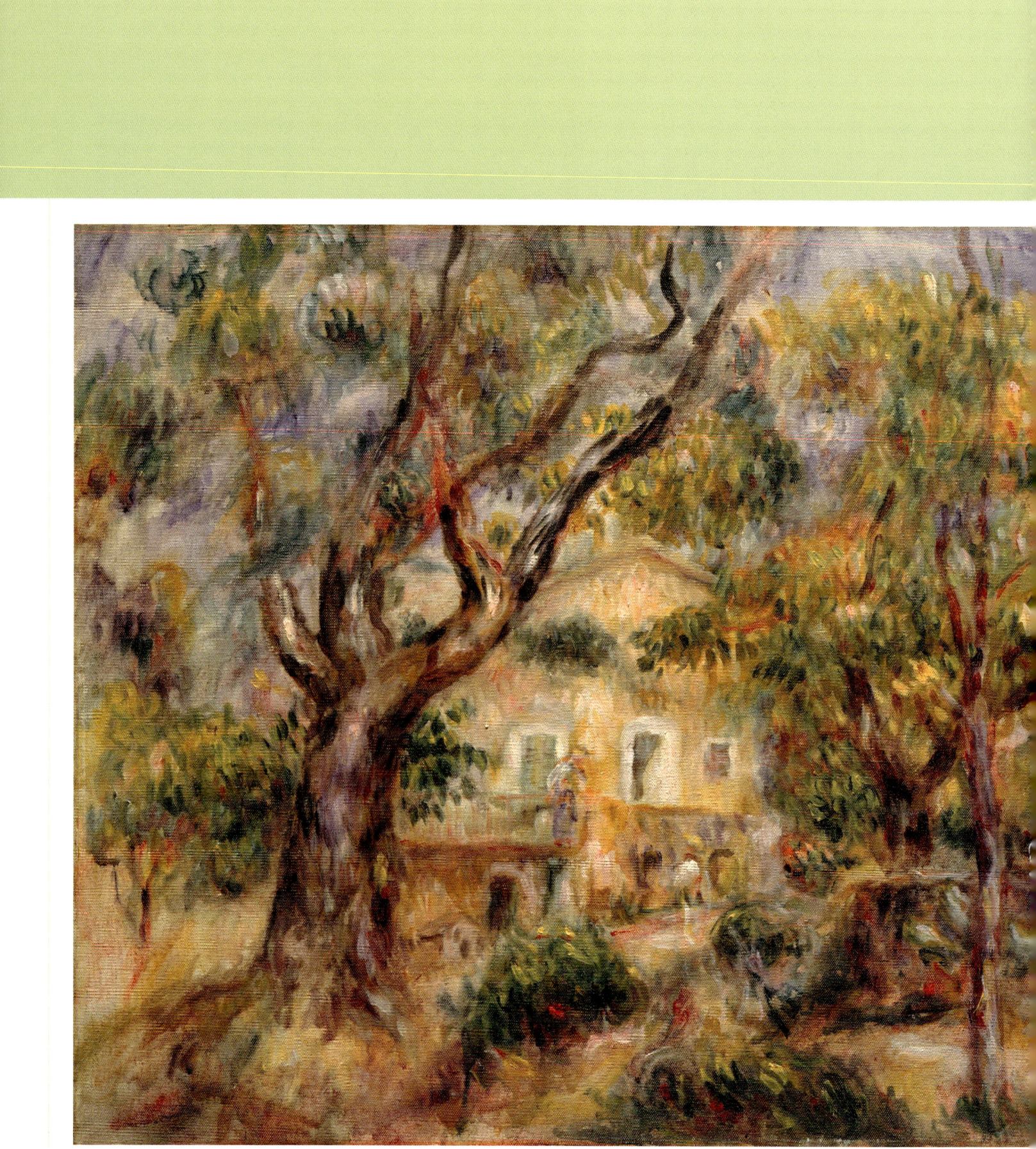

CHAPTER 5
The Final Years

In 1903, Renoir moved to Cagnes-sur-Mer near the city of Nice on the Mediterranean coast. At first he rented an apartment in a house (now the town hall) on the Rue de la Poste. In 1907, when he heard that several hectares of olive groves on a local estate were to be cut down and sold as timber, he bought the property to preserve them. It was here that he created his final home, Les Collettes, with its picturesque farmhouse and the views it afforded of beautiful, hilly countryside.

By 1910, Renoir's arthritis meant that he could no longer walk. He developed an elaborate mechanical system of a wheelchair and canvas support that were height-adjustable, which he used to reach every part of even large-scale paintings. His works from this period are joyful and give no hint of the frailty of the artist who created them.

Renoir seemed to recover the instinctive freshness of his art in the landscape and sunlight of the south of France. His final paintings are suffused with light, colour and vitality.

The Farm at Les Collettes, Cagnes, 1908–14. Renoir painted a number of views of the farmhouse and landscape at Les Collettes. In spite of his stiffened hands, the trees are painted with notable fluidity and expressiveness. Renoir's use of trees as a visual screen is reminiscent of Cézanne's technique of integrating foreground and background space.

'I WANT A RED TO BE SONOROUS, TO SOUND LIKE A BELL. IF IT DOESN'T TURN OUT THAT WAY, I ADD MORE REDS AND OTHER COLOURS UNTIL I GET IT.'

Pierre-Auguste Renoir

Claude Renoir in Clown Costume, 1909. *Dressed in red pantaloons and white ruff, Renoir's youngest son is painted standing next to a pillar, referencing the classical tradition.*

LIFE AT LES COLLETTES

Renoir's three boys were largely allowed to run free on the estate, although they were sometimes pressed into posing for portraits. In these, Renoir often experimented with methods learned from the masters, including Watteau and Velázquez. A series of paintings of Coco show the boy with a pink bow in his hair, inspired by a seventeenth-century Velázquez portrait of the Spanish infanta. Occasionally the children were required to model in complete costumes and in poses referencing paintings from earlier centuries. Renoir's commissions also reflect this: in 1910, he visited Germany to paint a portrait of the wife and daughter of Dr Fritz Thurneyssen. The fulsome result, *Madame Thurneyssen and Her Daughter*, is clearly influenced by Rubens.

Renoir's later years were afflicted by sadness. His two older sons, Pierre and Jean, were wounded while fighting in World War I, and Aline died in 1916. Despite all this, the artist ploughed on. His later nude paintings are highly sensual; they feature roses, symbolizing feminine beauty, and the palette is dominated by pinks, reds, ochres and golds. The excess of female flesh on display invited criticism from some quarters, which Renoir appeared to delight in, commenting: '[The model] is only there to inspire me, to

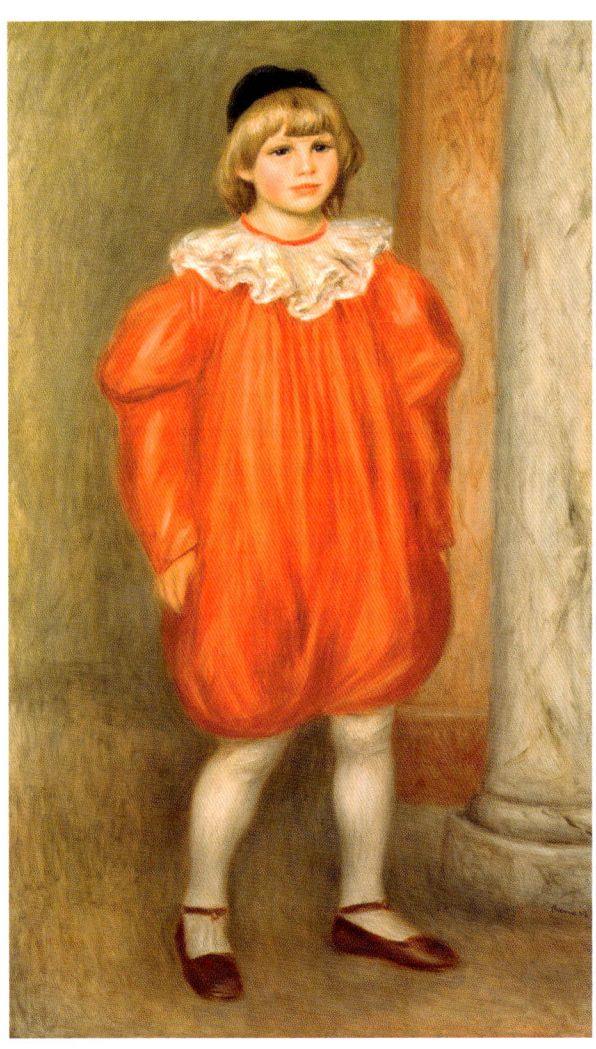

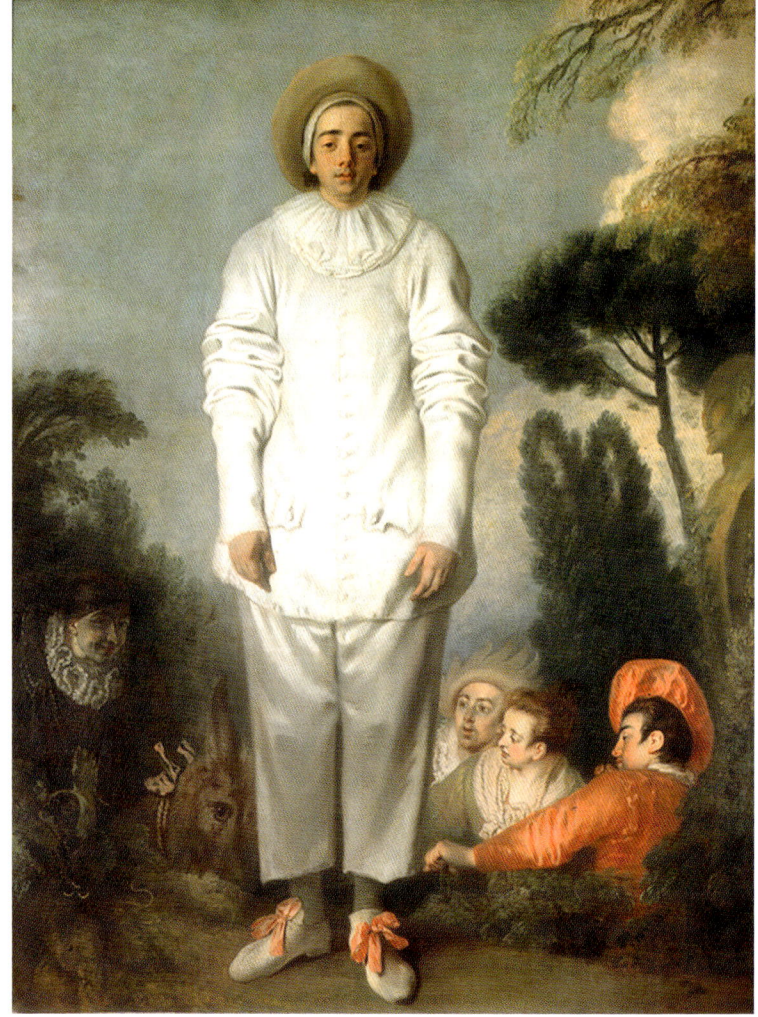

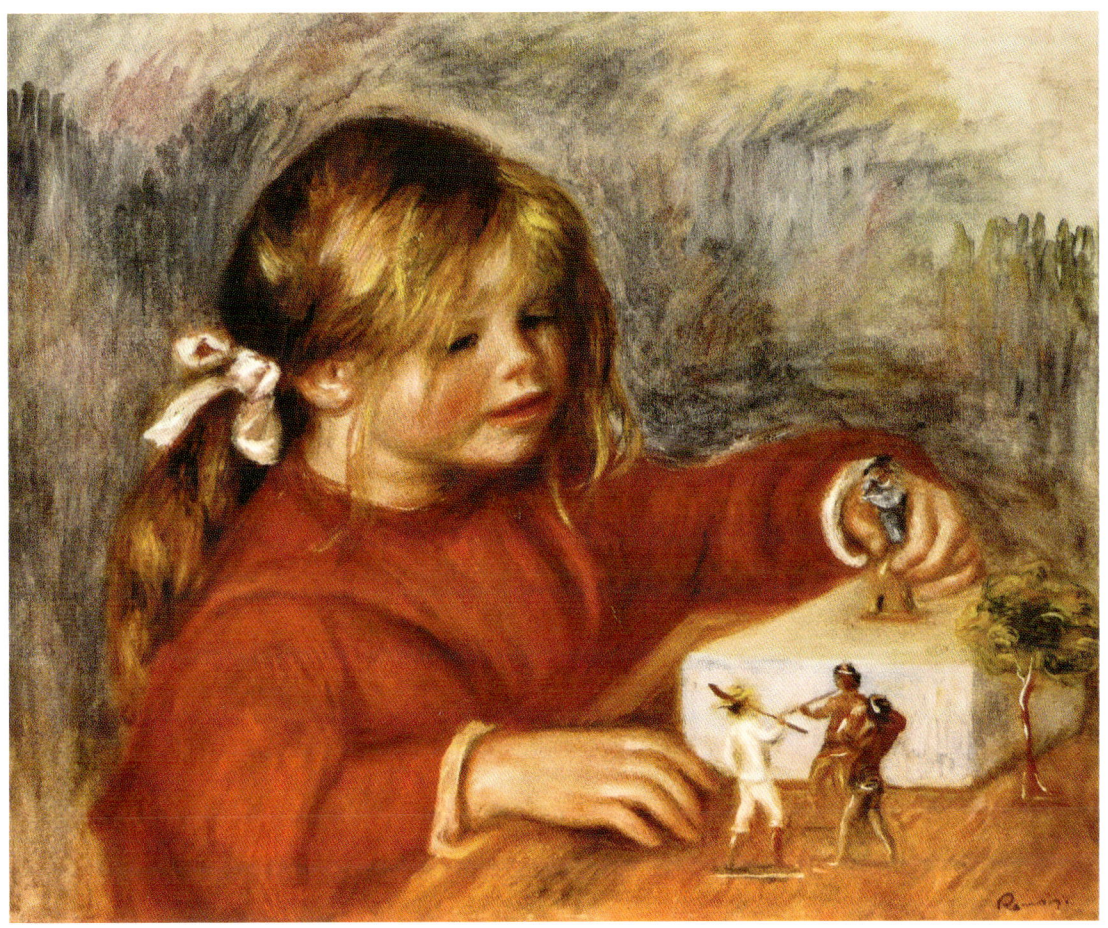

Claude Renoir, Playing, c.1905. An earlier painting of Claude shows a relaxed, long-haired child absorbed in imaginative play. Again Renoir references Velázquez, this time the great artist's painting of the Spanish infanta. But while Renoir reproduces the pink side bow in the hair, his portrait turns any notion of stiff formality on its head in a joyful celebration of childhood and creative freedom.

enable me to dare things which I would not be able to without her. . . . My models don't think . . . '

Renoir's perseverance in the face of physical infirmity astounded his friends. In 1916, Monet commented, 'As for Renoir, he is still amazing. He is supposed to be very sick, but then suddenly one hears that despite everything he is hard at work and forging ahead all the same. He's just simply awe-inspiring.' However, in a letter to Durand-Ruel in 1916 Renoir wrote, 'As for me, I'm in very, very bad shape. I have a ton of afflictions that make my life unbearable.' Yet bear them he did. In a short film made in 1919, the year of his death, he is seen painting at home, talking animatedly to friends and puffing on a cigarette.

Facing page: Gilles (Pierrot), *Jean-Antoine Watteau, c.1719. The central figure's melancholic expression conveys the idea of a sad, dreamy clown. Dramatic power is derived from the stasis of the subject in the face of public ridicule. Watteau's low viewpoint with the clown occupying the central space is echoed in Renoir's painting of Claude.*

Right: Infanta Margarita in a White Dress, *Diego Rodríguez de Silva y Velázquez, c.1656. Velázquez painted five portraits of Margaret Theresa of Spain, including this one which was sent to her uncle, Leopold I, in Vienna. Leopold later became Holy Roman Emperor. The Spanish infanta married him in 1666.*

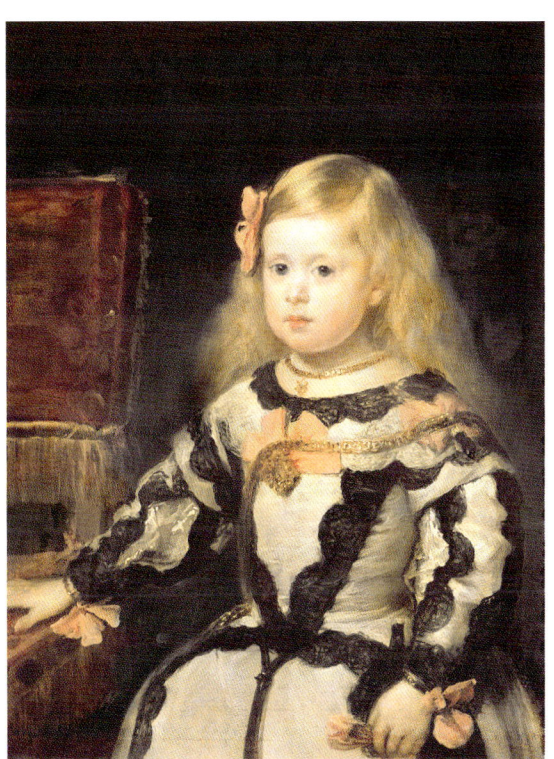

ARTIST AND ART DEALER

Few artists possess sufficient grasp of commercial matters to promote and sell their art themselves – most rely on the skills of an art dealer. Some dealers are of such importance that they become part of the story themselves, and Ambroise Vollard was one of these.

Born in 1866 on the island of Réunion, a French colony in the Indian Ocean, Vollard arrived in Paris at the age of twenty-one to study law. He soon changed career and became an 'amateur merchant', selling drawings and prints acquired from stalls on the banks of the Seine. The works of the Impressionists caught his eye and he started to collect them, initially buying unfinished paintings by Manet from the artist's widow. When he exhibited these in 1894 he was introduced to a circle of artists which included Cézanne, Morisot, Degas and Renoir.

In November 1895, Vollard staged a Cézanne retrospective of 150 paintings, although the artist's work was barely known in Paris at the time. Vollard's shrewd, perceptive eye and belief in his clients made him one of the most important art dealers of the early twentieth century. He not only launched the career of Cézanne, but also Picasso, and wrote several art books.

The outbreak of World War I caused Vollard to close his gallery on the Rue Laffitte in Paris. After the war, around 1924, he moved his business to his town house on the Rue de Martignac where most of his vast collection remained hidden behind closed doors. On 22 July 1939, twenty years after Renoir's death, Vollard was killed in an accident which took place when his chauffeur-driven car skidded off the road between Paris and his home at Le Tremblay-sur-Mauldre. He died without direct heirs and most of his collection was scattered between extended family and friends. The artist Jacques-Emile Blanche wrote: 'Have you heard how vast his legacy is? Finds are being made everywhere, valuable items are scattered around, none of them displayed or recorded, priceless things are being found under stacks of canvases.'

Some of Vollard's paintings were sent to the USA; hundreds more were eventually discovered in a farmhouse near a village in Serbia. Several of the paintings are still the subject of legal battles.

Ambroise Vollard's legacy includes the many books he wrote, among them *Auguste Renoir* (1841–1919) and *Renoir: An Intimate Record* (1925). They are still in print a century after the death of the artist, his long-time friend and client.

Portrait of Ambroise Vollard, *1917. In August 1917, Vollard visited Renoir in Essoyes. He had bought a toreador's costume on a trip to Spain and obliged Renoir by sitting for his portrait attired in it.*

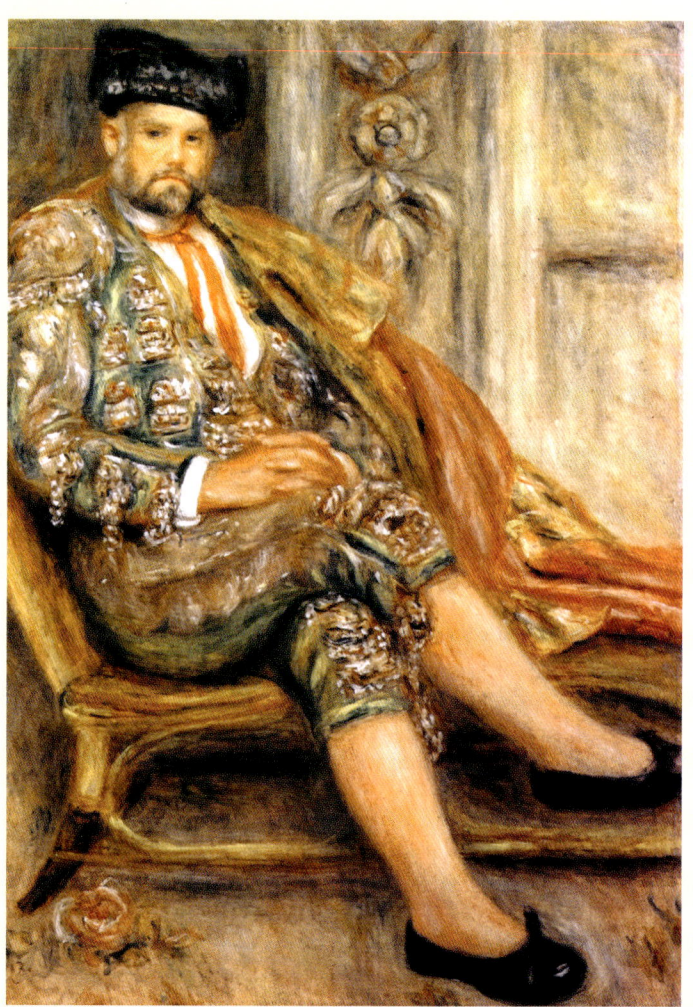

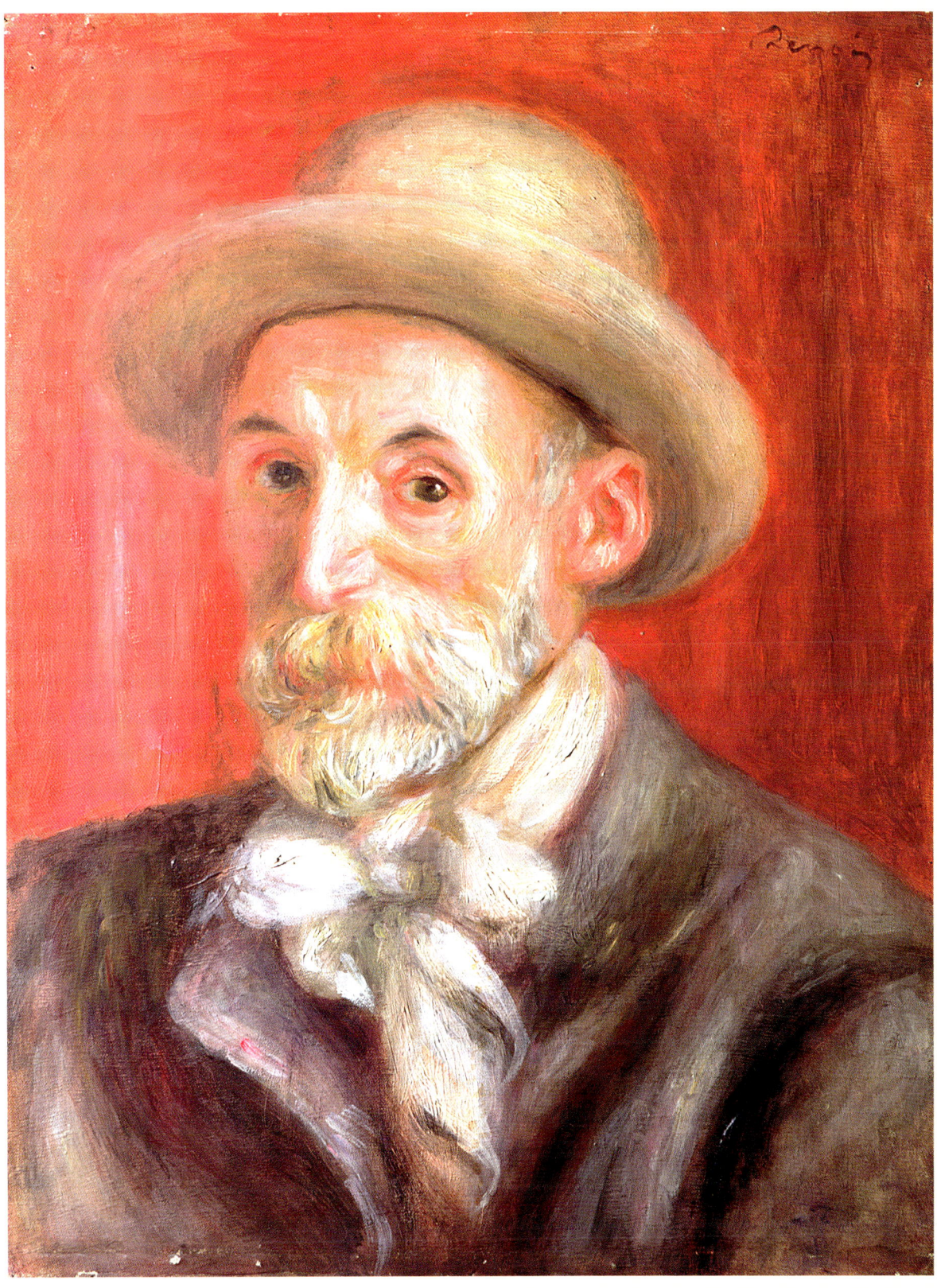

Self-portrait, 1910. Here Renoir portrays himself approaching the age of seventy. His steady gaze betrays none of his physical suffering. The red background underlines his defiant and resolutely positive frame of mind.

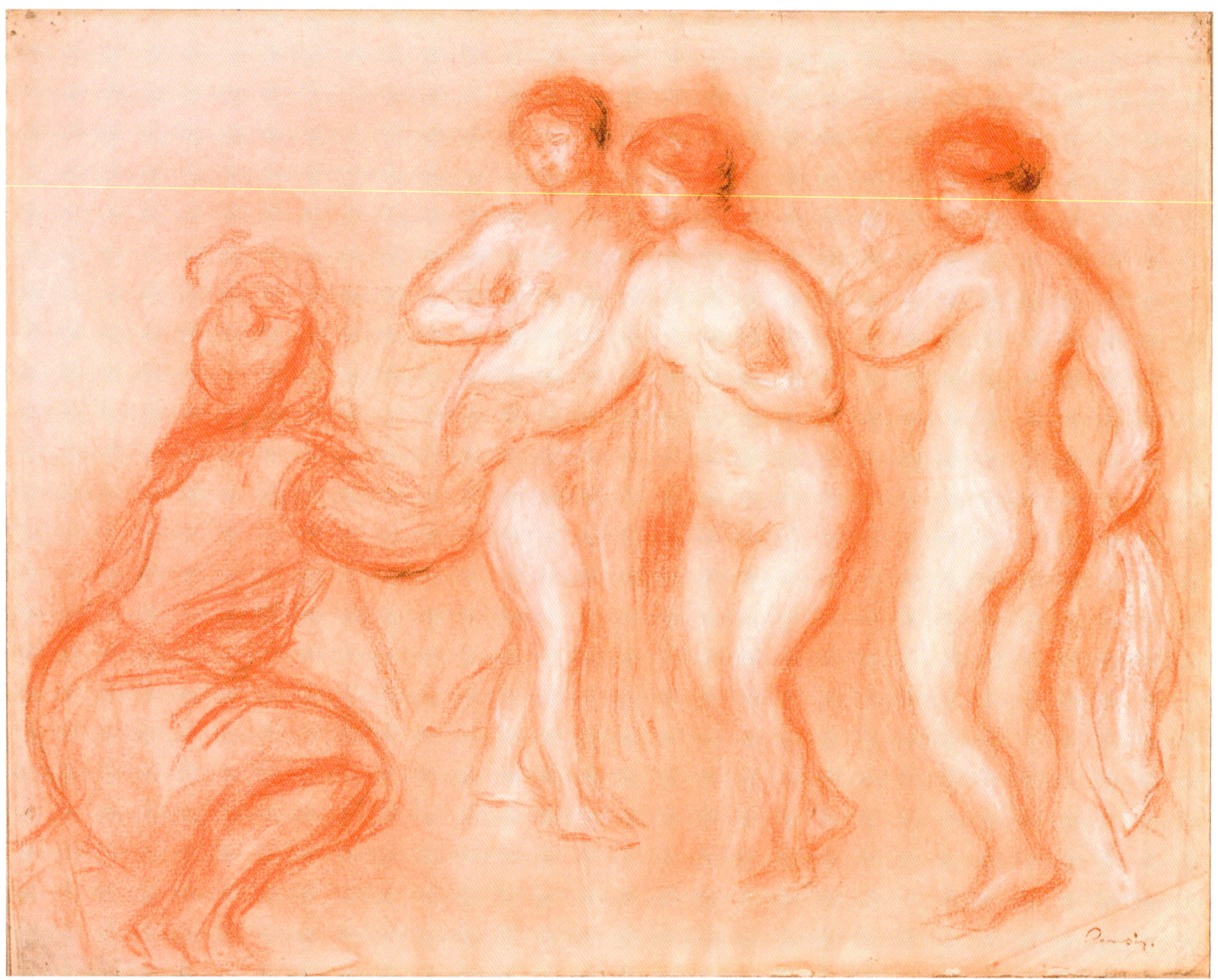

The Judgement of Paris, *c.1908. Renoir made this preliminary red and white chalk drawing on textured paper when he was planning to execute a sculpture of the subject.*

SCULPTURE

Renoir had once written to Paul Berard that sculptors have all the luck, as their statues stand in the sun and become part of the light itself – they exist in nature as does a tree. Later in life, he was to turn to this discipline himself. Vollard had been encouraged by Renoir's brief foray into sculpture in 1908, but he knew the artist could no longer physically manipulate any of the media for sculpting. He devised a plan for him to sculpt by proxy: Renoir would paint an image and then oversee a sculptor who would translate it into a three-dimensional object.

Vollard proposed Aristide Maillol for the collaboration, as he and Renoir were both preoccupied with the classical ideal and admired each other's work. But Maillol was busy with his own sculptures so he recommended the twenty-four-year-old Catalan artist Richard Guino who had acted as his assistant in Paris in 1910. Maillol had first seen Guino's work at an exhibition in Barcelona and described him as 'the most talented European sculptor of his generation'. Vollard introduced Renoir to Guino at

Les Collettes in 1913, with the promise: 'I have found your hands.' The two men, one nearing the end of his career and the other at the beginning of his, formed an intimate and intuitive relationship which resulted in thirty-eight sculptures, including nudes, busts and bas-reliefs. The most significant of these were interpretations of Renoir's 1908 drawing *The Judgement of Paris*, together with *Venus Victorious* (*c*.1914), *The Large Washerwoman* (1917) and *Maternity* (1916), the latter from a painting Renoir had made of Aline nursing their first-born son.

Although the sculptures were signed by Renoir, mystery has surrounded the nature of their process and a question hangs over who created them. It was in Vollard's interests to minimize Guino's part in their creation because he wanted exclusive control over the production of the bronzes. But Guino's family said the sculptor often worked alone in an outdoor studio at the bottom of the garden, making preparatory sketches and sculpting all the bronzes, while Renoir worked separately on paintings in his studio on the first floor of the house.

In 1965, decades after Renoir's death and with the selling price of his sculptures rising, Guino initiated a lawsuit against the Renoir estate. He claimed that as co-creator of the works he was entitled to 50 per cent royalties on past and future sales. The case took eight years to settle. In November 1973, nine months after Guino's death, his estate was granted an equal share of profits from the works together with part-ownership of the copyright (which was extended until 2043, seventy years from the date of Guino's death). From this point on, the sculptures bore the official stamp 'Renoir-Guino'.

According to Guino's son, Michel, the two families were never enemies. In 1982, it was agreed that all the original plaster casts for the sculptures be made the property of a trust, the Societé Civile Succession Richard Guino.

'IF I HAVE TRIED MY HAND AT SCULPTURE, IT WAS NOT WITH THE AIM OF ANNOYING MICHELANGELO, NOR WAS IT BECAUSE PAINTING WAS NO LONGER ENOUGH FOR ME, BUT BECAUSE MR VOLLARD VERY GENTLY FORCED ME INTO IT.'

Pierre-Auguste Renoir

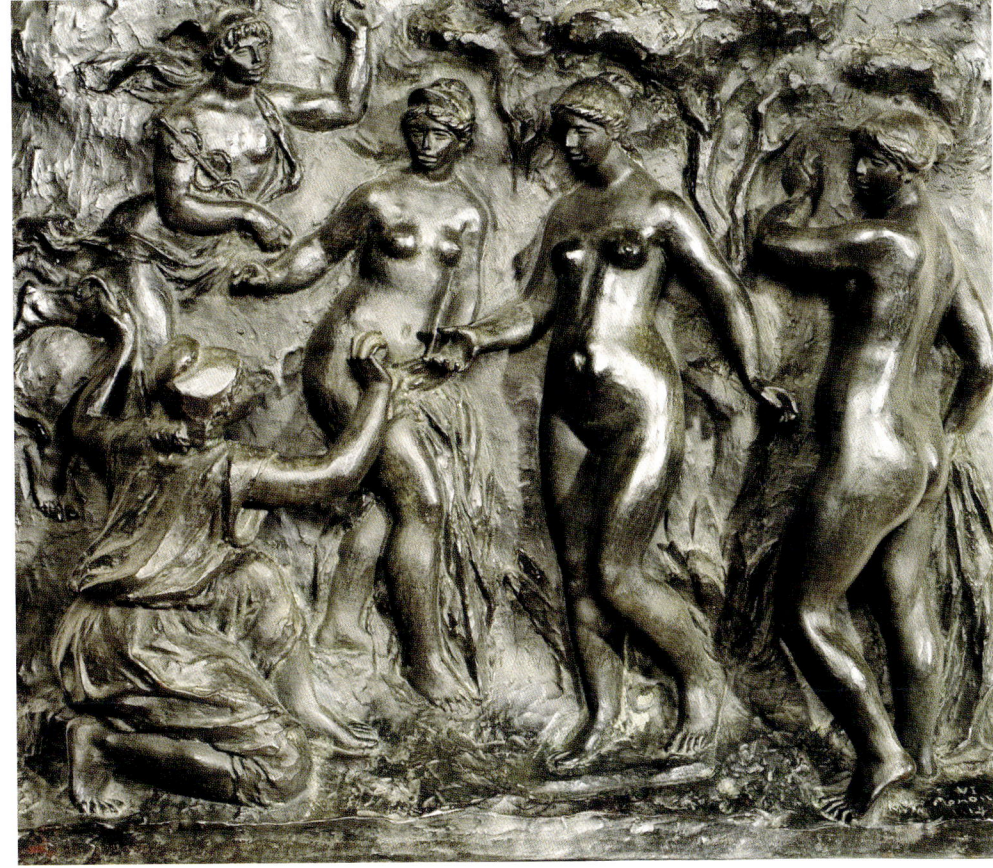

The Judgement of Paris, 1916. *Towards the end of his life, Renoir made several paintings of the judgement of Paris. He planned to use this bronze relief to decorate a large pedestal in a garden temple dedicated to the subject of love, but the project never came into being.*

'HE WORKED FROM
WITHIN HIS OWN NATURE
AND HAD THE CAPACITY
TO TAKE A MODEL OR
A LIGHT THAT AT TIMES
SEEMED DULL AND
IMPRINT IT WITH THE
MEMORY OF THRILLING
MOMENTS.'

Pierre Bonnard on Renoir

THE LAST GREAT WORK

In 1917, a new member of the Renoir household arrived in the
shape of Andrée Madeleine Heuschling (1900–79). Employed as a
servant, she would soon acquire a nickname, Dido, a new job, as
Renoir's model, and an admirer, Jean, who fell in love with her while
recuperating from his wartime injury. The couple married in 1920
and Dido was actively involved in Jean's career (he became a revered
film director, producer and writer). She was also one of the models
for Renoir's last great work, *The Bathers*. Painted in the garden at
Cagnes-sur-Mer, it owes a great deal to the nudes painted by Titian
and Rubens. Its timeless view of the natural world excludes any
features from modern life, but refers instead to the classical tradition
when, as Renoir put it, 'the earth was the paradise of the gods'.

On 3 December 1919, shortly after completing this painting,
Renoir died in his sleep, aged seventy-eight, following a bout of
pneumonia. His sons donated *The Bathers* to the state and it now
hangs in the Musée d'Orsay in Paris.

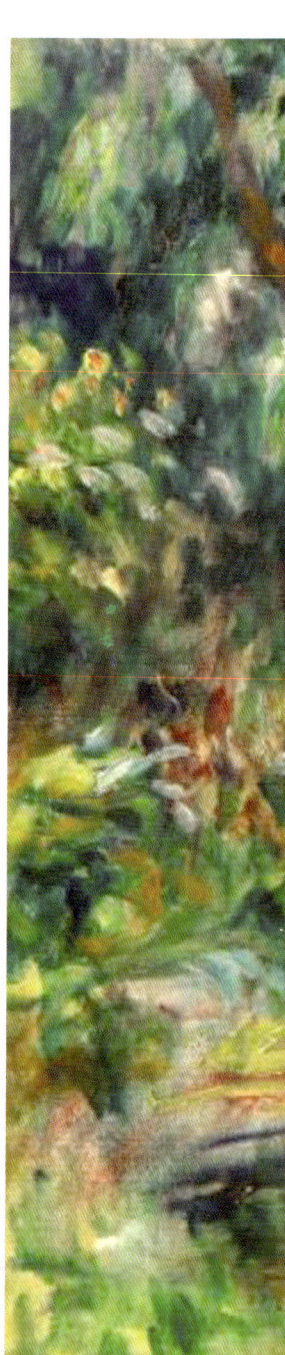

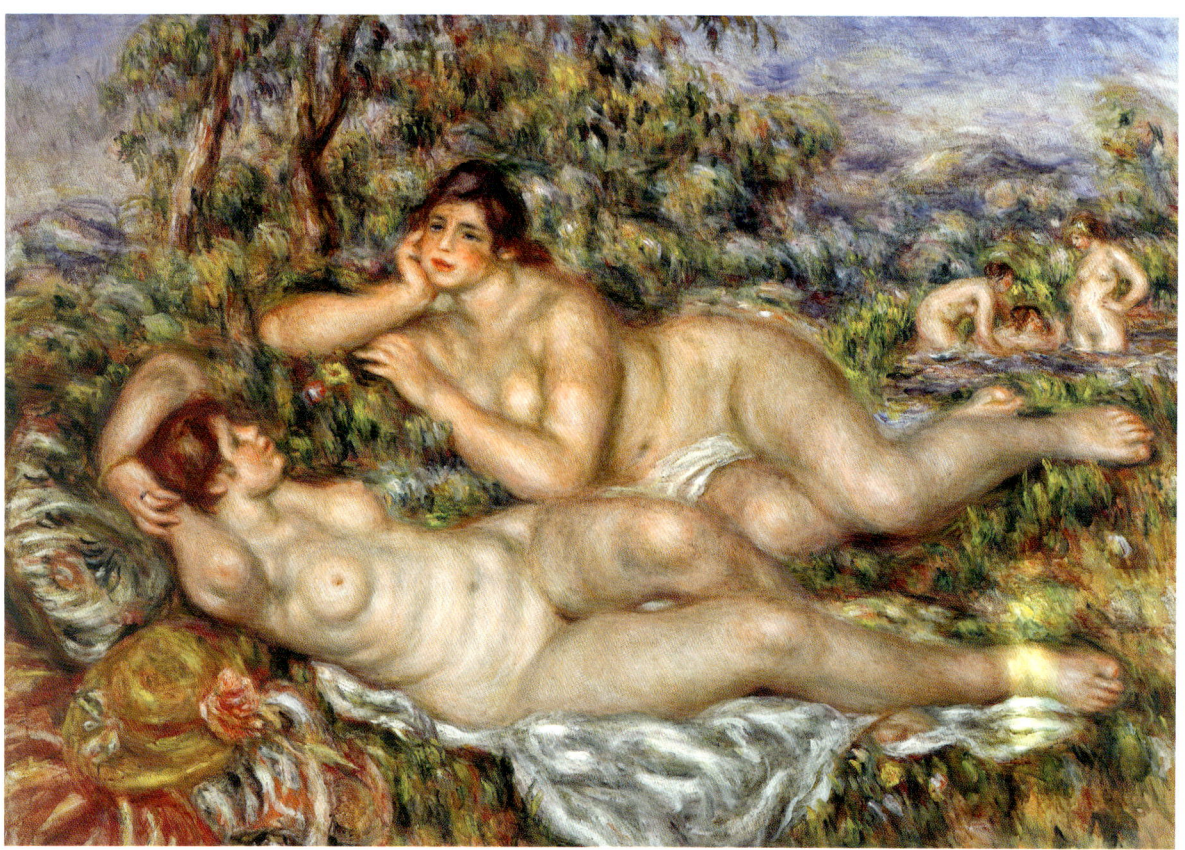

*The Bathers, 1918–19. This Arcadian scene shows two nudes in an attitude
of repose while three more figures frolic in a pool in the background. It is a
vision of sensuality in a Mediterranean landscape that draws influences from
the masters. 'It is a Watteau background,' said Renoir.*

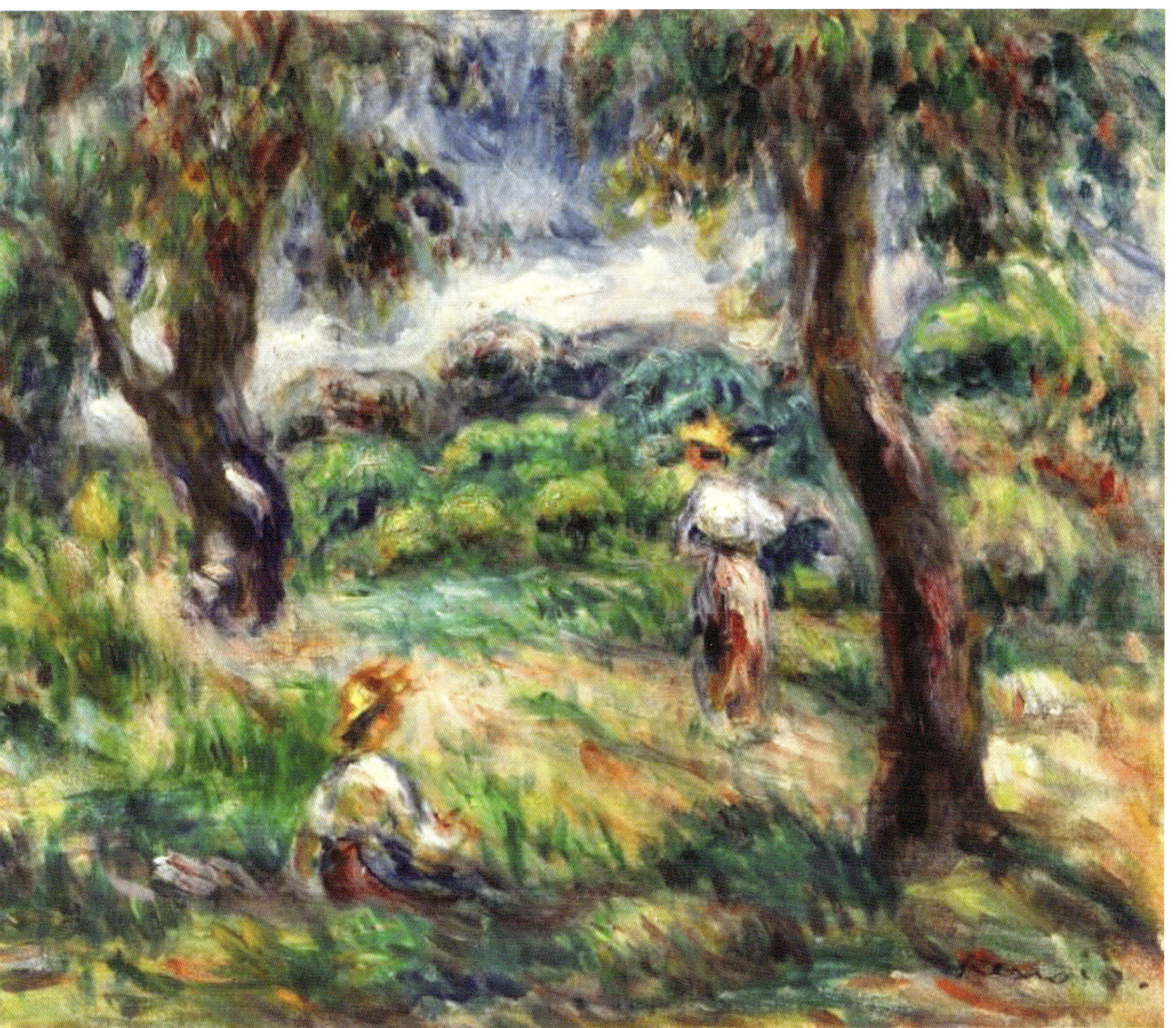

Paysage Bleu, *1915. Renoir's late landscapes are painted with rapid, fluid brushstrokes which suggest spontaneity. However, the composition and nuances of radiant colour indicate that this was not the case – the artist was drawing on a lifetime's experience to record a specific place and time.*

'IF I HAVE TO CHOOSE BETWEEN WALKING AND PAINTING, I'D MUCH RATHER PAINT.'

Pierre-Auguste Renoir

EPILOGUE: RENOIR'S LEGACY

In the final decade of his life, Renoir became a huge influence on two artists who would go on to dominate the early twentieth century – Henri Matisse and Pablo Picasso. Both owned paintings by Renoir and in 1917 they asked their art dealer, Paul Rosenberg, if he could arrange for them to meet the artist. In the event, only Matisse got to visit Renoir before he died. Living in Nice, just a short distance from the Renoir family home, he met with the artist several times during the last two years of his life.

Matisse declared Renoir's final work, *The Bathers*, a masterpiece. For his part, Renoir was keen to encourage younger artists, just as Manet had helped him when he was starting out. When Matisse asked the ailing Renoir why he kept pushing himself to paint, the artist replied, 'The pain passes, but beauty endures.' Renoir's influence, particularly his quest for beauty and truth, is evident in Matisse's work. His three-panel commission which included *The Dance* also featured a painting entitled *Bathers by a River*, clearly a nod to one of Renoir's favourite subjects. Matisse was also indomitable in old age, inventing a new medium of cut-outs to circumvent his increasing infirmity.

The Dance, Henri Matisse, *1910. Echoing the mood of pagan abandon evident in Renoir's The Bathers, Matisse uses a frenzied dance scene to express the rhythms of nature and the cosmos. A leading proponent of Fauvism, he takes up the banner of rampant 'crude' colour used by Renoir in his later years and unfurls it in this powerful depiction of humanity's wild, instinctive side. 'Rules', Matisse once said, 'have no existence outside of individuals.'*

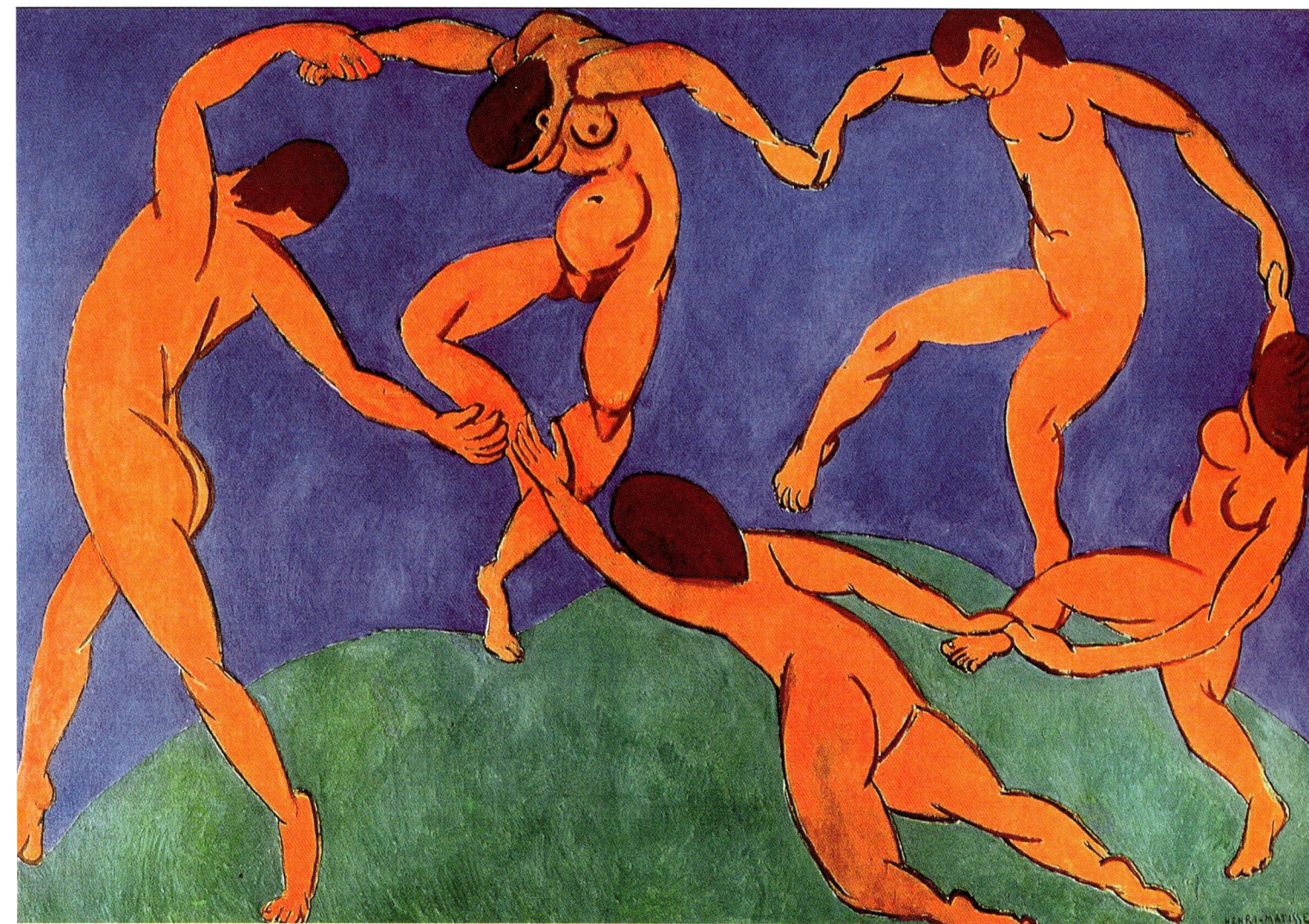

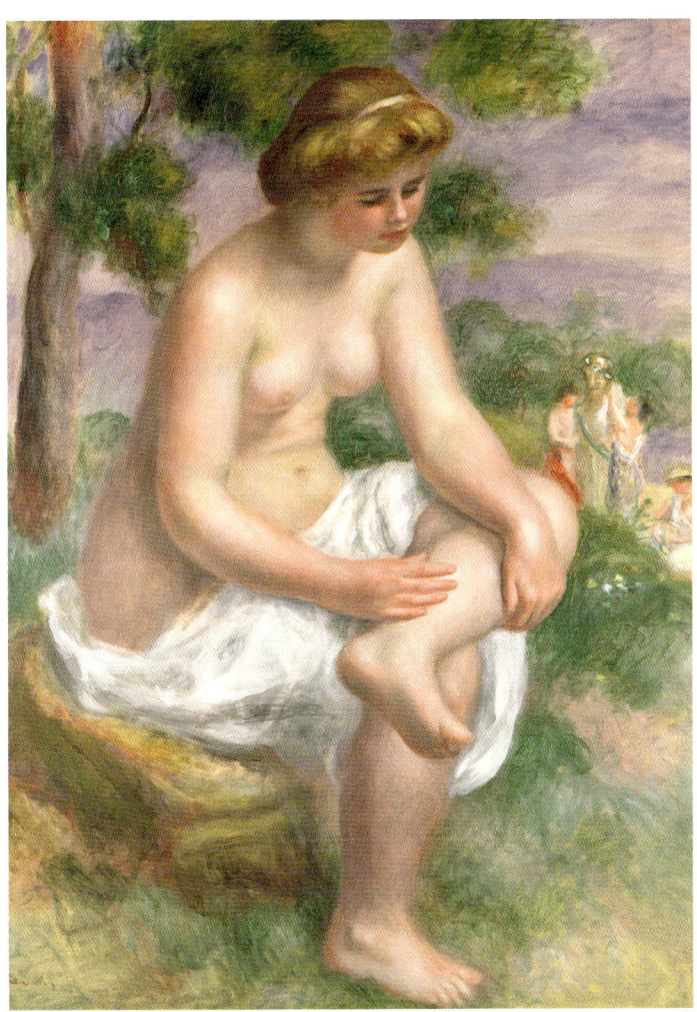

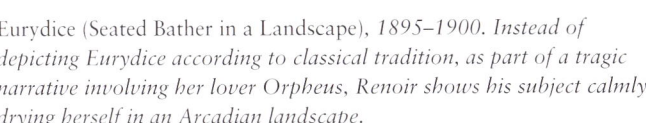

Eurydice (Seated Bather in a Landscape), *1895–1900. Instead of depicting Eurydice according to classical tradition, as part of a tragic narrative involving her lover Orpheus, Renoir shows his subject calmly drying herself in an Arcadian landscape.*

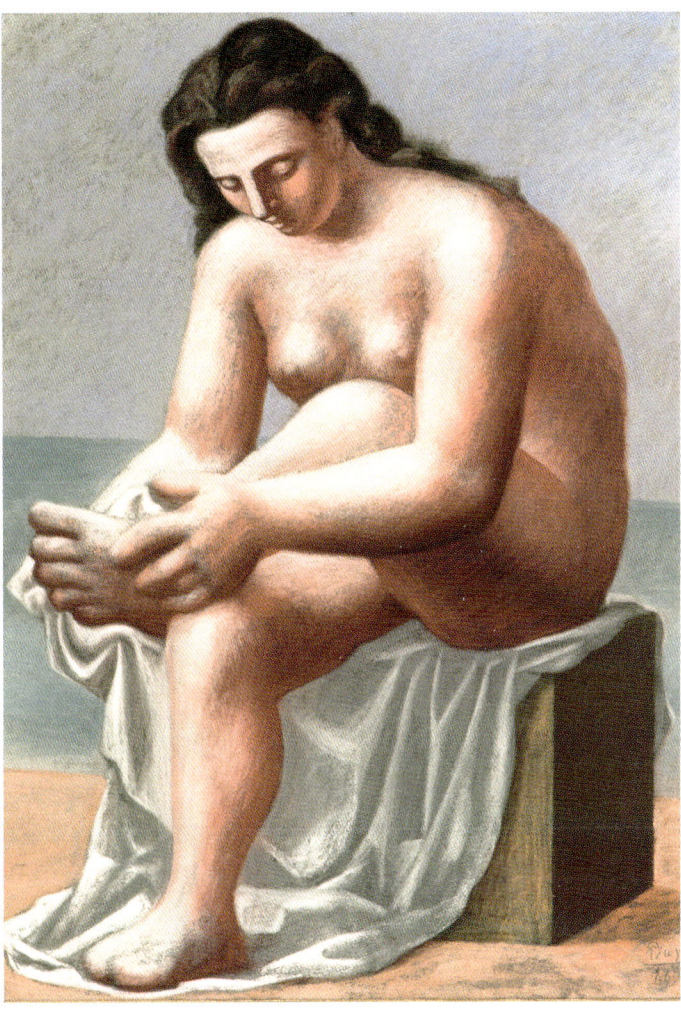

Seated Bather, Drying Her Feet, *Pablo Picasso, 1921. The reference to Renoir's seated bather is clear in this painting although Picasso exaggerates the physical form and simplifies the background to three uneven bands of ground, sea and sky.*

Picasso was influenced by Renoir and, more importantly, by Cézanne whose geometric style was a precursor to Cubism. Picasso bought seven of Renoir's later paintings and his *Seated Bather, Drying Her Feet* was directly inspired by Renoir's *Eurydice* (see above). Although the reaction to Renoir's later nudes was generally unfavourable and galleries considered them too dated to display alongside other collections of modern art, Picasso's positive response gives pause for thought. Renoir's influence can also be seen in the work of Pierre Bonnard (1867–1947), now admired for his innovatory use of colour and his intimate domestic scenes.

Renoir remains a hugely popular artist, loved for his sensual paintings of natural beauty, shimmering landscapes and the imaginative use of light, tone and colour. Any Renoir exhibition is guaranteed to be packed with visitors enchanted by the direct, life-affirming qualities of his work. Though some may regard his paintings as sentimental and unchallenging, many see him as an innovative trailblazer who was crucial to the development of modern art.

'GO AND SEE WHAT OTHERS HAVE PRODUCED, BUT NEVER COPY ANYTHING EXCEPT NATURE. YOU WOULD BE TRYING TO ENTER INTO A TEMPERAMENT THAT IS NOT YOURS AND NOTHING THAT YOU WOULD DO WOULD HAVE ANY CHARACTER.'

Pierre-Auguste Renoir

TIMELINE

1840s

'41 Pierre-August Renoir is born in Limoges, sixth of the seven children of Léonard and Marguerite Renoir, tailor and seamstress respectively.

'44 The family moves to Paris.

1850s

'54 Renoir becomes an apprentice at a porcelain workshop, painting china. He later turns to painting fans and blinds.

1860s

'61 Renoir enrols at Charles Gleyre's studio and then at the École des Beaux-Arts.

'62 Meets Pissarro, Cézanne, Diaz, Courbet, Corot and Daubigny; strikes up a close friendship with Jules Le Coeur.

'63 His painting *Nymph with a Faun* is rejected by the Salon; he destroys it.

'64 *La Esmeralda* is accepted at the Salon but he later destroys it, dissatisfied.

'65 Renoir meets Lise Tréhot.

William Sisley, his portrait of Alfred Sisley's father, is accepted for the Salon.

'68 Renoir shares a studio with Bazille near the Café Guerbois on Avenue de Clichy, a favourite spot for artists to gather.

He meets Manet, Degas and Zola.

1870s

'70 *Bather with a Griffon Dog* and *Woman of Algiers* are accepted by the Salon. When the Franco-Prussian War breaks out, Renoir enlists in the cavalry and succumbs to dysentery while posted in southwest France.

'72 Monet introduces him to Paul Durand-Ruel. The Salon rejects his submission *Interior of a Harem in Montmartre*.

'74 Exhibits six paintings at the First Impressionist Exhibition.

'75 At an auction of Impressionist paintings, Renoir sells twenty paintings for a total of 2,251 francs.

'77 Exhibits twenty-one canvases at the Third Impressionist Exhibition and sells fifteen and a pastel sketch for 2,005 francs.

'79 The portrait *Madame Charpentier and her Children* is given pride of place in the Salon.

1880s

'80 Aline Charigot becomes his frequent model and, eventually, his wife.

'81 Travels to Algeria and Italy, where he sees Raphael's frescoes in Rome.

'83 First major show at Durand-Ruel's gallery.

'86 Eight paintings are displayed in Brussels in the Les Vingt exhibition and Durand-Ruel shows thirty-eight in New York.

'88 First attack of arthritis.

1890s

'90 Aline and Renoir marry.

'92 The French government buys *Young Girls at the Piano*.

A retrospective of 110 works is held at Durand-Ruel's gallery in Paris.

'94 Gabrielle Renard joins the Renoir household to look after the children. She becomes a favourite model.

'98 Visits Cagnes for the first time and sees a Rembrandt exhibition in Amsterdam.

1900s

'00 Exhibitions of his work are shown in New York and at the Paris Exposition. He accepts the Légion d'honneur.

'03 Moves to Cagnes for a warmer climate as his arthritis worsens.

'04 Thirty-five paintings are exhibited in a Renoir Room at the Salon d'Automne.

'05 Fifty-nine works are shown at an Impressionist exhibition at the Grafton Gallery in London; nine appear at the Salon d'Automne, of which he is made honorary president.

'08 Moves to Les Collettes; exhibits in London, Paris and Rome.

'10 Travels to Munich to paint *Madame Thurneyssen and her Daughter*. A retrospective is held in Venice.

'13 Begins to collaborate with Richard Guino to make sculptures.

'14 Gabrielle leaves. Germany declares war on France and Renoir's sons Jean and Pierre are both wounded in battle.

'16 Jean is wounded for a second time; Aline dies.

'17 London's National Gallery buys *The Umbrellas*.

'19 Made a Commander of the Légion d'honneur and is carried through the Louvre in August to see his painting *Madame Charpentier*.

Dies in December.

FURTHER INFORMATION

Renoir: An Intimate Record, Ambroise Vollard, Dover Publications Inc., 2003 (new edition)

Renoir, My Father, Jean Renoir, New York Review Books, 2001 (new edition)

Renoir: An Intimate Biography, Barbara Ehrlich White, Thames and Hudson, 2017

Renoir: His Life and Works in 500 Images, Susie Hodge, Lorenz Books, 2011

Renoir: Intimacy, Guillermo Solana and Colin Bailey, Distributed Art Publishers, 2017

Renoir: Painter of Happiness, Gilles Neret, Taschen, 2017

Renoir (2012), a film based on the last years of the artist's life, directed by Gilles Bourdos and starring Michel Bouquet.

LIST OF ILLUSTRATIONS

Pages 6–7
The Grands Boulevards, 1875, oil on canvas, 52.1 × 63.5 cm (20½ × 25 in), Philadelphia Museum of Art, USA. The Henry P. McIlhenny Collection.

Pages 8–9
Odalisque, 1870, oil on canvas, 69.2 x 122.6 cm (27¼ x 48¼ in), National Gallery of Art, Washington D.C., USA. Chester Dale Collection.

Page 10
Hélenè Fourment and Her Children, c.1636, Peter Paul Rubens, oil on wood, 115 x 85 cm (45¼ x 33½ in), Musée du Louvre, Paris. akg-images/ André Held.

Page 11
Portrait of Hélène Fourment with Her Son, 1860–64, oil on canvas, 73 x 59.5 cm (28¾ x 23½ in), Musée du Louvre, Paris. akg-images.

Pages 12–13
Le Déjeuner sur l'Herbe, 1862–3, Édouard Manet, oil on canvas, 207 x 265 cm (81½ x 104¼ in), Musée d'Orsay, Paris.

Page 14
Lise Sewing, c.1866, oil on canvas, 55.88 x 45.72 cm (22 x 18 in), Dallas Museum of Art, Texas, USA, The Wendy and Emery Reves Collection.

Page 15
Lise with a Parasol, 1867, oil on canvas, 184 x 115.5 cm (72½ x 45½ in), Museum Folkwang, Essen, Germany. Leemage/UIG via Getty Images.

Pages 16–17
Portrait of Auguste Renoir, 1867, Frédéric Bazille, oil on canvas, 61.2 x 50 cm (24 x 19½ in), Musée Fabre, Montpellier, France. Photo: Musée d'Orsay, Paris, France.

Page 17
Frédéric Bazille at His Easel, 1867, oil on canvas, 105 x 73.5 cm (41¼ x 29 in), Musée Fabre, Montpellier, France.

Page 18
The Gust of Wind, c.1865, Gustave Courbet, oil on canvas, 146.7 x 230.8 cm (57¾ x 91 in), Museum of Fine Arts, Houston, USA. Museum purchase funded by Caroline Wiess Law.

Page 19
Jules Le Coeur in the Forest of Fontainebleau, 1866, oil on canvas, 106 x 80 cm (41¾ x 31½ in), Museu de Arte, Sao Paulo, Brazil. Bridgeman Images.

Page 20
'Revolution in painting! And a terrorizing beginning', 1874, engraving (b/w photo), Amedee Charles Henri de Noe Cham,

Bibliothèque Nationale, Paris, France. Archives Charmet/ Bridgeman Images.

Page 21
Snow-covered Landscape, 1875, oil on canvas, 51 x 66 cm (20 x 26 in), akg-images/ Erich Lessing.

Page 22
In Summer (The Bohemian), 1868, oil on canvas, 85 x 59 cm (33½ x 23¼), Alte Nationalgalerie, Berlin, Germany.

Page 23
Bather with a Griffon Dog, 1870, oil on canvas, 184 x 115 cm (72½ x 45¼), Museu de Arte, Sao Paulo, Brazil. akg-images.

Page 24
The Swing, 1876, oil on canvas, 92 x 73 cm (36¼ x 28¾ in), Musée d'Orsay, Paris, France. De Agostini/Getty Images.

Page 25
Self-portrait, c.1875, oil on canvas, 39.1 x 31.6 cm (15¼ x 13 in), The Sterling and Francine Clark Art Institute, Williamstown, Massachusetts, USA.

Pages 26–7
Skaters in the Bois de Boulogne, 1868, oil on canvas, 89.9 x 72.1 cm (35½ x 28½ in), Private Collection, Bridgeman Images.

Page 28, top
A Modern Olympia, 1870, Paul Cézanne, oil on canvas, 57 x 55 cm (22½ x 21¾ in), Private Collection. History and Art Collection/Alamy Stock Photo.

Page 28, bottom
A Modern Olympia, 1874, Paul Cézanne, oil on canvas, 46.2 x 55.5 cm (18 x 21¾ in), Musée d'Orsay, Paris, France. De Agostini/Getty Images.

Page 29
La Loge, 1874, oil on canvas, 127 x 92 cm (50 x 36 in), Courtauld Institute of Art, London, UK.

Page 30
Impression, Sunrise, 1872, Claude Monet, oil on canvas, 48 x 63 cm (19 x 24¾ in), Musée Marmottan Monet, Paris, France. Bridgeman Images.

Page 31
Study. Torso, Effect of Sunlight, c.1875–6, oil on canvas, 81 x 65 cm (31¾ x 25½ in), Musée d'Orsay, Paris, France. Archivart/ Alamy Stock Photo.

Pages 32–3
Dance at Le Moulin de la Galette, 1876, oil on canvas, 131.5 x 176.5 cm (51¾ x 69½ in), Musée d'Orsay, Paris, France. Alamy Stock Photo.

Page 34
Le Pont des Arts, 1867, oil on canvas, 60 x 110.3 cm (24 x 39½ in), Norton Simon Museum, Los Angeles, USA. The Norton Simon Foundation.

Page 35
Pont Neuf, Paris, 1872, oil on canvas, 75.3 x 93.7 cm (29¾ x 37 in), National Gallery of Art, Washington D.C., USA. Ailsa Mellon Bruce Collection.

Page 36
Dance at Bougival, 1883, oil on canvas, 181.9 x 98.1 cm (71½ x 38½ in), Museum of Fine Arts, Boston, USA.

Page 37
Madame Charpentier and Her Children, 1878, oil on canvas, 153.7 x 190.2 cm (60½ x 75 in), Metropolitan Museum of Art, New York, USA. Catharine Lorillard Wolfe Collection, Wolfe Fund 1907.

Page 38
By the Seashore, 1883, oil on canvas, 92.1 x 72.4 cm (36¼ x 28½ in), Metropolitan Museum of Art, New York, USA. H.O. Havemeyer Collection, bequest of Mrs H.O. Havemeyer, 1929. akg-images /Liszt Collection.

Page 39
Seascape (The Wave), 1879, oil on canvas, 72.6 x 91.6 cm (28½ x 36 in), Potter Palmer Collection, Art Institute of Chicago, USA.

Page 40
Two Sisters, 1881, oil on canvas, 100.4 x 80.9 cm (39½ x 32in), Art Institute of Chicago, USA. Mr and Mrs Lewis Larned Coburn Memorial Collection.

Page 41, top
Oarsmen at Chatou, 1879, oil on canvas, 81.2 x 100.2 cm (32 x 39½ in), National Gallery of Art, Washington D.C., USA. Gift of Sam A. Lewisohn. Shutterstock.

Page 41, bottom
Boating Couple, c.1881, pastel on paper, 45.1 x 58.4 cm (17¾ x 23 in), Museum of Fine Arts, Boston, USA. Given in memory of Governor Alvan T. Fuller by the Fuller Foundation.

Page 42
Luncheon of the Boating Party, 1881, oil on canvas, 129.54 x 172.72 cm (51 x 68 in), Phillips Collection, Washington D.C., USA.

Page 43
Lunch at the Restaurant Fournaise, 1875, oil on canvas, 55 x 65.9 cm (21½ x 26 in), Potter Palmer Collection, Art Institute of Chicago, USA.

Page 44
Piazza San Marco, Venice, 1881, oil on canvas, 89.5 x 104.4 cm (35¼ x 41 in), Minneapolis Institute of Arts, Minneapolis, USA. The John R. Van Derlip Fund/Bridgeman Images.

Page 45
Bay of Naples, Evening, 1881, oil on canvas, 57.9 x 80.8 cm (22¾ x 31¾ in), The Sterling and Francine Clark Art Institute, Williamstown, Massachusetts, USA.

Page 46
Blonde Bather, 1881, oil on canvas, 81.6 x 65.4 cm (32 x 25¾ in), The Sterling and Francine Clark Art Institute, Williamstown, Massachusetts, USA. Bridgeman Images.

Page 47
Madame Léon Clapisson, 1883, oil on canvas, 81.2 x 65.3 cm (32 x 25¾ in), Art Institute of Chicago, Chicago, Illinois, USA. Mr & Mrs Martin A. Ryerson Collection.

Page 48
Dance in the Country, 1883, oil on canvas, 180 x 90 cm (70¾ x 35½ in), Musée d'Orsay, Paris, France.

Page 49
Dance in the City, 1883, oil on canvas, 180 x 90 cm (70¾ x 35½ in), Musée d'Orsay, Paris, France. akg-images/ Laurent Lecat.

Page 50
La Grenouillère, 1869, oil on canvas, 66.5 x 81 cm (26 x 31¾ in), Nationalmuseum, Stockholm, Sweden.

Page 51
Bain à la Grenouillère, 1869, Claude Monet, oil on canvas, 74.6 x 99.7 cm (29½ x 39¼ in), Metropolitan Museum of Art, New York, USA.

Pages 52–3
Reclining Nude, 1883, oil on canvas, 65.1 x 81.3 cm (25¾ x 32 in), Metropolitan Museum of Art, New York, USA. The Walter H. and Leonore Annenberg Collection. Bequest of Walter H. Annenberg, 2002.

Page 54
The Umbrellas, 1886, oil on canvas, 180.3 x 114.9 cm (71 x 45¼ in), National Gallery, London, UK. Sir Hugh Lane Bequest, 1917. akg-images.

Page 55
The Bather ('Baigneuse Valpinçon'), 1808, Jean Auguste Dominique Ingres, oil on canvas, 146 x 97.5 cm (57½ x 38½ in), Louvre, Paris, France/ Bridgeman Images.

Pages 56–7
The Large Bathers, 1887, oil on canvas, 117.8 x 170.8 cm (46½ x 67¼ in), Philadelphia Museum of Art, USA. Mr and Mrs Carroll S. Tyson, Jr. Collection, 1963. akg-images.

Page 57, top
Two Young Peasant Women, 1891–2, Camille Pissarro, oil on canvas, 89.5 x 116.5 cm (35¼ x 46 in), Metropolitan Museum of Art, New York, USA. Gift of Mr and Mrs Charles Wrightsman, 1973.

Page 57, bottom
The Large Bathers – study, 1884–7, oil on canvas, Musée d'Art et d'Histoire, Palais Massena, Nice, France. Bridgeman Images.

Page 58
Mont Sainte-Victoire, 1889, oil on canvas, 53 x 64.1 cm (21 x 25¼ in), Yale University Art Gallery, Katharine Ordway Collection.

Page 59, top
Mont Sainte-Victoire, c.1902–6, Paul Cézanne, 57.2 x 97.2 cm (22½ x 38¼ in), Metropolitan Museum of Art, New York, USA. The Walter H. and Leonore Annenberg Collection, gift of Walter H. and Leonore Annenberg, 1994. Bequest of Walter H. Annenberg, 2002.

Page 59, bottom
Two Young Girls at the Piano, 1892, oil on canvas, 111.8 x 86.4 cm (44 x 34 in), Metropolitan Museum of Art, New York, USA. The Robert Lehman Collection, 1975. Shutterstock.

Page 60
Spring (in Chatou), c.1875, oil on canvas, 59 x 74 cm (23¼ x 29 in), Private Collection. Bridgeman Images.

Page 61
Path Leading Through Tall Grass, 1877, oil on canvas, 60 x 74 cm (23½ x 29 in), Musée d'Orsay, Paris, France. Bridgeman Images.

Pages 62–3
Figures on the Beach, 1890, oil on canvas, 52.7 x 64.1 cm (20¾ x 25¼ in), Metropolitan Museum of Art, New York, USA. Robert Lehman Collection, 1975. Shutterstock.

Page 64
The Floor Planers, 1875, Gustave Caillebotte, oil on canvas, 102 x 146 cm (40 x 18 in), Musée d'Orsay, Paris, France. Bridgeman Images.

Page 65
Woman at Her Toilette, 1875–80, Berthe Morisot, oil on canvas, 60.3 x 80.4 cm (23¾ x 32 in), Art Institute of Chicago, Chicago, Illinois, USA. Stickney Fund.

Page 66
Woman Reading, c.1895, oil on canvas, 41.6 x 32.7 cm (16½ x 13 in), The Sterling and Francine Clark Art Institute, Williamstown, Massachusetts, USA.

Page 67
A Woman Nursing a Child, 1894, oil on canvas, 41.2 x 32.5 cm (16¼ x 12¾ in), Scottish National Gallery, Edinburgh, UK.

Page 68
Nude in a Landscape, c.1887, oil on canvas, 21 x 31.7 cm (8¼ x 12½ in), The Henry and Rose Pearlman Foundation, on long term loan to the Princeton University Art Museum. The Picture Art Collection/Alamy Stock Photo.

Page 69
Bather Arranging Her Hair, 1885, oil on canvas, 91.9 x 73 cm (36¼ x 28¾ in), The Sterling and Francine Clark Art Institute, Williamstown, Massachusetts, USA.

Pages 70–71
Large Nude, 1907, oil on canvas, 70 x 155 cm (27½ x 61 in), Musée d'Orsay, Paris, France. Getty Images.

Pages 72–3
Peaches on a Plate, c.1905, oil on canvas, 22.2 x 35.6 cm (8¾ x 14 in), National Gallery of Art, Washington D.C., USA. Ailsa Mellon Bruce Collection.

Page 74
Jean and Coco, c.1902, pastel on paper laid on canvas, 45.5 x 41.5 cm (18 x 16¼ in), Private Collection. Photo © Christie's Images/Bridgeman Images.

Page 75, left
Jean as a Huntsman, 1910, oil on canvas, 172.72 x 88.9 cm (68 x 35 in), Los Angeles Collection of Modern Art, USA. Gift through the generosity of the late Mr Jean Renoir and Madame Dido Renoir.

Page 75, right
Prince Baltasar Carlos in Hunting Dress, 1635–6, Diego Rodríguez de Silva y Velázquez, oil on canvas, 191 x 103 cm (75 x 40½ in), Prado, Madrid, Spain/Bridgeman Images.

Page 76
Portrait of Madame Henriot, 1876, oil on canvas, 66 x 50 cm (26 x 19½ in), National Gallery of Art, Washington D.C., USA.

Page 77, left
La Parisienne, 1874, oil on canvas, 163.2 x 108.3 cm (64¼ x 42½ in), National Museum of Wales, Cardiff, UK. Bridgeman Images.

Page 77, right
Portrait of Victor Chocquet, c.1875, oil on canvas, 53 x 43.5 cm (21 x 17 in), Harvard Art Museums/Fogg Museum, Bequest of Grenville Lindall Winthrop.

Page 78
Woman at the Piano, 1875–6, oil on canvas, 93 x 74 cm (36½ x 29 in), Art Institute of Chicago, Chicago, Illinois, USA. Mr and Mrs Martin A. Ryerson Collection.

Page 79, left
Children Playing Ball, 1900, colour lithograph, 58.5 x 51.1 cm (23 x 20 in), National Gallery of Art, Washington D.C., USA. Rosenwald Collection.

Page 79, right
Portrait of Tilla Durieux, 1914, oil on canvas, 92.1 x 73.7 cm (36¼ x 29 in), Metropolitan Museum of Art, New York, USA. Bequest of Stephen C. Clark, 1960.

Pages 80–81
The Farm at Les Collettes, Cagnes, 1908–14, oil on canvas, 54.6 x 65.4 cm (21½ x 25¾ in), Metropolitan Museum of Art, New York, USA. Bequest of Charlotte Gina Abrams, in memory of her husband, Lucien Abrams, 1961.

Page 82, left
Claude Renoir in Clown Costume, 1909, oil on canvas, 120 x 77 cm (47¼ x 30¼ in), Musée de l'Orangerie, Paris, France. akg-images/De Agostini Picture Library/A. Dagli Orti.

Page 82, right
Gilles (Pierrot), 1718–19, Jean-Antoine Watteau, oil on canvas, 184.5 x 149.5 cm (72½ x 58¾ in), Louvre Museum, Bequest of Dr Louis La Caze, 1869. Heritage-Images/Art Media/akg-images.

Page 83, top
Claude Renoir, Playing, c.1905, oil on canvas, 46 x 55 cm (18 x 21½ in), Musée de l'Orangerie, Paris, France.

Page 83, bottom
Infanta Margarita in a White Dress, c.1656, attributed to Diego Rodríguez de Silva y Velázquez, oil on canvas, Lobkowicz Library, Prague, Czech Republic. Peter Horree/Alamy Stock Photo.

Page 84
Portrait of Ambroise Vollard, 1917, oil on canvas, 102 x 83 cm (40 x 32½ in), Private Collection.

Page 85
Self-portrait, 1910, oil on canvas, 45.7 x 38.1 cm (18 x 15 in), Private Collection. Bridgeman Images.

Page 86
The Judgement of Paris, c.1908, black, red and white chalk on off-white, medium-weight, medium-texture paper, 48.9 x 62.2 cm (19¼ x 24½ in), The Phillips Collection, Washington D.C., USA. akg-images/Album.

Page 87
The Judgement of Paris, 1916, bronze, 73.7 x 90.8 (29 x 35¾ in), Davis Museum and Cultural Center, Wellesley College, MA, USA/gift of Dr Ruth Morris Bakwin (Class of 1919)/Bridgeman Images.

Page 88
The Bathers, 1918–19, oil on canvas, 110 x 160 cm (43¼ x 63 in), Musée d'Orsay, Paris, France. akg-images/De Agostini/G. Nimatallah.

Pages 88–9
Paysage Bleu, 1915, oil on canvas, 30.4 x 45.3 cm (12 x 17¾ in), The Picture Art Collection/Alamy Stock Photo.

Page 90
The Dance, 1910, Henri Matisse, oil on canvas, 260 x 391 cm (102¼ x 154 in). The Hermitage Museum, St Petersburg. classicpaintings/Alamy Stock Photo.

Page 91, left
Eurydice (Seated Bather in a Landscape), 1895–1900, oil on canvas, 116 x 89 cm (45½ x 35 in), Musée Picasso, Paris, France. Bridgeman Images.

Page 91, right
Seated Bather, Drying Her Feet, 1921, Pablo Picasso, pastel on paper, 66 x 50.8 cm (26 x 20 in), Nationalgalerie, Berlin, Germany. akg-images.

INDEX